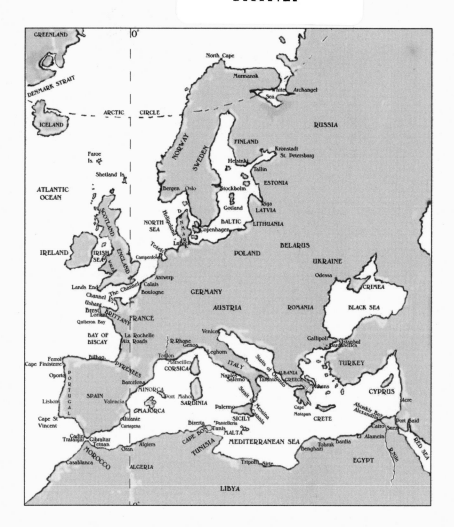

SCOTS AND THE SEA

To my wife Janet,
without whose encouragement and help
this book would not have been written.

SCOTS AND THE SEA

JAMES D.G. DAVIDSON

MAINSTREAM
PUBLISHING

EDINBURGH AND LONDON

First published in Great Britain in 2003 by
MAINSTREAM PUBLISHING COMPANY (EDINBURGH) LTD
7 Albany Street
Edinburgh EH1 5UG

ISBN 1 84018 694 1

Typeset in Book Antiqua, Carta and Van Djick

Printed in Great Britain by Mackays of Chatham plc

Contents

Preface

The story of *Scots and the Sea* is inevitably an intermittent one. Records of events at sea before the sixteenth century are sparse. There were long periods when the activities of Scots at sea were confined to fishing, limited trading restricted by England's Navigation Acts and the constant threat of piracy, warfare between galleys in the waters of the Hebrides and Western Isles and communication across firths and between islands and the mainland.

Since the Act of Union of 1707 Scots have served in Britain's royal and merchant navies, sharing the experiences of shipmates from other countries. From this point on the story becomes more concerned with the achievements of individuals than with the passage of history. My purpose has been to make the reader aware of the wealth, breadth and depth of Scotland's maritime tradition, which has constantly been overshadowed and sometimes appropriated by her neighbour's. For those who wish to put events in a chronological context, a framework has been provided as an appendix, using the dates of accession to the throne of kings and queens and well-known events.

Scots and the Sea is written for the general reader. It is not a work of original historical research, although every effort has been made to ensure accuracy. Where conflicting reports of events exist, I have used my own judgement. I have drawn freely on all sources of information available to me but, except for reported speech, I have not quoted directly from the work of other authors.

James D.G. Davidson
Newtonmore, 2003

⚓ CHAPTER 1 ⚓

The Rugged Peninsula

No point in Scotland is more than 45 miles from tidal salt waters to the west, north or east. No place in the hills south of Edinburgh or Glasgow lies more than 40 miles from the Firth of Forth, the Firth of Clyde or the Solway Firth. Beinn Dearg in the Forest of Atholl, in Highland Perthshire, is only 45 miles from the Firth of Tay and the city of Dundee. It is the same distance from the Moray Firth and the city of Inverness, and the same again from tidal Loch Linnhe and Fort William. One-sixth of Scotland's 790 islands are inhabited. They vary in size from rocks that remain above the high-water mark at spring tides to islands more than 50 miles long in the Shetlands and Hebrides. The sea has shaped Scotland and in turn Scots have helped to shape maritime history, trade and communications.

Most Scots live much closer to the sea than 45 miles. Seven of our ten biggest towns and cities are seaports, including Aberdeen, Dundee, Glasgow and Edinburgh, with Leith. Four-fifths of the population live in cities, towns and villages on firths, estuaries and navigable rivers or along the coast. Most cities except Glasgow and its satellites have beaches within easy reach and even from Glasgow going 'doon the watter', visiting Rothesay or the Ayrshire coast, is relatively easy. The trades' holidays bring thousands to the coasts of the South West or the North East. In the latter part of the twentieth century it was possible to find the rare individual, perhaps living in the west of Aberdeenshire or the centre of Inverness-shire or Perthshire, who had never seen the sea, but in the twenty-first century that would be unusual indeed.

The reasons why Scots went to sea were different from those which motivated Polynesians to explore the Pacific in their big double canoes, Arabs to risk their dhows in the Indian Ocean, or Vikings to beach their longships on the shores of the British Isles. A prime reason has always been . . . to get to the other side: from one island to another or between islands and mainland, and later to cross wider seas in order to trade, explore or emigrate. Basic subsistence was perhaps the main reason. Fishing has traditionally provided an important supply of food and income for Scots and the sea has also been a source of employment for men working as crew members of vessels whose purposes were not necessarily theirs, unless a share of prize money or a share of the fishing catch was part of the deal. There were predators who went to sea as pirates, or privateers with the official sanction of their respective sovereigns, lurking in international waters. Others set sail to defend their own territory or territorial waters from an invader, or to attack enemy merchant shipping or warships in retaliation. Lifeboat crews still risk their lives on errands of mercy. For more than a century amateur sailors, like Olympic gold and silver medallist Rodney Pattison, have gone to sea to compete in races, to challenge records or simply to cruise for pleasure.

Few countries on earth have a higher ratio of seacoast to landmass than Scotland. Our jagged coastline extends for more than 10,000 kilometres or 6,214 miles around a country deeply indented by arms of the sea, which itself covers only 78,813 square kilometres or 30,408 square miles. Exposed to the primeval forces of the North Atlantic, our climate is highly variable but we are not – or not yet – exposed to extremes of temperature. Not yet, but should the polar icecap melt beyond some unpredictable limit we may live to see the Gulf Stream change course and our climate transformed into a small-scale imitation of northern Canada.

The long and jagged coastline has always been vulnerable to predators, armed incursion, smugglers or illegal immigrants, but it also has tremendous potential for the generation of sustainable electrical power from wind, waves and currents, and from the ebb and flow of the tides. In the twenty-first century its vulnerability to the smuggling of illegal drugs, with their hideous potential for destruction of health and self-respect, is possibly the greatest single danger facing the Scottish nation.

⚓ ⚓ ⚓

Eight or nine thousand years ago the sea, swollen by meltwater from the retreating polar icecap, flooded the land between the hills of Antrim to the west and The Rhins of Galloway and the Mull of Kintyre to the east and north. Hunter-gatherers occupied the coastal areas and found much of their food in shallow waters and between high- and low-tide marks. By the millennium which spanned 5500 BC to 4500 BC there is evidence that settlers on the east coast were already catching fish from small vessels, and that the inhabitants of Skara Brae in Orkney ate pelagic and shell fish as a mainstay of their diet.

Around 1500 BC volcanic dust from an eruption of the Icelandic volcano Mount Hekla blotted out the sun, forcing the peoples of the Western Isles and the north of what became Scotland to migrate south by land and sea in search of habitable areas, where they came into conflict with those already living there.

The Scots' colonisation of south-west Caledonia started some five centuries after the first Roman attempt to subdue the country. The campaign of the Roman General Agricola, governor of Britain, had reached the Solway and the Tay in AD 80. In the following year Agricola's fleet embarked on an exploratory voyage around the Hebrides while his armies penetrated to the North East. Although he defeated the Picts at Mons Graupius – possibly Benachie in Aberdeenshire – in AD 84, he never gained control of the area north of the Forth and Clyde. Inchtuthill on the Tay became his most northerly British fortress.

In AD 208 Roman Emperor Septimus Severus attempted once again to subdue the Caledonian tribes and established a naval base at Cramond, just west of Edinburgh, to provide support for his armies in the north. Those armies, backed by supply ships and warships, still failed to subdue the Caledonii, either by land or sea.

As Roman power waned, raids by Scots from Ireland on the west coast of Caledonia increased – 'Scotti' was the Roman word for pirates. By the fifth century, the Scots were well established in Argyll and the southern Hebrides, which they called Dalriada after their native region of Ireland, and were pushing the Picts north and east.

In AD 563 Colum Cille, better known as St Columba, put to sea from the Antrim coast in a curragh made of wickerwork and hides and landed on the tiny island of Iona off the west coast of Mull, where he established a monastery. In the following century there is a record of six monks dying when their boat sank off the island.

Between AD 568 and AD 733 there were no less than eight naval expeditions from Dalriada to the islands and coasts – north, south and west. The Picts were active in the same waters. In AD 581 Aedan Mac Gabrain, King of the Scots, invaded Orkney – sea crossings were evidently no deterrent. In AD 617 a party of Picts from Skye raided the island of Eigg and massacred an Irish missionary and 150 of his followers, simply because they had usurped the sheep grazing rights of the local Pictish ruler. Then in AD 682 King Bridei of the Picts reclaimed the Orkney Islands from the Scots.

An ancient document *Senchus Fer N-Alban* suggests that by the middle of that century Dalriada had a comprehensive ship-levy system obliging groups of households to provide, and man, a warship each. They could assemble a fleet of some 170 vessels, each manned by 14 men, from more than 2,000 households, but the earliest known naval battle in British waters occurred in AD 719 in the Minches between rival factions from Dalriada, probably a dispute over territory.

A Viking attack in AD 795 on the monastery of Iona heralded two centuries of Viking raids on the coasts of the British Isles. Norse colonisation would have a profound effect upon the culture and genetics of the native population, and on crafts such as shipbuilding and the making of weapons and jewellery. By the start of the ninth century Norsemen had overrun Orkney and Shetland and in AD 806 they ravaged Iona again, killing 68 monks and laymen and burning the abbey. By the middle of that century they had occupied Caithness, Sutherland and the west coast as far south as Islay. The whole coast was constantly exposed to Viking raids. Eoganan, who became King of Dalriada in AD 834, reigned for only five years before he was killed at sea by Norsemen.

Kenneth MacAlpin, in alliance with the Norse, seized control of the central lowlands and in AD 843 declared himself King of Scots and Picts. Settlement of the islands and coasts by the Norse and their virtual command of the sea isolated Scotland and played a significant role in the process of uniting the mainland as one kingdom. The tide of domination and control ebbed and flowed many times before the boundaries of modern Scotland became accepted and defined, but the cleansing sea, constant in its inconstancy, exerted an overriding influence on every aspect of life in the islands and on the seaboard of the future Scotland.

⚓ ⚓ ⚓

Mobility at sea and superb seamanship were the keys to the success of the Vikings. They had perfected the construction of the longship, which enabled them to carry out long-distance raids from bases in Norway, and from settlements elsewhere.

Longships varied in length from 20 to 30 metres; they had a beam of about 6 metres and measured only 2 metres from keel to gunwale. When loaded and with a crew of 40 to 50, the longship still had a draught of just one metre. Extra cargo only increased this marginally, by 1 or 2 per cent. The hulls were clinker-built with overlapping oak planks 24 centimetres thick, fastened with wooden pegs. Furnished with a dipping lugsail, longships were capable of sailing fast with the wind astern or on the beam but as tacking into the wind was difficult they were equipped with oars for manoeuvrability and for propulsion when the wind was too light for sailing. There was a steering oar at the stern. Because a longship's keel only projected a few centimetres below the bottom strakes, the vessel could easily be beached and re-launched and could therefore be used as a landing craft, cargo-ship or warship, though there was a tendency to drift to leeward in a cross-wind. Nevertheless, their versatility made them equally suitable for carrying out hit-and-run raids, large-scale landings or for communication and supply. From the Viking longship the boat builders of the Western Isles and seaboard by stages developed the galley or birlinn, which was a half-decked vessel of similar hull conformation, propelled by oars and sail.

In AD 870 the rock of Dumbarton, fortress capital of the Britons of Strathclyde, was captured by Norse raiders. They arrived in 200 longships but only succeeded in capturing the fortress after cutting off the Britons' water supply, followed by a siege of four months. The Norse and Scots made an unsuccessful attack on the south side of the Solway Firth with 615 ships in AD 937. Following their defeat, the Norsemen escaped to Dublin while the Scots and Britons left behind had to acknowledge the supremacy of the English king, Edgar. (Meanwhile the Norse ruler of Orkney was using longships to transport peat from Tarbat Ness to Orkney, setting a fashion for 'bringing coals to Newcastle'.)

Edgar cruised up the English coast of the Irish Sea and, according to tradition, was rowed in state by the rulers of Wales, the Isle of Man, Galloway, Strathclyde and the Hebrides. A twelfth-century Anglo-Norman writer, Geoffrey Gaimer, claimed that Edgar 'held the land as an emperor. He alone ruled over all the kings and over the Scots and the Welsh. Never, since Arthur, had any king such power.' It did not last, if indeed it ever existed.

In AD 971 when Danish longships entered the Firth of Tay and landed at Luncarty they were confronted by a Scottish army under King Kenneth II. On this occasion the Scandinavians were defeated and forced to re-embark. In 1054 an English naval and military expedition was sent to Scotland in support of Malcolm Canmore (Bighead) – Malcolm III – against Macbeth. Malcolm finally slew Macbeth in 1057 and, after the brief reign of Lulach, regained the throne of his father, Duncan.

When the English were defeated at Hastings in 1066 by the invading Normans, the Saxon princess Margaret fled to Scotland. Malcolm Canmore married Margaret and fell under her religious and cultural influence. It was she who instituted a ferry across the Forth – at Queensferry – for the benefit of those making pilgrimage to the priories at Dunfermline and St Andrews. Malcolm invaded Northumbria in 1093 after a naval fleet blockading Scotland had been destroyed in a gale. He was killed along with his eldest son during the raid and Margaret died some days later, apparently of a broken heart. In 1098 King Edgar, the second son of Malcolm III and Margaret, negotiated an alliance with King Magnus Barefoot of Norway, formally ceding the Western Isles and Kintyre to him, despite having no real control over Scotland's western seaboard himself.

In 1121 Alexander I, another son of Malcolm III and Margaret, founded the first Scottish royal burgh at Berwick-on-Tweed and gave special privileges to merchants in order to stimulate trade with the European continent. He was succeeded in 1124 by his younger brother David I, who founded royal burghs for the same purpose in Dunfermline, Edinburgh, Perth and Stirling. Ten years later David I regained the islands of Man, Arran and Bute from the Norwegians and conferred them on Somerled, the first chief of the great Clan Donald. (MacDonald is still the commonest name after Smith in twenty-first-century Scotland.)

Somerled became Lord of the Isles from North Uist and part of Skye to Islay and the Mull of Kintyre, and sometimes as far south as the Isle of Man. So important was sea power to the MacDonalds that a galley, with oars and sails, featured prominently in the coats of arms of all their leading families. They were not the only major clan to exercise power by sea. The coats of arms of the Campbells and more than a dozen other prominent western clans also incorporate galleys or boats on their escutcheons to emphasise their close links with the sea. The galleys of the west coast and Western Isles were less sophisticated versions of the longship, but fulfilled the same functions on a more parochial scale.

In 1156 Dugall, son of Somerled, and Thorfinn, a powerful noble, sailed through all the islands as far south as Kintyre. The inhabitants accepted Dugall as their overlord, but Godred, son of the Norwegian King of the Isles, did not. He sailed north from the Isle of Man with a powerful fleet of longships to be met by a fleet of 80 galleys commanded by Somerled, with Dugall and Thorfinn in company. A bloody but indecisive naval action was fought, after which a treaty was signed between Godred and Somerled. The Norwegian ceded the Mull of Kintyre and the Hebridean islands south of Ardnamurchan to Somerled but retained the northern isles and the Isle of Man. In 1158, despite the treaty, Somerled invaded Man and defeated Godred. The Norwegian fled home and Somerled became King or Lord of the Isles from the Outer Hebrides to the Irish Sea. On his death the Isle of Man reverted to Godred and in 1210 King Haakon IV of Norway re-established his overlordship of Orkney and the Western Isles.

Alexander II succeeded William to the Scottish throne in 1214. William had reigned for nearly 50 years and had established royal burghs at Dundee,

Ayr and elsewhere. The royal burghs were becoming Scotland's new trade centres, their merchants having legal rights to trade in raw materials such as wood and leather from the surrounding countryside. A healthy trade with Flanders was also being developed.

Alexander II declared that he would set his standard on the cliffs of Thurso and rule over all the territory claimed by King Haakon of Norway to the west, as well as the Orkney Islands. Norse invaders were expelled from Bute by Alan, Lord of Galloway, a supporter of Alexander with a reputation as a great warrior. Alan had a large army and 200 ships, which enabled him to dominate the Irish Sea and its coasts. In 1237 a truce was signed between Alexander and Henry III of England, fixing the Scottish border along a line between Berwick and Gretna Green, but sovereignty over the islands off the north and west coasts eluded him. He died on the little island of Kerrera while on his way to attempt to establish Scottish control over Argyll and the Western Isles and was succeeded in 1249 by his son, Alexander III.

Two years after his accession ten-year-old Alexander III was married to Margaret, the eleven-year-old daughter of Henry III of England. This marriage established good relations with England for a generation and allowed merchants and craftsmen to thrive. By now there were some 50 royal burghs in Scotland, some linked by roads, bridges and ferries.

In 1263, despite his youth, Alexander decided to assert his sovereignty over the Western Isles, but King Haakon sailed from Norway in July with a force of 160 ships and 20,000 men to challenge him. Haakon led the expedition in a ship specially built entirely from oak, with a gilded dragon's head and neck at the prow and a square sail on a swinging yard. This ship alone carried 240 warriors and 60 oarsmen.

The Norwegians' course took them by way of the Shetland Islands, north of the Orkneys and Sutherland (Norse Suderland) and south through the Minches. They stopped to pillage some 20 settlements on the way and stayed to enjoy their spoils. It was nearly autumn by the time Haakon anchored his fleet in Lamlash Bay on the east coast of the Isle of Arran. Alexander could not raise sufficient forces to give battle and sent emissaries to negotiate, to win time until the onset of winter. When the stormy weather began, he withdrew from the negotiations. King Haakon was losing patience and running out of supplies. He moved his ships up the Clyde to the Fairlie Roads, the channel between the Cumbrae islands and the Ayrshire coast, and challenged Alexander to negotiate a treaty or meet him in battle. To reinforce his demands he sent a quarter of his fleet up Loch Long to plunder and pillage. Alexander, however, continued to play for time.

On 30 September, the first of the expected gales blew up from the south-west, trapping the Norwegian fleet in the firth, scattering and battering the longships, which could not make way into the wind. Haakon's own ship dragged its anchors and was driven up the Clyde, while four other ships were driven ashore on the beach near Largs, including one of the supply ships. Haakon himself led a force ashore to rescue them but was attacked by a Scottish army and driven back to the water's edge. Those trying to escape overloaded the boats, many of which sank. The storm prevented Norwegian reinforcements from landing until dusk, by which time they were only able to cover the withdrawal of those of their compatriots who had not died on the beaches. When the storm subsided, King Haakon sailed away from the Firth of Clyde, defeated. He rounded the Mull of Kintyre and navigated his battered fleet through the Minches, cleared Cape Wrath, and sought haven in Orkney.

In 1264, Alexander III assembled an army and a fleet in the Western Isles to overawe the island chiefs and weaken their loyalty to their Norwegian rulers. His strategy was at least partly successful. King Haakon, who had been very old at the time of the Battle of Largs, had died in Orkney two months after the confrontation and was buried in Kirkwall in what is now St Magnus Cathedral. His son Magnus made peace and in 1266 signed the Treaty of Perth by which the Western Isles and the Isle of Man were sold to Alexander III. Magnus's son, Eric, married Alexander's daughter in 1281.

On the afternoon of 19 March 1286 a tempest with heavy rain was scouring the Firth of Forth. Alexander had been conferring with his Council in Edinburgh Castle and against their advice he decided to cross the firth and ride to Kinghorn in Fife to spend the night with his French queen Yolande. His first wife, the English princess Margaret, had died in 1275. Alexander and three followers crossed the Forth by the Queen's Ferry and safely reached Inverkeithing. There, two guides were engaged to conduct him along the storm-lashed coast to his destination. In the dark he lost touch with his guides. The following morning his battered body was found on the beach at Kinghorn. Whether he had fallen over the cliff or been thrown from his horse was never established. His premature death was a tragedy for Scotland. He had exercised strong and able government, maintained peace with England, developed links between the royal burghs and won some control over the western coast and islands. Scotland lost a king whose children had all predeceased him. His granddaughter, the child of Margaret and King Eric of Norway, became heir to the throne.

The Maid of Norway stayed with her father in Norway until she was seven. Then in 1290, on passage to Scotland to be betrothed to the infant son of the English king, Edward I, she became ill in rough seas and died shortly after her ship reached Orkney, both seasick and homesick. Soon afterwards the English captured the Isle of Man and Edward, later to become 'the hammer of the Scots', who had been on superficially good terms with Alexander III, became increasingly arrogant. The untimely deaths of Alexander III and his little granddaughter had far-reaching effects, triggering a struggle between 13 claimants to the Scottish throne and involving the English in support of whichever claimant appeared to offer the best prospect for English interests. The latent antipathy between north and south was stirred into a series of conflicts which, although they were part of the evolutionary progress towards a United Kingdom of Great Britain and Northern Ireland, would cost countless lives at sea as well as on land and immeasurable pain over a period of five centuries.

♏ CHAPTER 2 ♏

The War of Independence at Sea

So Scotland's maritime traditions emerged from prehistory: from the fishermen who made their livelihood using coracles and dugout canoes in coastal waters; from the galleys which rowed and sailed between the Western Isles, raiding and trading; from Norse and Viking predators who bequeathed their place names, their genes and their seafaring and shipbuilding skills to many island and coastal communities; and more recently from the merchants who traded with Europe and beyond and who were not above a bit of piracy on the way.

At the beginning of the fourteenth century the countries of southern and western Europe were not building warships. Instead, ships that could be used for either trade or warfare were preferred. Forts and castles had long been used to defend land or to consolidate territorial gain; the concept was now simply adapted to the deck of a trading or merchant ship and forecastles (fo'c'sles) and aftercastles were built at each end. It was easier to board an enemy ship from an aftercastle or fo'c'sle and it enabled the superior vessel to shoot down on the enemy from above when the two were grappled together in combat. The tactic of lines of battleships firing broadsides at each other from a distance came much later; that of going alongside and boarding the enemy survived into the twentieth century.

Before the death of Alexander III in 1286 and the invasion of Scotland by Edward I of England ten years later, there had been little in the way of naval warfare between the two nations except for sporadic actions involving individual merchants and pirates. Edward I's aggression set the pattern for the next two centuries and had repercussions long after that.

There were few naval incidents in the period between Edward I's invasion and the English defeat at the Battle of Bannockburn in 1314. Edward I took Berwick in 1296 and used the port for transports with replenishments. The English army campaigned in Galloway with the support of some 80 ships off the west coast. Half of these were Irish but some belonged to Hebridean island chiefs allied to the English. In 1303 the English crossed the Forth to Fife, not far from Rosyth, using prefabricated assault bridges brought from Lynn in Norfolk in a convoy of 29 ships with 2 escorts. On the west coast a fleet of 173 ships carrying 3,500 men from Ulster, paid by the English, captured Rothesay Castle on the island of Bute, while Edward I wintered in Dunfermline.

Before Robert the Bruce, rival of England's acolyte John Balliol, was crowned King of Scotland in 1306, his first uprising was defeated and he took refuge in the Western Isles. Ships from England were joined by some from Ireland in the search for him. Bruce was, however, supported by Angus, Lord of the Isles, whose galleys enabled supplies to reach him on remote islands. In 1306 English ships captured Dunaverty Castle in Kintyre with the assistance of a Scots 'admiral', John of Menteith, and a squadron of galleys commanded by Hugh Bisset from Antrim, while Eoin MacDougall of Lorne patrolled the North Channel in an attempt to prevent Bruce's escape from Rathlin Island. However, Bruce contrived to get a boat across to Ayrshire while Scots ships retook the Isle of Man, which changed hands twice more over the next four years.

In 1314, the year of Bannockburn, Scottish and Flemish privateers were active on the east coast of England and English merchant ships had to be convoyed. Ships from Yarmouth were dispatched to intercept Scots cogs – flat-bottomed cargo boats that had been adapted as warships in Holland. While Bruce was campaigning in Ireland, in the Irish Sea an English admiral, John of Athy, defeated a Scottish squadron under Thomas Dun who was killed. In 1316 the merchantman *St James* from Bayonne was attacked by Scottish and Flemish ships – presumably pirates – whose crews killed all but three of the Frenchmen, but when a superior squadron under the English admiral Sir John Botetort appeared, the attackers sailed away.

After his campaign in Ireland, Robert the Bruce turned his attention to developing a Scots naval force and, in keeping with the trend at the time, he wanted ships that could be used for trade or converted for fighting. He built ships designed like Viking longships on the Clyde at Cardross near Dumbarton and the Exchequer Rolls of 1326 indicate that some of his west-coast subjects made their ships and crews available to him. Individuals, sometimes in the pay of their respective sovereigns, commanded squadrons comprising merchant ships either armed or temporarily converted for war, or else they operated as privateers with letters of authority from a sovereign or government; or sometimes as pirates without anybody's authority. To give one example from a later century, in 1561 a Captain Patrick Blackadder was taking prizes 'authorised' by a letter from James III dated 1476.

By the time of the Declaration of Arbroath in 1320, trade between the royal burghs of Scotland and continental Europe was beginning to thrive. By 1327 exports of wool had reached a record high of 5,000 sacks.

In 1328 Edward III of England recognised Bruce as Robert I of Scotland, but when Robert died in 1329, an attempt by Edward Balliol, son of John, to regain the Scottish throne met initially with success. Supported by an English fleet and some discontented Scottish exiles, he sailed from the Humber and landed at Kinghorn in Fife. He defeated a small Scottish army near Perth and was crowned King of Scots at Scone. Almost his first act was to cede most of lowland Scotland to the English and in 1333 a Scottish army was defeated at Halidon Hill near Berwick, which had been blockaded by English ships. A group of 20 Flemish ships under Captain John Crab was hired to drive off the English vessels but they were defeated and burned. The English then re-occupied Berwick and the Isle of Man. David II, Robert's legitimate successor, fled to France.

The following year galleys from the Western Isles brought clansmen across the Clyde, where they were joined by patriots from Ayrshire and Renfrewshire in a campaign against Balliol. Although the English army penetrated as far as the Clyde and the Tay, the Scots remained active at sea, raiding East Anglia in 1334. Meanwhile, an English seaborne force captured Dunnottar Castle on the coast two miles south of Stonehaven but it was retaken soon afterwards by the Scottish regent, Sir Andrew de Moray. Five hundred miles to the south, Scottish ships were raiding the Channel Islands and the Isle of Wight and all English merchant shipping had to move in convoy.

Eventually Balliol was forced to flee. The English mobilised all available ships over 40 tons for war against the Scots but in 1335 Edward III abandoned his campaign in the Borders and disbanded his fleet of converted merchant ships, retaining only 'cruisers' to intercept trade between Scotland and mainland Europe. The same year an Irish attack by sea against Rothesay was repelled. In August 1336 French and Scottish cruisers captured English ships off the coasts of Suffolk and the Isle of Wight. With French support Scottish ships harassed the English and in 1341 the English garrison was expelled from Edinburgh and David II returned from France as king – only to be captured by the English in 1346. A decade later Berwick yet again changed hands, twice in quick succession, but after the Truce of Berwick in 1367 David II was released. He was succeeded by Robert II in

1371. The reigns of both Robert II and Robert III, who succeeded him in 1390, were decades of dissension and sporadic warfare with England and internal disruption.

John Mercer, a wealthy burgess and merchant of Perth, was wrecked on the coast of Northumbria in 1376. His merchandise was seized and he was imprisoned. His son Andrew fitted out a squadron of privateers and, in revenge, plundered Scarborough. However, in 1378 a privateer squadron commanded by a London merchant, John Philpot, attacked a Scottish merchant convoy under Captain Andrew Mercer and captured him.

In 1380 the Scots parliament purchased two ships specifically for operations against English pirates, but in 1384, following a Scots raid on Cumberland, the English retaliated, reached Edinburgh and sacked the city.

In 1406 King Robert III died in Rothesay Castle on the Isle of Bute less than a fortnight after hearing that his son James, heir to the throne, had been captured off the east coast of England by pirates from Great Yarmouth. The 11-year-old prince was being sent to France for safety in *The Maryenknyght* when it was intercepted. Overwhelmed, Robert lost the will to live and refused to eat. The pirates sold their prize to the English king, who promptly imprisoned the young prince in the Tower of London despite there being a truce in force between Scotland and England at the time.

Over the next 70 years Scotland was governed, initially by a regent (the Duke of Albany) and then by the first three Jameses of the Stewart dynasty. It was a period when the influence of the English monarchy over southern Scotland waxed and waned, while the power of Donald, Lord of the Isles, and his successors over the Western Isles and the north mainland was at its peak. Not until 1424, by which time he was nearly 30 years old, was James I able to organise a tax to raise sufficient money to pay a ransom to Henry V and secure his own release from the Tower of London. On his return he established a shipbuilding yard, marine workshop and storehouse at Leith, where he built ships adaptable for commerce or warfare. In 1428, parliament, meeting in Perth, enacted a law that each four merk of land within six miles of the sea was to provide 'one oar' to serve the king. Later the same year James called a meeting of Highland chiefs in Inverness and had more than 50 of them arrested on arrival, including Alexander, the current Lord of the Isles, though he and most of the others were released after a short imprisonment. Alexander responded by sacking Inverness. James marched north to Lochaber, where he captured Alexander and then imprisoned him in Tantallon Castle, far away on the south side of the Firth of Forth. He was released two years later and immediately took up arms against the king again, defeating the royal army at Inverlochy, at the north end of Loch Linnhe, and regaining domination of the Western Isles.

In February 1437 James I was assassinated in Perth and a month later his seven-year-old son James II was crowned in Holyrood Abbey in Edinburgh. His coronation marked the start of a 23-year reign punctuated by executions, kidnapping, treachery, murder and warfare – principally between the supporters of James and the powerful Douglas family. The Lord of the Isles ravaged the islands in the Clyde in 1454 and in the same year the Archbishop of Dublin was captured by Scots pirates in Dublin Bay and ransomed. The Lord of the Isles was, however, bribed with grants of land to support the king and when the last Douglas stronghold, Threave Castle, fell to James II in 1455, the king had virtually made himself master of his own kingdom. An artillery enthusiast, he introduced gunpowder and cannon to Scotland, which had a major effect upon the design of ships.

Bishop Kennedy of St Andrews, the most influential bishop in fifteenth-century Scotland, was a pioneer of ship design. He built a ship for trade and war at the enormous cost of ten thousand pounds Scots and named her *St Salvator*. She was eventually wrecked on the Northumbrian coast. Amongst the owners of the latest type of dual-purpose vessel were Sir Andrew Wood of Largo, shipowner and merchant; the Barton family; and William Brownhill of Leith.

In 1460, while besieging Roxburgh Castle – held by the English, who still claimed overlordship of Scotland – James II was killed by one of his own guns which 'brak in the fyring'. James III succeeded at the age of eight and Bishop Kennedy of St Andrews assumed the regency.

Shortly afterwards, John MacDonald, Lord of the Isles, concluded the Treaty of Ardtornish with Edward IV of England. Under the terms of the treaty the power of the Earl of Douglas was to be restored in the south of Scotland and MacDonald and Douglas were to rule all Scotland north of the Forth, whilst acknowledging Edward IV of England as their superior. But MacDonald had to buy his peace with the regent, Bishop Kennedy, by ceding most of his mainland territories to the Scottish crown. John MacDonald's natural son, Angus Og, reacted by raiding far and wide to show his resentment of his father. James III was then caught up in a struggle for power and domination between the English king and his supporters on the one hand and the Scottish aristocrats who opposed the pro-English faction on the other.

In 1469 the 17-year-old king was married to 12-year-old Princess Margaret of Norway. Was it young James who, according to the *Ballad of Sir Patrick Spens*, 'sat in Dunfermline toon, drinking the blude-red wine', who sent this 'skeely skipper' to fetch the princess? His ship reached Norway in two days but sank in a 'deadly storm' on the return voyage. Luckily Margaret must have crossed in another ship, as she made the journey safely.

Orkney and Shetland were gifted to Scotland as her dowry and in 1473 the 16-year-old princess gave birth to a son who, as James IV, would become one of Scotland's most able monarchs. John, Lord of the Isles, who had just had the earldom of Ross confiscated because of his treasonable dealings with Edward IV, finally submitted to James III in 1476, but four years later fighting broke out in the Borders. English naval squadrons were operating against Scotland on both coasts. Sir Andrew Wood first came into prominence in May of 1481 when he commanded *Yellow Carvel* and defeated an English squadron which had entered the Firth of Forth with the intention of sacking Edinburgh.

Meanwhile, on the opposite coast of Scotland, the quarrel between John, Lord of the Isles, and his son, Angus Og, came to a head. In 1481 they met with opposing fleets of galleys in the Sound of Mull near Tobermory, ostensibly to negotiate. John had the support of the Macleods, Macleans and MacNeils. Angus had powerful backing in the persons of John Stewart of Atholl and Colin Campbell of Argyll. The negotiations collapsed in angry dispute and a fierce battle commenced – so ferocious that it became known as the Battle of Bloody Bay. It ended in a decisive victory for Angus Og, confirming him as effective chief of the Clan Donald with his seat in Duart Castle on the east coast of Mull, nullifying the Treaty of Ardtornish between John and Edward IV of England and renewing the dispute between the Lords of the Isles and the Scottish crown over the lands claimed by Clan Donald on the west coast. Angus Og and his followers twice sailed to the Isle of Arran and plundered crown lands, making further conflict with the Stewart kings unavoidable.

In 1482 Scottish ships were active against the English and their supporters in both the Irish Sea and the English Channel, forcing the English to form a fishery protection squadron to guard East Anglian fishermen against raids by Scottish and Scandinavian predators. In 1484 ships with the authority of Richard III of England got the better of an inferior squadron of Scottish ships in the North Sea.

After more than a decade of turbulence, during which James III nearly lost his throne more than once, he was finally murdered in 1488 as he lay wounded in a mill by the Bannock burn after the battle of Sauchieburn: a battle against rebels nominally commanded by his 15-year-old son, the Duke of Rothesay, who then became James IV. Ironically, James III had made his last stand with the sword of Robert the Bruce, his renowned forebear and victor of the battle of Bannockburn, only to die beside the Bannock burn himself.

⚓ CHAPTER 3 ⚓

A Scottish Navy Conceived

James IV fathered a Scottish navy but his brainchild did not survive beyond infancy. Born at his father's favourite residence, Stirling Castle, in 1473, he was gifted with intelligence, initiative, an adventurous spirit and cheerful disposition, but the Scotland he was born into was neither a comfortable nor prosperous country. It was wild and lawless, with a dearth of harbours or port facilities and few roads, bridges, or even inns. The first English Navigation Act of 1381, which obliged the English to restrict their exports and imports to English ships, had forced Scotland into a trading partnership with France and her continental neighbours and added impetus to piracy and smuggling. Although the royal burghs were beginning to develop trade with the European continent, not many foreign merchants visited Scotland. In winter – from the end of October until February – few Scottish merchant ships left harbour. Wool, hides, woollen cloth, salted fish and meat for export had to wait until the spring before they could be shipped to a continental port from the east coast.

At the beginning of the sixteenth century there were some 40 royal or free burghs varying in size from Edinburgh and Dundee (then the second city in Scotland) to little seaports such as Crail, Cullen or Inverkeithing, which exported a few 'laths' of herring and paid a pound or two to the king's Customs. Only royal burghs were allowed to engage in foreign trade and customs dues were paid on the export of hides, wool, salt, coal and fish. The royal burghs with their emblems of tolbooth, mercat cross and tron (or weighing machine) had the sole right to hold weekly markets and annual fairs, to exact tolls on all goods brought into the burgh and to send ships to foreign countries. In those days even abbots went fishing: Thomas Crystal,

Abbot of Kinloss in Morayshire, 'toiled with oars and sail' for the good of his monastery, presumably to catch fish for consumption or sale.

In James IV's time royal ships would have been used for trading when not required for warlike purposes. This would have helped to cover the costs of maintenance and manning. New designs and fashions in ship construction from elsewhere in Europe were constantly being adopted and adapted. James IV had a carvel built in 1449: probably a galley with a single deck and flush planking, designed for either rowing or sailing, with one sail per mast, suspended from a yard which could be dipped either side of the mast. The Bishop of Aberdeen owned one in 1457. A 500-ton barge built for Bishop Kennedy of St Andrews was then one of the largest merchantmen afloat. In the Hebrides, the basic ship design of the Vikings survived in the shape of the high-prowed open galley or longship, fleets of which were maintained by the Lords of the Isles.

When James IV was crowned king at Scone, 15 days after his father's death, he crossed the Forth from Leith to Dunfermline and then travelled on to Dundee, where he made Lord Hailes Great Admiral of Scotland, although there is no record of this admiral ever going to sea, or indeed an explanation of why he was appointed.

In the same year a Danish pirate, Lutkyn Mere, was attacking merchant vessels in Scottish waters. Even the loyal Sir Andrew Wood had been unable to protect the merchantmen, but Lutkyn Mere's ship was eventually captured by a royal vessel. While nine of the crew who agreed to go in the king's ship to Duchal Castle were spared and given clothing, thirty-six of them who did not were executed. Later that summer, five heavily armed English ships which had repeatedly attacked and plundered Scottish merchant ships – despite a peace treaty between England and Scotland – were finally brought to action off Dunbar by Sir Andrew Wood's two ships, *Yellow Carvel* and *Flower*. After a long and hard-fought battle the English ships surrendered and were triumphantly escorted into Leith harbour by Sir Andrew.

Hostility between Scots and English seamen persisted. In February 1490 one of King James's ships was chased by English ships in the Firth of Clyde and had to take refuge under the guns of Dumbarton Castle. In August of the same year, a well-armed English squadron of three privateers with royal authority, commanded by Stephen Bull, lay off the Isle of May in the Firth of Forth, waiting in early morning light to attack Sir Andrew Wood as he returned to Leith, his two ships loaded with merchandise from Flanders. The action which followed was imaginatively described by the sixteenth-century historian Robert Lindesay of Pitscottie in his *History and Cronicles of Scotland*.

Stephen Bull captured some local fishermen. When he saw two ships approaching from the south-east, he made his captives climb the mast to see if they could identify the approaching vessels. At first the fishermen pretended not to recognise them but when promised their freedom they confirmed that the ships were *Yellow Carvel* and *Flower*. The English captain was delighted. Confident that he was about to win two valuable prizes and the approbation of the English monarch, he had a barrel of wine broached and invited his subordinate captains to 'take good courage for the enemies is at hand'. Sir Andrew, seeing three great ships, heavily gunned, approaching on an interception course, ordered his crews to their action stations. The gunners were ordered to load and the sailors to make ready their crossbows and to take up their two-handed swords. Then he 'caussit to fill the wyne' and the men all drank to each other. At that moment the sun began to rise and 'shined bright upon the sails'.

The English, with guns of longer range, opened fire first. The wind was steady from the south-east. Sir Andrew, knowing his ships were outgunned, beat to windward of Bull's squadron then closed the range. All through a long summer's day, farmers and fisherfolk on the coast of Fife watched the battle 'which was very terrible to see'. When darkness fell, action was temporarily broken off, but the contestants stayed in close touch and when the day began to break 'trumpets blew on every side' and a furious battle recommenced. While it was in progress all five ships were drifting past Fife Ness and north-west towards the estuary of the Tay. Sir Andrew cleverly stayed to windward and eventually the English ships ran aground on sandbanks. All three were forced to surrender. They were then boarded and towed into Dundee by Sir Andrew as prizes and handed over to King James.

The king gave money to the defeated crews and in due course sent both ships and men back to the English monarch, Henry VII. Before they were returned to England, however, Sir Andrew made use of the crews to build houses and fortifications 'to resist and expel those pirates and raiders who have often attacked from the sea our kingdom and subjects'. Sir Andrew, who had been knighted by James III, was now made an admiral and a free baron with lands at Largo by James IV.

Henry VII was not impressed by James's magnanimity. The English parliament issued a decree on 17 October 1491 banishing all Scots from England unless they became 'denizens' (were naturalised) within 40 days. James responded by sending ambassadors to France and Spain in the royal ship *Katherine* to renew alliances and to find a princess to wed. They were accompanied by the poet William Dunbar, perhaps to compose a royal proposal if a suitable princess were found, but he was violently seasick even before the ship reached the Bass Rock. A treaty with France was renewed in March 1492 and in May of the following year Sir James Ogilvie sailed across the North Sea as the king's emissary to conclude an offensive and defensive treaty with Denmark.

While James was strengthening foreign alliances he was continually irked by the unpredictability of the clans of the north and west – in particular by Clan Donald and other clans subordinate to the Lord of the Isles, who virtually controlled the west coast and Hebrides. In effect, these areas formed a separate kingdom. It became clear to the young king that the Lord of the Isles had to be brought under the control of the crown if Scotland was ever to be a united kingdom. The Scots parliament of 1493 passed legislation requiring all coastal burghs to maintain 20-ton vessels to be manned by unemployed able-bodied men. The purpose was not only to improve fisheries but also to form a body of seamen who could man the nation's ships when needed. Parliament then passed a sentence of forfeiture, depriving the Lord of the Isles of both lands and power, and in August James sailed for the Western Isles with an impressive fleet.

The arrival of a royal fleet appeared to overawe the island chiefs. Most of them accepted the king's edict and came to Dunstaffnage Castle, impressively sited on the coast north of Oban. They made their submission to the king, who then granted them new charters of the lands they had previously held as vassals to successive Lords of the Isles. He even knighted the two who offered the greatest threat to him – Alexander of Lochalsh and John of Islay, both MacDonalds. However, James's troubles were far from over and he had to return twice in 1494 in his ship *Christopher*, accompanied by a barge and two smaller vessels, to reinforce his authority.

On the second occasion he summoned all the most powerful chiefs and lords of the kingdom to the royal castle at Tarbert, situated strategically between Loch Fyne and West Loch Tarbert on the Atlantic coast. He fortified the castle, then sailed to the south of the peninsula and captured Dunaverty Castle, which he garrisoned to control his western approaches. His recent knighthood meant nothing to John of Islay, who stormed Dunaverty soon after the king's departure and hanged the governor from the walls, but a clan chieftain loyal to the king, MacIan of Ardnamurchan (a forebear of the MacDonalds of Glencoe), captured John and his four sons. Towards the end of the year they were tried and hanged.

In preparation for another venture in the west, James had his ship refitted and suitable boats built, including a royal barge. Convoyed by the faithful Sir Andrew Wood in the royal ship *Flower* and accompanied by *Yellow Carvel*, in May 1495 he sailed up the Firth of Lorn and the Sound of Mull to Mingary Castle, seat of MacIan of Ardnamurchan. There he received the submission of four powerful chiefs whose loyalty to the crown had still been in doubt: MacDonald of Sleat, Maclean of Duart, the Chief of the Camerons and MacNeil of Barra. Later he put the chiefs of Mackenzie and Mackintosh, whose loyalty was also in question, under guard in Edinburgh Castle. He then felt able to turn his attention to other things – things as varied as literature, poetry, languages and the arts of war. He had a prodigious memory and was reputed to speak eight languages: Latin, Danish, German, Flemish, Italian, French, English and Gaelic.

Unfortunately James's judgement was less reliable than his memory and he unwisely supported the so-called Duke of York, Perkin Warbeck, claimant to the English throne, who arrived in Scotland in November 1495. An ill-starred invasion of England in his support petered out in the following year. Warbeck left Ayr for Ireland in July 1497 in the merchant ship *Cuckoo*, hired by King James from the Barton brothers.

James's earlier attempts to introduce law and order into the Western Isles and clan lands had only been partially successful. Early in 1496 Bute was devastated by Western Islemen and so in March 1498 James decided he should visit the isles again to re-establish his authority. He sailed from Ayr on a week's cruise, visiting first Arran and then his fortified castles at Kilkerran – now Campbeltown – and Tarbert. He visited Kilkerran twice again that year, spending two months there in June. In return for promises that they would make their galleys available to him when required, he gave grants of land to the Macleods of Dunvegan and Lewis, but his confidence in them was misplaced. In April 1500 James gave his loyal supporter, Archibald Campbell, Earl of Argyll, vice-regal powers over the former Lordship of the Isles but Macleod of Lewis declined to obey the earl and as a result was outlawed. Macleod supported the claim of Donald Owre to Lordship of the Isles and secured the support of the Macleans and Camerons. They plundered Bute and attacked those western clans that had been loyal to the king.

In 1501 James sent two ships and two thousand men to Denmark to support his uncle, King John, against the 'rebellious Swedes'. Early in the following year, he embarked on what was to be a final expedition to subdue the Lord of the Isles, Donald Dubh, son of Angus Og. Parliament, meeting in Edinburgh, agreed that while the Earl of Huntly attacked rebel strongholds on the mainland such as Eilean Donan at the head of Loch Alsh and Strome on Loch Carron, the royal ships should besiege the rebels' base in the Treshnish Isles some miles west of Mull – the castle of Cairn na Burgh.

After spending several days inspecting his ships, which were being fitted out for the expedition under Sir Andrew Wood at Dumbarton, James embarked heavy guns. On 11 May he transferred the command from Sir Andrew to the Earl of Arran, who supposedly had more experience of artillery. The squadron put to sea and proceeded to bombard the recalcitrant island chiefs into submission. The castle of Cairn na Burgh was bombarded until it surrendered. Maclean of Lochbuie, MacQuarrie of Ulva and MacNeil of Barra were brought to stand trial for treason. The squadron returned to Dumbarton before the end of June having accomplished its task, though one of the king's ships had to return in August to show the royal standard around the islands and stayed there on patrol until the end of the year.

This artillery experiment led to the development of guns specifically designed for mounting on ships. Soon afterwards James demonstrated his continued interest in sea-going by visiting the Isle of May in the small barque *Colomb*, whence he was rowed the six miles to Anstruther on the Fife coast.

In the spring of 1505 the royal squadron sailed from Dumbarton carrying guns borrowed from Edinburgh Castle. It headed for Arran and successfully recaptured the earl's castle from a rebel named Walter Stewart. Opposition to the king by Torquil Macleod of Lewis and several of the powerful island and west-coast chiefs continued for another two years but in the autumn of 1507, after a series of operations involving William Brownhill's ship and others commanded by John Smollett, burgess of Dumbarton, and William Brown in cooperation with the Earl of Huntly, Stornoway Castle in Lewis – Torquil Macleod's stronghold and the last rebel base in the Western Isles – surrendered to Huntly and his force which included a ship named the *Raven*. Donald Dubh, the last claimant to the Lordship of the Isles, was captured but Torquil Macleod escaped.

In May 1505 the construction of a dockyard for shipbuilding was started at Newhaven near Leith under James IV's direction. He had visions of himself leading the 'crusade against the infidel', taking a great fleet to the shores of Palestine and advancing thence against the Turks. To this end he sought bases in the Mediterranean. Already several ships and boats had been built for him. Some of the timber came from Fife, from the shores of Loch Lomond and from the surviving areas of the great Caledonian forest, but much had to be imported. He sent agents all over western Europe to purchase the necessary timber and cordage to supplement whatever could be obtained locally.

Margaret was built in the Pool of Airth on the south bank of the Forth between Stirling and Falkirk. It took two and a half years to build her and cost about six thousand pounds Scots – approximately a quarter of the king's annual revenue. She displaced between 600 and 700 tons and was armed with 21 guns. One of the king's most experienced sea captains, John Barton, was given command of her. It was he who in 1507 was entrusted with taking the young Archbishop of St Andrews on a diplomatic mission to the continent. John and his brothers, Robert and Andrew, were shipowners and shipmasters from Leith. Their father, John, had been a favourite captain of the king's father, James III. In 1481 when a royal ship had been captured by a superior force of Portuguese vessels and some of his men had been killed, repeated appeals to the Portuguese for compensation had failed – until James III had issued letters of marque licensing John Barton's ship as a royal privateer.

James IV now held the three Barton brothers in high regard. He gave lands in Fife to Andrew, paid friendly visits to Robert's house and entrusted him with conveying a silver model of a ship to the shrine of St James in Spain. When *Margaret* was launched, James renewed the letters of marque and sent a herald to the Portuguese court to proclaim that the letters were again in force. This soon landed him in trouble. Robert Barton in *Lion* captured a Portuguese ship but was imprisoned when he called at the friendly Dutch port of Veere because of legal action by some Portuguese merchants. It took representations at the highest level to obtain his release. Not long after this incident John, who had borrowed *Lion* from his brother, captured another Portuguese vessel and was sued by the owners of the cargo. Between 1508 and 1510, both Andrew and Robert Barton were sent by King James to assist the Danes against the city-state of Lubeck. Robert returned in 1510 and urgently requested more ships and men to help the Danes. However, a third complaint in June 1510, this time from the Portuguese king, forced James to suspend the letters of marque, but with James's agreement King John of Denmark issued similar letters to the Barton brothers, who then continued their depredations. When Andrew captured a Breton ship, complaints were lodged with the Lords of Council in Edinburgh by Margaret of Savoy on behalf of the Antwerp merchants who owned the cargo. By failing to appear before the Court, Andrew lost official sympathy and the Lords of Council declared that if he were to be captured 'justice sald be ministrat'.

Andrew Barton returned to Denmark and James unwisely renewed his letters of marque, inevitably antagonising the English as well as the Portuguese. Andrew thereupon sailed south with *Lion* and *Jenny Pirwin* towards the English Channel and into the merchant shipping lanes, claiming cavalierly that the King of Scots was at war with the Portuguese. He proceeded to intercept and plunder every ship which did not outsail him. The plundered merchants decided to appeal to Henry VIII of England, who, according to the treaty then in force, should have asked James IV of

Scotland for redress. Instead he ordered the Admiral of England, Sir Edward Howard, and his brother, Lord Thomas Howard, to seek out and destroy Andrew Barton. Two ships were fitted out for the operation and put to sea in June 1511.

The two English vessels became separated by bad weather. Lord Thomas was lying in The Downs, a safe anchorage off the Kent coast, when he sighted *Lion*. He gave chase and soon overhauled her. Barton, though massively outgunned, fought back. Lord Thomas's ship came alongside and boarded *Lion*, but Andrew's crew fought on courageously. Only when Andrew himself was mortally wounded, shot through the heart by an English archer, did the survivors surrender. Meanwhile Sir Edward Howard had fallen in with *Jenny Pirwin*. He pursued and boarded her. All her crew were killed or captured and the two ships were brought into Blackwall on the Thames on 2 August. When James IV demanded redress from Henry VIII, he received the supercilious reply that 'the fate of pirates was never an object of dispute among princes'. Henry freed the Scottish sailors but kept the ships. *Lion* became the second man-of-war in the English navy, which added to James's chagrin. He was already incensed by the death of one of his most able sea captains at English hands.

The keel of the four-masted *Michael*, arguably the greatest warship in the world at the time of her launch on 12 October 1511, had been laid down at Newhaven, Leith, in 1507. Sir Andrew Wood supervised her construction. She cost nearly thirty thousand pounds Scots – millions of pounds sterling in today's money. *Michael*'s length is reported variously as 180 feet (55 metres) or 240 feet (75 metres) and she had a beam of 35 feet (11 metres). According to Robert Lindesay of Pitscottie, her sides were 10-feet (3-metres) thick, which sounds extraordinary in a timber-built ship. She probably displaced about 2,000 tons. Her main armament comprised twelve guns on each side, and three bronze guns of longer range – two aft and one forward – all cast by the king's master melter in Edinburgh Castle and each needing six wagons to carry it down to the ship. *Michael* also had 300 smaller guns. Apart from officers, her complement comprised some 300 mariners, in addition to specialist gunners and 'men of war'. The ship was victualled with 3,000 gallons of ale, 240 salted beef carcasses, 5,300 salted fish, 13,000 loaves of bread and 200 stones of cheese as well as fresh provisions. After *Michael* was launched and lying at anchor, James tested her by firing a cannon ball at her side. According to Pitscottie, it 'shook her not and did her little scathe'.

The year 1512 proved to be eventful but ominous for the Scottish king. On 10 April his queen, Margaret – sister of Henry VIII – gave birth to a son and heir, another James. In the following month his ship *Margaret*, commanded by John Barton, captured several Flemish privateers. Barton sent him a ghoulish gift of the pirates' heads in barrels. In May the French ambassador, de la Motte, sailed into Ayr harbour with a fleet of captured merchant ships and fishing boats which he proceeded to sell to the inhabitants. He also brought with him an amended form of a draft treaty, which guaranteed mutual support and contained an undertaking that neither party would make a truce with England without the other's consent. De la Motte left the following day in a ship belonging to William Brownhill. She was escorted by the ships of Robert Barton and David Falconer but, unluckily, they were intercepted by an English squadron. Falconer's ship was sunk but the other ships got away to France. The amended treaty was finally confirmed by Louis XII on 12 September 1512.

Meanwhile James visited Newhaven daily to monitor the progress of his shipbuilding programme. At Leith he was reported to have 13 large ships, 19 smaller ships and a captured English vessel. It was later claimed by the English ambassador that in reality there were only ten small ships there, one of them rigged as a warship, several smaller craft and a galley which was being built to act as a tender to *Michael*, now renamed *The Great Michael*. Henry VIII, aware of James's preparations, was determined not to become embroiled in a war with Scotland when already at war with France. He was told that the Scots would keep the peace provided their ambassadors were given safe conduct to France and their merchant ships were given safe passage but there was no conclusive settlement. The English ambassador was in Edinburgh on the day John Barton's ship returned from France loaded with wheat, gunpowder and cannonballs.

James played for time whilst trying to persuade Louis to send ships, men and artillery from France. Henry still had no son and heir and James's eye was fixed firmly on the English throne. James's ambassador to France was the ambitious, two-faced Andrew Forman, Bishop of Moray, for whom loyalty to God, king and country was secondary to personal advancement. He sailed for France in John Barton's ship at the end of March 1512, well provided with bread, capons, salmon and ale from the king's stores. Around the same time a letter reached James from Henry, 'well and lovingly written', asking for *The Great Michael* to be given to him and assuring him that Scottish ships would not be molested provided they did not consort with French ships. Henry also informed his brother-in-law that compensation had been paid for the two Scottish ships captured the previous year. James understandably, however, declined to give away his greatest warship.

On a stormy day at the end of November 1512 a French ship ran up the Firth of Forth before an easterly gale and anchored off Leith. On board was the French ambassador, de La Motte, with promises and gifts for the Scottish king. The ship dragged its anchor and was blown up river to Blackness, where *The Great Michael* lay at anchor. James was rowed out to his flagship and received the French ambassador on board. The Frenchman had brought gifts – wine, cannon, gunpowder and shot – and cloth of gold for Queen Margaret. James was asked to take action 'to diminish the arrogance of the English', who had joined with Ferdinand of Aragon and the Pope in a 'Holy League'. Louis of France offered James a bribe of fifty thousand francs and made vague promises to assist him in a crusade against the Turks when the war in Europe was over. James did make one final attempt to avert war by trying to persuade Henry to enter a truce with France but he got no answer.

In mid-February 1513 *Petite Louise* sailed out of the Forth with the French ambassador and James's emissary James Ogilvie on board, bearing letters to the French king and to the Pope. These contained the ominous news that James had decided to invade England at midsummer. To the Pope, James argued that he had tried to keep the peace but that Henry VIII's refusal to give safe-conduct to his ships or to his ambassadors obliged him to resort to force. Work on his ships at Newhaven continued and brass cannons were being cast in Edinburgh Castle.

The French ambassador did not reach Scotland until the middle of May with Louis's agreement to James's invasion plans. He declined to send any form of assistance until the Scottish fleet joined the French fleet off the French coast. Louis particularly wanted *The Great Michael* on his side. The fleet of which James had boasted fell far short of expectations. Its nucleus comprised three ships which were short of guns and a fourth which was under-manned. The rest had failed to materialise.

On 25 July, while troops were mustering in the Borders for an attack on England and Henry VIII and the greater part of his army had embarked for France, the Scottish ships sailed down the Firth of Forth with orders to rendezvous with the French fleet. There is some doubt as to the final composition of the Scottish squadron, but at most it numbered eleven vessels: the four royal warships and seven others belonging variously to John Barton, William Brownhill, Captain Chalmers and others. *The Great Michael* now had a complement of 303 seamen and 7 gunners, *Margaret* had 60, *James* 55, *Barque Mytoune* 13 and *Barque of Abbeville* 83. Chalmers' barque had a complement of 60 and the others perhaps 40 each. The crews comprised fighting men as well as sailors.

Ominously the fleet was commanded not by John Barton or by a man of the calibre of Sir Andrew Wood, but by the relatively inexperienced Earl of Arran, James Hamilton, who had been made Admiral of Scotland in recognition of his knightly accomplishments. For reasons best known to himself, the earl steered north-east instead of south-east, cleared Fife Ness and Buchan Ness, then set course for the Pentland Firth. After skirting the north coast of Scotland, he sailed through the Minches, more intent upon defending the Isle of Arran and the Clyde from any English threat than on linking up with the French navy.

On 9 September 1513, James IV, with the flower of Scotland, was killed at Flodden – the most disastrous military defeat in the nation's history – while the under-manned, inadequately equipped, poorly commanded and inexperienced Scottish fleet sailed south through the Irish Sea. The Earl of Arran had pointlessly stopped en route to ransack the town of Carrickfergus on the Antrim coast, garrisoned by the English, instead of hastening to make contact with the French fleet. Louis had expected the Scottish squadron to arrive off Brest in the middle of August. He had intended it to link up with seven ships from Brittany and that the combined fleet would then join a squadron of Norman ships lying in the estuary of the Seine.

Petite Louise lay off Villerville throughout the second half of August, ready to conduct the Scottish fleet into Honfleur where they were awaited by a ship newly completed in a French yard for Robert Barton. In the event, the Scottish ships did not appear off the French coast until after Flodden. Early in November the squadron, depleted by three ships which Arran took it upon himself to lend to Louis, returned ingloriously to the Firth of Forth without having exchanged a single shot with the enemy. *The Great Michael* never returned to Scotland but was sold the following year to Louis for forty thousand francs. It was an ignominious end to James IV's navy. On 13 November, John Barton was carried ashore to die in Kirkcudbright and in August 1514 Scotland joined France in a treaty with England.

♒ CHAPTER 4 ♒

Sectarian Warfare

After James IV's death at Flodden, his infant son James V, aged just 17 months, was crowned king at Stirling. The death of an exceptionally able, if unpredictable monarch, together with some 30 of his theocracy and aristocracy, and 10,000 of the flower of the nation, left Scotland rudderless in an uncharted sea. The English had been merciless. The few who were captured were killed and every corpse was stripped naked. Two years after the battle, Sir Andrew Wood died and was buried in Upper Largo parish church after a distinguished and loyal career in the service of both James III and James IV.

The widowed Queen Margaret, who was only 23 years old, now became regent of Scotland. She married Archibald Douglas, the Earl of Angus, but her regency lasted less than two years before John, Duke of Albany, supplanted her. In 1517 Albany renewed the 'auld alliance' with France and it was agreed that in due course James V should marry a French princess. Scotland was still a predominantly Catholic country whereas Henry VIII of England, brother of Queen Margaret and thereby uncle of James V, had severed England's ties with Rome as a result of his divorce from Catherine of Aragon and encouraged the Protestants, setting the scene for sectarian warfare. Scottish Protestants tended to look to England for support.

Scottish ships continued to raid the east coast of England and to harry English merchant shipping. In 1522 a punitive English expedition raided the Firth of Forth and attacked Leith and Kinghorn in Fife with gunfire. They left when four French ships arrived with reinforcements for the Scottish defences. The following year, while Scots ships blockaded the Humber, English troops burned the abbeys at Kelso and Jedburgh and an

English captain, Christopher Coe, captured seven merchant ships homeward-bound for Scotland, but Scottish ships managed to retake *Jenny Pirwin*.

While the regent Albany was away in France making arrangements for James V's marriage, Queen Margaret and her pro-English supporters regained power but in May 1528 the young king, now 16 years old, escaped from the clutches of the Douglas family to Stirling Castle. There he rallied support and in July entered Edinburgh with an army to assert his right to rule.

Before long, trouble in the western Highlands and islands engaged his attention. The Earl of Argyll, the king's lieutenant in the west, had been feathering his own nest at the expense of the MacDonalds and was feuding with the Macleans. Lauchlan Maclean of Duart had married the daughter of the Earl of Argyll but in 1523, growing tired of her, he put her on a rock at low tide and left her to drown. She was rescued by a passing boat. The Campbells then took every opportunity to exact reprisals from the Macleans. In the spring of 1531, James decided to lead an army north to impose his authority and he managed to enforce a temporary peace.

In 1532 Scottish ships interrupted trade off Start Point in the English Channel and from February to April the east coast of England was virtually blockaded. Off the Scottish west coast, the English warship *Mary Willoughby*, which had been sent to 'punish wild Scots', was captured in 1533 by the galleys of Hector Maclean of Duart. She became part of the Scottish navy and was apparently busy and successful in Scotland's interests for 15 years. Similarly, in 1534 the *Mary Walsingham* of Yarmouth was captured by the galleys of a local chief while fishing off the Shetlands.

In 1536 James V sailed from Kirkcaldy to Dieppe to marry Princess Madeleine, the delicate 16-year-old daughter of the King of France – only for her to die seven months later. Almost immediately James was married by proxy to Mary of Guise. She had been considered as a possible fourth wife for Henry VIII, who had described her as 'a lady of majestic stature and graceful proportions'. She had turned him down, perhaps because of his reputation, but her marriage to James V was yet another cause of Henry's increasing antagonism towards his nephew and the country he ruled.

Trouble between his supporters and rebellious clans obliged James to visit the west coast once more with a display of force. He sailed from the Firth of Forth in May 1540 with a large and heavily armed fleet piloted by Alexander Lindsay, who had learned his skills in the brilliant Huguenot school of navigators and explorers based in Dieppe and Le Havre. Many Scots had accompanied these French adventurers on raids to the Caribbean and beyond. Lindsay compiled a sophisticated 'rutter' or pilot book of the coasts as he accompanied James to Orkney, Lewis, Skye, Mull, Islay and Kintyre before putting into the Clyde and disembarking at Dumbarton. James brought back with him any local chiefs who were suspected of causing trouble. Those who promised obedience were released in exchange for hostages but some were confined until the king's death two and a half years later. This royal cruise had the desired effect: there was 'great quietness and obedience' in the isles and the rents for crown lands began to be paid with regularity.

In 1542 the English vice-admiral John Cary blockaded Scottish commerce and fisheries for the whole of the winter while Scottish ships in the Bay of Biscay unsuccessfully attempted to intercept an English convoy sailing north from Bordeaux. An English squadron put to sea from the east coast to attack the Scots but returned to harbour on learning that 21 Scottish warships had been sighted off Holy Island, 15 miles south-east of Berwick. In fact this was the *Mary Willoughby* and *Salamander* returning to the Firth of Forth with 19 English prizes. The intermittent hostilities continued when English admiral William Woodhouse patrolled the North Sea between Berwick and the Humber, taking prizes and forcing a French squadron to return home. However, the French did succeed in bringing troops and supplies to the west coast and the relief of Dumbarton, which was under siege.

Warfare broke out in the Borders before James, under pressure from the Roman Church, which feared the spread of Protestantism from England, raised a reluctant army. It was heavily defeated on 24 November 1542 at Solway Moss to the west of Carlisle. Two weeks later James's queen, Mary of Guise, gave birth to the baby who would become Mary Queen of Scots. James had set his heart on a male successor and only a week passed before he died at Falkland Palace in Fife, heartbroken. In a period of less than two years both his sons had died, his foreign policy had failed to achieve stability or prosperity, internally Scotland was riven between the pro-French and pro-English factions and their Catholic and Protestant supporters. Finally his army had been routed while his navy barely existed. Although James was aged only 30, it was all too much.

Henry VIII managed to secure a peace treaty with Scotland on the understanding that the infant Mary Queen of Scots would be betrothed to his son, Edward. He demanded that she be placed in his custody and in breach of the treaty he seized a number of Scottish merchant ships. A French convoy had brought money and supplies to Scotland in June. The treaty, which was highly unpopular in Scotland, was annulled by the Scottish parliament in December and the alliance with France was renewed.

Henry VIII, furious, sent his fleet into the Firth of Forth and landed armies at Leith. They captured Edinburgh, looted and destroyed much of the city in what became known as 'the rough wooing'. The Scots retaliated with a victory at Ancrum Moor in February 1545. Four months later French ships landed 3,500 troops in the Clyde in support of the Scots. While this was happening the last Lord of the Isles, Donald Dubh, made an unsuccessful attempt with a fleet of 180 galleys to invade Ireland and bolster his sovereignty over the isles.

Henry VIII died in January 1547 but the war with Scotland continued. In March three Scottish ships – *Lion*, *Lioness* and *Marie-Celeste* – were captured off Yarmouth. Meanwhile, although the pro-French Catholic faction were still in power bolstered by Cardinal Beaton of St Andrews, persecution of the Protestants, culminating in the martyrdom of George Wishart in 1546, united the opposition. John Knox grasped 'the sword of the Lord' and was party to the assassination of Cardinal Beaton in his castle at St Andrews. At the end of July 1547, however, the Protestant garrison of the castle, where Knox had been made chaplain, surrendered to the Earl of Arran, Governor of Scotland, after bombardment by a French fleet. John Knox was among those captured and sentenced to row in the French galleys. Only six weeks later Arran commanded a Scottish army which was heavily defeated at Pinkie, near Musselburgh. The English put garrisons on islands in the Forth and occupied Dundee and Arbroath. In January 1548 French ships managed again to land supplies for the Scottish garrison at Dumbarton. The six-year-old Mary Queen of Scots was sent for safety to the island of Inchmahome in the Lake of Menteith and a year later, to avoid capture, she sailed from Dumbarton for France where she was to be brought up by the family of her mother, Mary of Guise.

In June 1548 over 6,000 French troops had been landed at Leith to prevent a takeover by the Protestant army of the Duke of Somerset. Their presence, coupled with an attempt by Mary of Guise to raise a tax to support the French troops and strengthen defences against the English, had the effect of fanning the flame of Scottish nationalism – particularly strong amongst those of the population who were Protestant. February 1550, however, saw the English evacuation of Broughty near Dundee, the last English garrison in Scotland, and in 1554 Mary of Guise replaced the Earl of Arran as Regent of Scotland.

In May 1559 John Knox returned from exile and landed at Leith, having been refused permission to travel through England. Later in the same year thousands more French troops were also landed at Leith. An English squadron was ordered to attack any French ships en route to Scotland and early in 1560 it arrived in the Forth and blockaded the French in Leith while an Anglo-Scottish Protestant army besieged them. Mary of Guise died in June and after her death the Treaty of Edinburgh was signed, whereby both England and France withdrew their troops, leaving Scotland to settle its own religious future. Two months later the Scottish parliament renounced the Pope and adopted Protestantism but on 19 August 1561 the 18-year-old Catholic Mary Queen of Scots, widow of the French Dauphin, followed in John Knox's footsteps and returned to Scotland, disembarking at Leith after a five-day voyage from Calais.

The circumstances of Mary's journey were not uneventful. The decision to return to Scotland had been her own but the arrangements had been undertaken jointly by representatives of France and Scotland. The titular Lord High Admiral of Scotland, the conceited young James Hepburn, Earl of Bothwell, was involved. He arrived in Paris accompanied by the sea-going Bishop of Orkney and Lord Eglinton, who was known to be involved in piracy on the high seas, in order to complete the arrangements.

Queen Elizabeth of England, who feared both the young Scottish queen's Catholicism and her well-founded claim to the English throne, had been debating whether or not she should send ships to intercept her cousin en route to Scotland. She had ships patrolling the North Sea, ostensibly to control piracy. By the time she decided against interfering and wrote to Mary to give her that assurance, the Queen of Scots was already at sea on her way to Leith. It had been suggested to Mary by a French cardinal that she should leave her jewellery behind in France because of the dangers she faced. Her riposte was to ask why it was safe for her if it was dangerous for her possessions.

The day of embarkation failed to produce fair weather. It was dull, with poor visibility. The two royal galleys left Calais harbour under oars at about noon on Thursday, 14 August, convoyed by two warships. As they cleared the harbour, the Queen and her entourage were witnesses to an unfortunate accident: a fishing boat went down with all hands. 'What a sad augury for a journey!' the young queen was heard to exclaim. There is no record of any attempt to pick up any of the drowning fishermen.

The young queen's retinue comprised three of her French uncles as well as the four Scots Marys famous in song – Mary Beaton, Mary Seton, Mary Livingston and Mary Fleming – and a company of poets, musicians and chroniclers. Their departure was observed by the English ambassador's servant, who reported to his master that he had seen two great galleys, one white and one red, accompanied by two other vessels. The news was immediately communicated to England – presumably by fast boat across the Channel.

On board the white galley, Mary was in tears. She had lived in France since early childhood and although the decision to return to Scotland had been her own – albeit under pressure – it was wholly understandable if she dreaded what lay ahead.

The ships were just north of Flamborough Head on Sunday, 17 August when they were intercepted by English ships, which saluted the royal galleys but arrogantly boarded and examined the accompanying ships, making the excuse that they were looking for pirates. Lord Eglinton was detained and his ship, which was carrying the queen's stable of horses and mules, was forced to put into Tynemouth. Eglinton was later released and allowed to return to Scotland but the animals were held by the warden for a month or more on the spurious grounds that they had no permit to proceed across the border. The remaining ships, shadowed by the English fleet, proceeded through mist and haze on a course north by north-west, then west until the Berwickshire coast loomed through the fog.

The passage had taken two days less than expected. The queen had forbidden whipping of the oarsmen, which was customary practice, but the light wind had been favourable. No doubt each galley was fitted with a dipping lugsail, which would have doubled their average speed to three or four knots in a following breeze. As the little convoy entered the Firth of Forth, the mist thickened to fog, which John Knox interpreted as an omen of the 'sorrow, dolour, darkness and impiety' the young Catholic queen would bring to her native land. Nevertheless, despite the gloomy weather and the low spirits of those who accompanied her, Mary disembarked, reportedly smiling, to spend her first night on Scottish soil for 13 years. A fresh chapter in Scotland's history had begun.

⚓ CHAPTER 5 ⚓

Prize Money, Privateers, Piracy and Trade

During the Middle Ages prize money was a major, if not the main, motivation for a young man to go to sea in a warship, privateer or pirate vessel: money from the sale of booty, captured ships, or the ransom of prisoners. The scale of distribution between officers and crew became an established convention or, in the case of pirates, a subject of witnessed agreement between captain and crew member at the outset of a predatory voyage. For the able seaman, the attraction of serving in a privateer, in preference to a ship of a royal or republican navy, was overwhelming: discipline was less harsh and his potential share of prize money was greater. It was not depleted by an admiralty prize court or embezzled by corrupt dockyard officials or senior officers. This kind of corruption was a major source of resentment amongst those who did the fighting and took the prizes.

The dividing line between privateers and pirates was ill-defined. While pirates acted on their own account, privateers were licensed by letter of marque, issued by a government or sovereign to attack and if possible capture ships of any nation carrying merchandise to or from countries at war with their own. Many moved from semi-legality into piracy and back again as fate and fortune dictated. So-called 'international law' – even today no more than a loosely defined collection of principles, conventions and agreements – scarcely existed. The English cousins, Sir Francis Drake and Sir John Hawkins, fell into this double-dealing category as did John Barton and his sons, serving James III and James IV of Scotland part-time, half a century earlier. The notorious seventeenth-century Scottish pirate, Captain William Kidd, set out as a privateer licensed by the English

Admiralty but succumbed to piracy as his career regressed. Some merchant shipowners got the best of both worlds by obtaining letters of marque from their governments, while still trading on their own account.

Although privateering was not formally abolished until the Declaration of Paris in 1856, prize money from the sale of ships and cargo captured by ships of the Royal Navy was distributed on a scale which varied over the centuries, right up to the end of the Second World War. After a prize had been 'condemned' (the official word meaning 'approved as a legitimate prize') by the Prize Court, the sovereign – later the Admiralty – was entitled to a half share; the rest was in theory distributed on an agreed scale to all those in the ship that had captured the prize. Admiral Anson, in the course of his voyage round the world from 1740 to 1744, took over a million pounds in prize money, of which his own share was one hundred and twenty-five thousand pounds – an enormous sum in that era. At the end of the Second World War the amounts distributed after various legitimate deductions by the government were drastically reduced: an admiral of the fleet got forty pounds and an able seaman just four pounds. After 1945 the practice of awarding prize money was terminated.

The dependence of both Scotland and England on foreign trade meant pirates and privateers had ample targets for their profession. Scotland's exports were limited to those of an exclusively rural economy. Even mining for coal or iron ore was a rural occupation and smelting was practised in areas where timber was readily available. In the sixteenth century, Scotland's main exports were raw wool, linen, hides, some knitwear, smoked and dried fish and meat, salt and coal. Home production of grain, timber and iron barely met demand and much had to be imported, together with pitch, tar and almost all luxury goods such as wine and fine cloth. Scottish exports and imports were mostly shipped across the North Sea, to and from the Low Countries, France and the Baltic, constantly running the gauntlet of pirates.

Records of piracy are as old as the records of trade. Robert Davidson, the Provost of Aberdeen who died leading his citizens against the Lord of the Isles at the Battle of Harlaw in 1411, had nearly met his death as a pirate – narrowly escaping being hanged on the seashore. As an innkeeper, wine merchant and customs inspector, he provided information to the commander of the Scottish fleet, the Earl of Mar, who was authorised as a privateer to take 'enemy' ships. In 1410 Robert Davidson went to Harfleur in Normandy as Mar's agent to sell the cargo of a captured Dutch merchant vessel. He carried a French safe conduct, which protected him from any action by the ship's owners. Unfortunately for him, it transpired that the cargo belonged to the powerful Hanseatic League and when he got home he was charged with piracy. His death at Harlaw in the following year possibly saved him from a less honourable fate.

A Captain John Davidson, who was eventually hanged for piracy 'within the floodmark at Leith' in 1551, was first arrested with members of the Barton family from Fife in 1548. He was told to produce 'an English prisoner taken in woman's clothes' at Queensferry, or pay a one-thousand-pound fine and to bring his prize – presumably a ship – to Leith. In 1549 John Davidson, a Captain John Hume and the Bartons were ordered to 'help attack English ships in Aberlady Bay', 'to bring his booty from Montrose' and in 1550 to bring a 'Spanish prize from Burntisland'. After being arrested for a debt to a Frenchman, he was convicted of piracy for taking a French ship at Bordeaux in October and hanged the following year.

Ruari Og MacNeil of Barra made a successful career of piracy. Galleys from the Hebrides raided as far south as the Bristol Channel. In 1580 they captured a cargo worth thousands of pounds from the *White Hart* (not a pub!) of Bridgwater in Somerset. The lucrative business of piracy became a Scottish tradition, practised by many up and down England's coasts, though it must be remembered that – using the Navigation Acts – the English would not allow Scottish ships to trade normally with English ports.

When the Spanish Armada set sail in May of 1588 bound for England, Francis Drake and John Hawkins took a holiday from privateering with the authority of England's queen to help her lord high admiral, Lord Howard of Effingham, repel the would-be invaders. Scottish ships were not involved but Scottish Catholics prayed for the Armada's success. As late as December 1592, documents were intercepted in the hands of a Scottish Catholic emissary about to sail from the Clyde, inviting the Spaniards to use Scottish soil for a Spanish invasion of England.

The poorly planned and incompetently commanded Spanish expedition of 1588 was beaten by a combination of bad weather, hesitancy and well-handled English ships. Following indecisive action off Gravelines, strong winds became a gale, and by 3 August the Armada, still 100 ships strong, was being driven northwards with the English fleet in pursuit. The Spaniards attempted to enter the Firth of Forth but most were dispersed by violent storms and scattered across the waters around the Orkney and Shetland islands. The flagship of the Armada, *El Gran Grifon*, ran aground on Fair Isle. The sailors, reported as being 'for the most part young beardless men', were transported to Anstruther in Fife where they were given food and shelter while their repatriation was being negotiated.

Admiral Medina Sidonia attempted to marshal his scattered fleet and to lead them on a southwesterly course through the Hebrides and down the west coast of Ireland but the weather was foul. More of his ships were blown ashore on Hebridean islands and at least a quarter of the remainder wrecked on the Irish coast. In the same storm the Scottish merchant ship *Girona* was shipwrecked at Dunluce. Less than half of the original 132 ships of the Armada eventually got back to Spain, their crews weakened by starvation, thirst and disease. One Spanish ship which reached Tobermory, *San Juan de Sicilia*, was blown up – possibly with the connivance of Sir Lachlan Mor Maclean of Duart, who was an enemy of the MacDonalds and an ally of Queen Elizabeth of England. The Earl of Argyll, who had been living in Spain, returned with intelligence that the ship contained a stupendous treasure in gold coin and ingots but a prolonged treasure hunt lasting 400 years has brought little to light beyond a few guns, candlesticks, coins and only a single piece of Spanish gold, now in the British Museum.

In 1589 a marriage was arranged between the Scottish king, James VI and 14-year-old Princess Anne, younger daughter of the Protestant King Frederick II of Denmark. On her voyage to Scotland in November, the princess became stormbound in Oslo. The ardent young king could not wait and sailed across the North Sea in May 1590 to fetch her, impatiently writing passionate poetry to shorten the journey. On arrival in Oslo he was so impressed by her beauty that he arranged to wed her without delay. They stayed in Norway for a prolonged honeymoon, until April of the following year. During the return voyage to Leith, whilst sailing past the Bass Rock a mile or so off the Berwickshire coast, a freak storm suddenly arose, threatening the safety of the royal vessel although she did not founder. The storm coincided with the holding of a 'black mass' on the foreshore at North Berwick by Francis Hepburn, the new Earl of Bothwell, who for reasons unknown was inimically disposed towards the young king. Bothwell was involved in further incidents in Edinburgh, including an attempt to break into the Palace of Holyrood. In April 1591 he was put on trial for witchcraft and jailed.

On 26 March 1603 James VI heard the news that Queen Elizabeth had died and that he had become James I of England, uniting the crowns of the two rival kingdoms. In October 1604 it was decided to introduce a common currency and to abolish customs tariffs between the two countries.

One of the king's earliest acts after his accession was to condemn the use of tobacco. He called it 'a custom loathsome to the eye, hateful to the nose, harmful to the brain, dangerous to the lungs, and in the black stinking fume thereof nearest resembles the horrible Stygian smoke of the pit that is bottomless'. This powerfully expressed opinion had less effect on maritime trade than might have been expected in an age when kings were thought by many to rule by divine right. James would have been surprised if he had known that the import of tobacco and cigarette manufacture, together with shipbuilding and engineering, would one day generate much of the prosperity of Scotland's largest city.

In 1606 the king ordered a 'union flag', combining the crosses of St Andrew and St George, to be flown by all ships of both nations. Although his motive was probably to strengthen his hold upon the crowns of both England and Scotland, his directive must have been welcomed by merchant shipowners because it made their merchandise less vulnerable to pirates flying the flag of the rival nation. In 1608 it was decided that all Scots and English born since James's accession in 1603 should have dual nationality.

While politicians debated the issue of political union between Scotland and England, the Western Isles and seaboard continued to be a source of concern. Settlement in the islands in 1600 by the so-called Gentlemen Adventurers of Fife, with the purpose of making the inhabitants more law-abiding, had little effect, although in 1609 the clan chiefs did accept the Statutes of Iona, binding them to take responsibility for their followers. When Lord Ochiltree was sent in 1610 to pacify turbulent islanders, his troops were transported from Ayr in ships hired locally. In the same year three merchant ships from Leith were armed and fitted out by the Privy Council to subdue two English pirate ships operating among the Orkney Islands. Both ships were captured and their crews tried. Thirty men were hanged on 26 July 1610 on the sands of Leith.

Another English naval expedition, which included the royal ship *Phoenix*, sailed to the Western Isles in 1614 to assist the Earl of Argyll in suppressing the MacDonalds of Islay. They succeeded in destroying a few galleys and capturing Dunyvaig Castle. Soon afterwards English ships were sent from London to protect Scots merchantmen from pirates and Scottish ships were commandeered to suppress a local rebellion in Orkney. In 1616 the Earl of Argyll, supported by English warships, suppressed another rising in the Western Isles and the Privy Council sent Captain David Murray, in a ship provided by the English, to clear Scottish waters of pirates, wherever they came from. The royal ship *Charles* was also sent to Orkney to levy rent from foreigners fishing in Orkney waters.

England found herself at war with Spain again in 1626 and Spanish ships operating from the Netherlands and Dunkirk preyed on both English and Scottish shipping. Letters of marque were issued to skippers of ships from Fife and the Lothians to act as privateers against the Spaniards. They were effective but it was found necessary to commission a squadron of three warships – commanded by Captain David Murray and two subordinates – to reinforce the privateers. The ships from Dunkirk continued to wreak havoc while the three warships, under the overall command of the Earl

Marischal, lay 'idle and unprofitable in dry harbours without any purpose . . . to go to sea'. According to one report, the Earl Marischal stayed ashore while his three captains 'drank and made good cheer'. When ordered to leave harbour, the sailors refused because their pay was in arrears.

Consequent upon the union of the crowns and the urgent need to control piracy off the coasts of the British Isles, a system was introduced which was to continue until the Act of Union in 1707: the 'levying' through the Scots Privy Council of Scots seamen to man ships of the English navy. On 11 July 1626 an order was issued for a levy of 500 mariners from 20 Scottish coastal burghs. During the two Dutch wars later in the century Scots seamen were regularly 'pressed' into the English fleet and when the Dutch closed the Baltic to the English, masts for English warships were requisitioned from Scotland. In 1664 Charles II levied 500 Scots seamen for the English navy, paying a bounty of forty shillings per man in addition to English naval pay, but the Scots were keener by far to serve in privateers, where the pay, conditions and prize money were markedly better. To some extent the system of 'levying' protected Scots seamen from the press gang, because the responsibility for finding men was delegated to the coastal burghs, which could afford to take more time and may have found it a useful way of getting rid of undesirables. Charles freely offered privateering commissions to Scots skippers. It is thought that between 30 and 50 Scottish skippers received letters of marque to operate as privateers between 1664 and 1674.

The signing of the National Covenant in Greyfriars Kirkyard, Edinburgh, in 1638 was virtually a declaration of war — but a war which had little do with the sea. Rather the issue was again religion. By 1638 Charles I had managed to alienate two powerful factions in Scottish society. First, there were the Presbyterians, who believed that Christ, not the king, was the head of the Kirk. Secondly, by introducing bishops into government, Charles had weakened the traditional role of the Scots nobility. Matters were brought to a head in 1637 when Charles insisted, without consultation, on introducing an English-style prayerbook into Scotland. It incited a revolution and set in motion the events that would lead to the outbreak of civil war. With regard to maritime matters during the Civil War, in general the parliamentarians and Protestants had the support of the merchant classes, and therefore had access to merchant shipping. The Royal Navy also supported parliament and in 1640 an English fleet mounted an effective blockade of the Firth of Forth but had to return south when the Scots royalist army occupied Durham.

In June 1650 the young Charles II, setting a pattern for his Stewart descendants, sailed from the continent, where he had been in exile after his father's execution, and landed at Garmouth, a tiny fishing village on the south side of the Moray Firth at the mouth of the Spey. He swore an oath of loyalty to the Covenanters and made his way to Dunfermline.

On New Year's Day 1651 Archibald Campbell, Marquis of Argyll, now the most prominent signatory of the Covenant, crowned Charles II at Scone as King of Scotland, England, Ireland and France, but on 20 July Cromwell's troops defeated an army of Charles's supporters at Inverkeithing, close to the modern naval base of Rosyth. By May 1652 Charles's supporters' last stronghold, Dunnottar Castle on the Kincardineshire coast, surrendered, followed in August by the surrender of the Marquis of Argyll. Charles had escaped back to France in the previous September.

⚓ ⚓ ⚓

The infamous Captain William Kidd, son of a Presbyterian minister, was born in 1645 in Greenock, which had been a thriving seaport for a century or more, trading with Ireland and exporting large quantities of herring to France and the Baltic. Greenock had taken the motto, 'Let herring swim that trade maintain'; there was no better place to learn the seaman's trade.

William Kidd's name first appears as a member of the mixed British and French crew of a ship at anchor in the Leeward Islands off St Kitts in 1689, which was then French-occupied. England and France were at war. He and the other British sailors hijacked their 20-gun brig and sailed it to the neighbouring English-held island of Nevis where Kidd, who had a dominating personality and physique, was appointed captain. The ship was re-named *Blessed William* after the English monarch in order to please the authorities. Captain Kidd earned a substantial reward for his part in an attempt to land troops on the French island of St Martin before helping to defeat a French squadron of five ships. The expedition's commander reported that Kidd had 'fought as well as any man I ever saw . . . and was a mighty man'. The crew of the *Blessed William* were not so pleased. They had expected prize money and loot. A sea battle with no prizes taken was not their idea of a good deal and they objected to Kidd's domineering attitude. One night while he was ashore the crew weighed anchor and sailed away with everything Kidd possessed.

The sympathetic Captain-General of the Leeward Islands presented Kidd with the recently captured French vessel *Antigua*. He chased *Blessed William* to New York but found she had departed for the St Lawrence. New York appealed to William Kidd. Illegally acquired cargoes could be sold and refits undertaken with no questions asked. A struggle was in progress to oust the self-appointed leader of the English colony. Once again William

Kidd earned the gratitude of the authorities by helping to remove the interloper. He was voted a handsome sum of money by the provincial assembly and decided to stay in New York. He married a wealthy widow and, for a time, settled down to a domestic life, using *Antigua* for a bit of privateering on the side. He kept well in with leading citizens such as fellow Scots Robert Livingston, a merchant, and James Graham, who was Attorney-General.

After four years of domesticity William Kidd eventually became bored. He decided to sail to London and seek a royal commission as a privateer. The political climate was far from ideal. The Royal Navy was desperate for seamen to fight the French and objected to competition from privateers who could pay them better. The press gangs were active everywhere. However, Robert Livingston got him an introduction to the Earl of Bellomont, a zealous and influential Whig who was a member of the Irish peerage, a Member of Parliament and about to be appointed governor of the Massachusetts Bay Colony. Bellomont prevailed on Kidd to accept command of a vessel fitted out to intercept pirate ships returning with valuable cargoes from the Indian Ocean to New York. The booty could then be sold profitably to the benefit of a consortium comprising Bellomont, his friends (among them King William) and Kidd himself. There was no difficulty in obtaining the requisite commission. Kidd was to recruit seamen on a 'no prey – no pay' basis which would appeal to their gambling and aggressive instincts.

By early February 1696 Kidd's new ship, *Adventure Galley*, launched from Castle Yard, Deptford, was fitted out and ready for sea. She displaced 287 tons, carried 34 guns and could be propelled by oars or sail. His multi-racial crew of about 140 men were 70 per cent English, 18 per cent Dutch and included only seven Scots. On the way down the Thames, Kidd's vanity prevented him from showing the customary courtesies to a king's ship. As a result he was stopped and some of his best men were press-ganged for the Royal Navy.

By August, *Adventure Galley* was in New York, loading her hold for a voyage to the Indian Ocean. Kidd's objectives had changed. He had decided to sail for Madagascar, from where pirate ships sailed laden with priceless cargoes and he could hope to seize greater riches and keep a bigger share.

Adventure Galley sailed for Madeira, where Kidd embarked wine and replenished his supplies of water and fresh provisions. About a week later he anchored in the Cape Verde Islands to load salt for preserving food and more water and fresh food before the South Atlantic crossing. In mid-December, after weeks alone in the vastness of the ocean and temporarily becalmed, they were overtaken by three English warships under

Commodore Thomas Warren. This was no planned interception. The squadron's sailing master had died and due to an astonishing lack of professionalism they had lost both their way and the ships they were convoying, and run out of fresh food. Scurvy had broken out. Warren ordered Captain Kidd to navigate them to Cape Town. Kidd, acutely aware that his healthy crew might be conscripted, could not refuse. Instead he tried to ingratiate himself with the commodore and his captains, dining and drinking with them. Returning to his ship one morning in the small hours, he quietly ordered his crew to get their oars out and silently pulled away from the squadron. The three warships had no oars to follow. When dawn broke *Adventure Galley* was over the horizon and Kidd had convinced the commodore that he was up to no good.

Adventure Galley headed for the pirate base on the south-west coast of Madagascar where beef, rice, fruit, timber and fresh water were plentiful. After the long Atlantic crossing the ship was in need of careening: scraping off the accumulated marine growths. This task, completed while the ship was beached on a small island, took five weeks, during which Kidd lost a fifth of his crew through tropical disease. When ready, he decided to head for the Red Sea where the pilgrim fleet to and from Mecca was said to offer rich rewards. In his mind he had already crossed the hazy boundary between privateering and piracy.

Perim Island is situated in the straits where the Red Sea joins the Gulf of Aden. Ships have to pass through a 20-mile-wide channel outside the island's anchorage and this is where Kidd decided to await suitable victims. The crew suffered intense heat for a fortnight while he sent his quartermaster to reconnoitre the harbour of Mocha, 50 miles to the north. There lay 17 merchantmen ready to embark pilgrims on return from Mecca. In the course of two expeditions to Perim Island, to grab scarce water and meat, Kidd's crew killed some local inhabitants. News travels quickly in the desert. The ships at Mocha were warned. Kidd made an attack on the convoy when it left Mocha on 11 August but was beaten off by armed escorts and achieved nothing except to alert shipping in the area to his presence.

Captain Kidd's crew were beginning to become mutinous. They were short of water, the hull had begun to rot and leak, they had won no prize money and had lost confidence in a captain who was clearly intent on outright piracy. The risks had increased without an increased prospect of reward. When a small ship was sighted flying the cross of St George, a shot was fired across her bows. She hove to and her captain, Thomas Parker, came on board. While Kidd and his quartermaster were cross-examining him, men from *Adventure Galley* boarded Parker's ship against Kidd's orders, tortured some of her crew to find out if they had any treasure concealed and extorted just enough gold coins to buy urgently needed supplies. Kidd kept Parker prisoner because of his knowledge of the coast and seized a Portuguese sailor to act as interpreter.

Kidd set course for Carwar, bypassing Bombay. There some of his men took a ship's boat and tried to get away. Those who were recaptured were flogged, but ten men succeeded in reaching the East India Company's agent. He reported that Kidd was maintaining control 'by his own strength, being a very lusty man, fighting with his men on any little occasion, often calling for his pistols and threatening any one that durst speak anything contrary to his mind to knock out their brains . . .' When *Adventure Galley* left Carwar she was intercepted by two Portuguese warships of 22 and 44 guns, sent from Portuguese Goa to hunt him down. Kidd ran from them. When the smaller and faster ship overtook him, he crippled her with his guns before the other came within range. Then he outsailed the larger ship and later declared arrogantly, 'No Portuguese will ever attack the king's colours again!'

With his ship again in need of careening, Kidd sailed to the Laccadive Islands and remained there for some weeks. His crew treated the local inhabitants disgracefully, forcing them to do the hard work, using their boats for firewood and raping several women. When the natives responded by slitting the throat of the ship's cooper, the crew attacked a village, killing and wounding many inhabitants.

Until leaving these islands, Kidd's policy had been not to attack ships of the powerful and influential East India Company. When he had previously intercepted a merchantman and discovered she was a company ship, Kidd demonstrated his personal courage by refusing to issue arms to his crew, who were desperate for loot, and preventing them from leaving their own ship – but mutiny was simmering. On 20 October the ship's gunner, William Moore, became the catalyst. Kidd heard him discussing ways of taking a Dutch ship – the Dutch were England's allies at the time – and called him 'a lousy dog'.

'If I am a lousy dog, you have made me so,' Moore replied. 'You have brought me to ruin and many more!'

'Have I ruined ye, ye dog?' Kidd retorted. He picked up a heavy wooden bucket, whirled it round and brought it down on Moore's head. The gunner collapsed and was carried below, where he died the next day, his skull fractured. Kidd had destroyed the last vestige of loyalty between himself and his ship's company. Thereafter discipline was only maintained by fear.

For three more months *Adventure Galley* cruised the Arabian Sea while her mutinous crew slaved at the pumps in enervating heat. Flying French colours, they waylaid a Dutch-owned ship but Kidd was able to justify her capture when her captain presented a French pass. She was renamed *November* and taken in tow. Her cargo was sold to a renegade East India Company employee and at last Kidd was able to distribute some prize money to his crew. Two more small prizes were taken but their cargoes were only of sufficient value to augment *Adventure Galley*'s stores. Then, at the end of January 1698, Captain Kidd hit the jackpot in piratical terms: a capture which would make several small fortunes but would ultimately secure his conviction for piracy.

With French colours at the masthead, they intercepted the 400-ton *Quedah* off Cochin on the Malabar Coast. She had an English captain but belonged to an Indian mogul who regularly traded with the East India Company and was carrying a very valuable cargo of silk, rare textiles, sugar, opium, iron and saltpeter. Kidd sold some of the cargo to a crooked agent to enable enough prize money to be distributed to his crew to keep them quiet. Then he renamed the ship *Adventure Prize* and took her in tow, while another small prize was taken in tow by *November*, and manned with prize crews drawn from men he could still trust. As the monsoon season was imminent, Kidd's flotilla of four vessels set sail for Ile Sainte Marie, a recognised pirate base off the north-east coast of Madagascar. *Adventure Galley* was barely seaworthy and the pumps had to be manned day and night. When they entered the anchorage they were approached by a boatload of ruffians who knew that Kidd had a commission to capture pirates. With disarming honesty Kidd assured them that he 'was as bad as they'. His transformation to pirate was complete.

From this moment, Captain William Kidd's fate was sealed. First, he had to accept that *Adventure Galley* was now incapable of rounding the Cape and weathering the Atlantic. She was beached and burned so that her iron fittings could be recovered. He delayed several weeks at Ile Sainte Marie, faced with crossing two oceans in the clumsy, Indian-built *Adventure Prize*. Eventually, with a crew comprising men who wanted to return to America rather than prolong a career in piracy, he sailed for the West Indies, reaching Anguilla in the Leeward Islands in April 1699. There he heard that he had been declared a pirate by the London government and was being hunted. A renegade customs officer helped him to sell enough of the cargo to enable him to buy a sloop big enough to carry the remainder and to abandon the unseaworthy *Adventure Prize*. He managed to sell some of the most valuable and bulky merchandise before setting sail in the sloop for Boston, visiting various harbours en route to deposit returning sailors, sell more loot profitably and garner intelligence about his likely reception on arrival. He had fabricated a story that his only illegal acts had been performed under threat from his officers and crew and that he had killed William Moore in self-defence.

The sloop reached Delaware Bay in early June, where he discharged more men and cargo and met his wife and daughters, whom he had not seen for three years. After receiving a letter from the treacherous Bellomont, which amounted to a guarantee of safe conduct, he sailed round Cape Cod to Boston with the intention of reaching some compromise with his original partners. From Kidd's arrival in Boston until his execution in London 18 months later, the story is one of deceit, greed, self-interest and political jockeying by all concerned – and very little to do with the sea. He was grabbed when he appeared before the Massachusetts Council to explain himself, brought back to London and incarcerated in Newgate Jail. Following a prolonged juridical charade, it took just two days – 8 and 9 May 1701 – for William Kidd to be tried and convicted of murder and piracy. He had no lawyer to defend him. He never gained access to the papers he had sought for his defence. He arrived drunk at the gallows and delivered a tirade against those who had given evidence for the prosecution. At the first attempt to hang him the rope broke. Given a second chance, William Kidd expressed repentance. This time the rope held and his neck was broken.

It is difficult to identify any good emanating from the life of William Kidd. Although he was an accomplished seaman and navigator, not lacking in personal courage, he was undoubtedly greedy, vain, violent, dishonest and guilty of both piracy and murder. He was made a scapegoat for the sins of many others but perhaps he helped to focus the attention of European governments on the need to give higher priority to eradicating piracy and better protection to ships on the high seas plying a legitimate trade.

⚓ CHAPTER 6 ⚓

Stormy Passage to Union

The second half of the seventeenth century saw a continuation of religious rivalry, civil strife, sporadic skirmishing across the border between Scotland and England, intermittent war between England and her continental trade rivals, the Great Fire of London, plague and piracy at sea. There were Scots sailors in English merchant ships and in warships which participated in a series of battles. Scots were excluded from trade with the Americas, Africa and the East by the English, who had at least five times the population and around forty times the revenue of Scotland. It was a period of decline in the size and quality of England's Royal Navy – from 76 ships and 12,000 men in 1679 to 24 ships and 3,000 men by 1684. Discipline, morale and professionalism had sunk to their nadir. It was largely due to the dedication of the remarkable Samuel Pepys, Secretary of the Admiralty, that the trend began to be reversed as the seventeenth century drew to a close.

Few individual Scots achieved sufficient distinction to be recorded in the maritime history of the half-century before the Act of Union in 1707. Captain Kidd and Alexander Selkirk were exceptions. The latter was not the first sailor from Largo in Fife to earn a niche in history. Sir Andrew Wood had won a place two centuries earlier with far greater credit. Alexander Selkirk first went to sea in 1695. He became an experienced, if ill-disciplined, seaman and was sailing master or navigator of the *Cinque-Portes* on a privateering expedition in the South Pacific when he quarrelled with the captain. He was put ashore in 1704 on the uninhabited Pacific island of Juan Fernandez, some 400 miles from the coast of Chile, by some accounts at his own request. There the 28-year-old sailor survived by ingenuity for five years, until rescued by a ship of the Royal Navy. His adventures gave Daniel Defoe the inspiration for *Robinson Crusoe*.

The inhumanity of abandoning a man on a deserted island was nothing compared to the brutality of a society which, two decades earlier, had allowed two women to be drowned from a Wigtownshire beach because of their religious beliefs. Margaret McLauchlan, a woman in her 60s, and an 18-year-old girl, Margaret Wilson, were sentenced to death for refusing to forsake their adherence to the extreme Presbyterian Cameronian sect. They were tied to stakes at low water, the older woman further out in deeper water. No doubt it was expected that her inundation by the incoming tide would persuade the young girl to recant. Neither did so and Margaret Wilson's head was finally forced beneath the waves by a soldier so that she would drown more quickly.

Another horrendous example of brutality was the massacre of Glencoe on 13 February 1692, when 35 MacDonald men and an unknown number of women and children were slaughtered by soldiers of the Argyll regiment, commanded by Robert Campbell of Glenlyon. Glencoe opens into Loch Leven, a sea loch linked to the Atlantic by Loch Linnhe, the Firth of Lorn and the Sound of Mull. It is a spectacular but infertile glen whose inhabitants would have been as dependent on fishing and the sea as they were upon cattle and the land. They had no materials for manufacture and no goods to trade other than cattle, smoked or salted fish, hides and possibly wool, although sheep were of far less importance to the Highlander than cattle.

The order for the brutal massacre was signed by King William, although it was drafted by a lowland Scot, Sir John Dalrymple. His flimsy excuse was that the chief of the MacDonalds of Glencoe had failed to take the oath of loyalty to King William before the New Year's Day deadline – although he had made an attempt to do so and been delayed by bad weather. Revenge was possibly the underlying reason for the massacre by men commanded by Campbell of Glenlyon – Campbells against MacDonalds, an echo of the conflict that had disrupted the western coast and islands for centuries.

At first glance this atrocity may seem to have little to do with the stormy passage to political union between Scotland and England and even less to do with the story of Scots and the sea. This view, however, ignores the reaction to the atrocity of Jacobites, Catholics and Episcopalians, who comprised a major part of Scotland's population. Whatever their attitude to the MacDonalds as a clan, many saw the massacre as an act of despotic punishment or cruel revenge, authorised by an alien king. It helped to crystallise opinion for or against union with England and undoubtedly reinforced support for the Jacobite cause, which would erupt more than once in the following century. In the two decades after the massacre, only the Darien disaster would have a greater influence upon Scottish attitudes to their southern neighbour. The Act of Union, when enacted in 1707, would profoundly affect future activities of Scots in maritime trade, fisheries, exploration, emigration, shipbuilding and service in the royal and merchant navies.

In 1695 the Company of Scotland was founded with the object of encouraging trade with North America, Africa and any accessible parts of Asia. These were years of famine in both Highlands and Lowlands after a succession of disastrous harvests. The company was founded more in hope than faith because English merchants were determined to corner all trade and obstruct their Scottish and continental rivals.

An attempt had been made in 1621 to establish a Scottish colony across the Atlantic to rival New England and New France on the east side of North America. King James gave William Alexander from Stirling the titular proprietorship of Nova Scotia and what are now the Maritime Provinces of Canada. French colonists, who were already established in the area, called their colony Acadia. James awarded baronetcies to any Scots willing to promote emigration to Nova Scotia. William Alexander's son, also William, sailed with seventy men and two women to settle there. However, when Charles succeeded James to the throne four years later he became involved in a disastrous war with France which undermined the colony's chances of success.

Scottish revenues were being used to re-establish a small navy but there was insufficient tax revenue to deploy ships to assist the colonists across the Atlantic. Although a Scots sea captain, David Kirks, captured Quebec from the French in July 1629, a month later the Scottish settlement of Fort Ochiltree in Nova Scotia was taken by the French, and Acadia, which had been occupied by Scots, had to be returned to them in 1632 in payment of a debt by the crown. William Alexander and his colonists were left deep in debt.

Scotland's need for overseas investment and maritime trade had become paramount. It was realised that the country's backward economy, crippled by famine, was in desperate need of stimulus. Even in fishing villages on the east coast, where witchcraft was often blamed for disasters at sea, witches could hardly be blamed for the shortages of oatmeal, barleymeal and flour, and a dearth of exports to exchange for basic necessities.

It was a Scot, William Paterson, the founder of the Bank of England in 1694, who put forward a plan that may have been good in theory but in practice became a disaster. He argued that if the English parliament had given trading monopolies to English companies, the Scottish parliament should do the same for Scotland. He had his eye on 'the Door of the seas, the Key of the universe' – the Isthmus of Darien, 200 miles east of where the Panama Canal now links the Atlantic with the Pacific. The concept was splendid, the market research and execution abysmal.

Darien was in the Spanish sphere of influence. It was also within striking distance of English and French colonies in the West Indies. Paterson's hope was that it could be settled by Scots, then developed into a profitable trans-shipment area and entrepôt between the two oceans, but he had reckoned without the debilitating climate, the jealousy of other nations and the total lack of sympathy on the part of King William.

In June 1695 the Scottish parliament passed an act which established the Company of Scotland, trading to Africa and the Indies with half of its capital to be subscribed by Scottish shareholders and the balance by investors from England or elsewhere. Initially the shares were well subscribed, but the powerful English East India Company immediately saw a threat to its monopoly. Its directors lobbied the English parliament, which declared that it would impeach any English subscribers. They were forced to withdraw their investments, which had the immediate effect of lowering the value of shares. King William also opposed the scheme because it would have broken the English trade monopoly. Without his approval, foreign merchants would not invest in the Scottish company. By now, however, national pride had been thoroughly roused and an enormous effort was made to raise two-thirds of the capital in Scotland, instead of the original aim of just half. This was eventually achieved and in July 1698 the three ships *Caledonia*, *St Andrew* and *Unicorn* set sail from Leith with 1,200 emigrants on board and an odd assortment of cargo including wigs, stockings and bibles. William Paterson went with them. The voyage, which took four months, seems to have been uneventful but took a heavy toll on the emigrants' health.

First impressions on arrival in the Gulf of Darien were favourable. The natives were friendly, if not over keen to offer valuables in exchange for items from the Scots' strange cargo. One colonist described the soil as rich, the air good and temperate and the water sweet. The captain of *St Andrew* claimed that the harbour could accommodate 1,000 of the greatest merchantmen in the world. A fort was built on a small promontory, huts erected and clearings made for the cultivation of yams and maize. However, no foreign merchant ships appeared – only one or two spy ships. Provisions began to run low and fever broke out. One in four cases proved fatal – among them William Paterson's wife. An attempt to get provisions from Jamaica was foiled by a royal proclamation forbidding any English colonist in the Caribbean or Americas to have any dealings with the Scottish settlers, who were also threatened by the Spaniards.

By July of 1699 it had become clear that the venture was heading for disaster. The survivors re-embarked, some of them already infected with fever, and set sail for the east coast of North America. Only about half of the original colonists survived sickness and starvation; a quarter eventually returned home, among them the widowed William Paterson, but the rumours of their failure reached Scotland 12 days too late. A second party of 300 would-be colonists had already set sail for Darien. They arrived in November to find an over-crowded graveyard, a partly ruined fort and a few empty huts. They lost one of their two ships through fire but re-embarked in the other and made for Jamaica.

The commander of a third expedition unwisely did not wait for confirmation of the previous expedition's arrival but set sail with 1,400 emigrants on board at the end of September. They arrived at Darien to find a scene of desolation. Perhaps fortunately, they had not brought enough axes or saws to rebuild the ruined settlement, but they re-occupied Fort St Andrew. The Spaniards in the area were aggressively 'dog in the manger'. A Spanish army and fleet moved to attack the fort. Campbell of Fonab, a leader of the expedition, delayed them by attacking their encampment early in the New Year, but the fort was soon blockaded by land and sea. The Scots defended it for more than a month. Only when the number of men fit to hold a musket was down to less than 300 did they surrender. The Spaniards, admiring their courage, allowed the remnants of the Scottish expedition to march out, carrying their sick and wounded, with drums beating and colours flying. On 1 April they re-embarked in three ships, finally abandoning the colony. They called at Jamaica but the English settlers refused to help them. One of the Scottish ships was wrecked off Cuba. The other two set course for New York but fate dealt the venture a final blow: the ships ran into a hurricane and both were lost with all hands.

Darien was a bitter and expensive lesson. Two thousand men and women and a huge sum of money, which Scotland could ill afford, had been lost. The realisation dawned that until Scottish merchants had free access to overseas markets, the Scottish economy could not thrive. Despite the political and emotional opposition to union with England, Scottish merchants and those to whom money was more important than traditional independence began to lean towards the concept of a united kingdom.

In March 1702, Queen Anne succeeded to the throne. Uninspiring but determined, her ambition was to rule a United Kingdom of England and Scotland where freedom of religion could be practised. After prolonged and bitter argument, the English parliament passed the Alien Act which prohibited the import of cattle, coal and linen from Scotland into England – a lethal blow to trade – and simultaneously declared that unless Scotland ratified the Act of Settlement, or alternatively entered into negotiations leading to union, then all Scots would be classed as aliens. The English Admiralty then issued an edict that ships of the Scottish Navy should strike their national colours and salute ships of the English Navy. When Captain Thomas Gordon, senior captain of the two Scottish frigates *Royal William* and *Royal Mary*, put into Tynemouth in June 1706, he was fired on by the English ship *Dunwich* for failing to do this. He wrote to complain and ask guidance from the Earl of Wemyss, Lord High Admiral of Scotland. He received a somewhat ambiguous reply to the effect that since both countries had the same sovereign he should act 'as one English man of war comes to another'.

While this political battle was in progress, the English continued to disrupt Scottish trade. Following the collapse of the Darien venture, the Company of Scotland attempted to send merchant ships to Africa and India. The English captured and retained one of these, *Annandale*, whilst another, *Speedy Return*, belied its name and disappeared. In August 1704 the English merchant ship *Worcester* was obliged to take shelter in the Firth of Forth. She was immediately seized to compensate for *Annandale*. The rumour spread that *Worcester* was a pirate ship and that she had sunk *Speedy Return*. In actual fact *Speedy Return* had herself turned pirate, but this did not prevent Captain Green of *Worcester* and his crew from being arrested, tried and found guilty. Meanwhile, members of the crew of *Speedy Return* had landed in England. Despite an order from Queen Anne that Captain Green and his crew should be reprieved, the judges, who were threatened and intimidated by an Edinburgh mob, issued a death sentence. The captain and two of his crew were hanged between high- and low-water mark, on the sands of Leith. The incident was so serious, and English indignation so violent, that war almost broke out. However, the Duke of Argyll was persuaded, as High Commissioner with virtually presidential power, to intervene and persuade the Scottish parliament, albeit reluctantly, to start negotiations anent a treaty of union.

The Alien Act was repealed. The Scottish demand for a federal union succumbed to the promise of 'full freedom and intercourse of trade and navigation', with Scottish representation in the Westminster parliament. Customs duties had to be raised to the English level but the English government handed over a relatively large sum to be paid in compensation to the shareholders who had invested in the Darien venture. Scotland retained its legal and educational system – and its established church.

The politics of the negotiations and the narrowness of the victory for those in the Scottish parliament who favoured Union are irrelevant to maritime history but the outcome was of tremendous significance both to the development of the Scottish economy and the future of maritime trade. Union simultaneously opened up the opportunity for Scots to join the Royal Navy and other crown services, to serve in the East India Company and other trading companies, to emigrate to the colonies or to occupy senior political and government posts in the United Kingdom and the empire. England gained Scottish technical, commercial and administrative skills and a catchment area for recruitment which provided a high proportion of all the soldiers and sailors who fought in the Napoleonic and colonial wars from a population representing little over 10 per cent of the British Isles as a whole. The royal assent to the Act of Union was given on 6 March 1707.

⚓ CHAPTER 7 ⚓

United Kingdom and United States

The century between the creation of the United Kingdom by the Act of Union in 1707 and the outbreak of the Peninsular War in 1808 was a period of immense significance for the development of the Scottish economy and the country's relationship with the sea. From 1707 the Royal Navy of England became the Royal Navy of Great Britain and the Scottish royal navy simply disappeared. There had been Scots serving in both navies for many years, but in the eighteenth century the Royal Navy became a way of life for many from north of the border.

Article IV of the Act of Union allowed Scottish exports to enter English and colonial markets without payment of customs duties and Article V gave Scots the privileges of the Navigation Acts, which afforded Scottish-owned merchant ships the protection of the Royal Navy and allowed them to carry merchandise between Great Britain and its colonies. However, these privileges were bought at a high price. Scots became allies in England's wars to wrest trade and economic supremacy from the Spanish, French and Dutch and were obliged to support the London government's attempts to extract taxation from the American colonies.

The Hanoverian dynasty only reigned by sufferance over those Scots who were not Presbyterian and more than once the Jacobite sentiment of the supporters of the exiled Stewarts erupted into military action. In 1708, when their hopes were still very much alive, James Stewart, the only legitimate son of James VII of Scotland and II of England and called by some 'the Old Pretender', sailed from France with a convoy of French ships carrying an invasion force organised by Louis XIV, in an attempt to meet up with some of his supporters who were waiting for him on the shores of the

Firth of Forth. They reached the Firth but when an English squadron appeared the French force turned back.

Following Queen Anne's death, James Stewart again sailed from France in October 1715 and, having avoided Royal Navy patrols, landed at Peterhead. The Jacobites, who comprised Episcopalians from the North East as well as Catholics from the Highlands and elsewhere, occupied Aberdeen, Inverness, Perth and Dundee, but were held up at Stirling. When news came in January that the Duke of Argyll was marching on Perth with government troops, James Stewart and John Erskine, Earl of Mar, who had raised James Stewart's standard at Braemar, fled ignominiously, without telling their army, and took ship from Montrose back to France. The Jacobite clansmen – betrayed as they would be repeatedly by the Stewart dynasty – dispersed north and west to their glens.

In 1745, Prince Charles Edward Stewart, the Old Pretender's son, set sail from France and landed on the Isle of Eriskay in the Outer Hebrides with seven companions. Six weeks later, on 4 September 1745, he entered Perth with a small army comprising some Jacobite clansmen and Catholics from Ireland. The rising pursued its futile course from Prestonpans via Derby to disaster at Culloden. His escape to France, aided by Flora MacDonald, is commemorated in the haunting 'Skye Boat Song', which disguises reality in a mist of romanticism.

Following the Jacobite defeat in 1746, the British government exploited their fighting skills. Just 13 years after Culloden, soldiers recruited in the Highlands, commanded by General James Wolfe, who had been present at that battle, and supported by the Royal Navy, scaled the Heights of Abraham and took Quebec, overcoming fierce French resistance. Wolfe's Highlanders were among the earliest of a flood of Scottish recruits to the British Army and Navy throughout the second half of the eighteenth century and beyond. By the time of the Napoleonic wars it has been estimated that very nearly one in four of the male population of the Highlands was serving in either the Army or the Navy. This was as much the result of government reprisals, deprivation of land, poverty and unemployment – not to mention the press gangs – as of fighting spirit.

Daniel Defoe, best known as the author of *Robinson Crusoe*, had been a secret agent in Scotland before the Union, working to promote it. He had developed an affection for the country, although he tended to regard it as an English possession. He wrote a travel book, disguised as fiction, which throws an interesting light on Scotland two decades after Union.

Everywhere he went he was made welcome. He adjudged the Scottish gentry the most civilised in Europe. He described the area between Leith and Edinburgh, now occupied by the New Town, as 'a spacious, rich and pleasant plain'. The Canongate appeared to him 'perhaps the largest, longest and finest street for buildings and numbers of inhabitants, not only in Britain but in the whole world', but he also said, 'I believe that in no city in the world so many people live in so little room'. In Dumfries he observed that 'the benefits of commerce . . . appear visible' but in Kirkcudbright he saw ' a harbour without ships, a port without trade, a fishery without nets, a people without business'.

He described Glasgow as 'the cleanest, beautifullest and best built city in Britain . . . a very fine city . . . its four principal streets are the fairest for breadth and the finest built that I have seen in one city together'. From a Londoner, this was astonishing praise. However, in casting a verdict upon the city's growing imports of cotton, sugar and tobacco from across the Atlantic and the export of indentured servants, he commented: 'these they have in greater plenty and upon better terms than the English, the poor people offering themselves fast enough, thinking it their advantage to go'. This might be regarded as an urban forerunner of 'the clearances' which were soon to desolate the Highlands. Destitute Scots sold themselves into virtual slavery in the West Indies by legal indentures with a term. When the term expired the individual had seldom accumulated enough capital or possessions to become free and either continued as a servant in return for board and lodging or else became absorbed into the native community. This, rather than slaves taking the surnames of their masters, is the most likely origin of the many Scottish surnames borne by natives of the Caribbean islands. The English encouraged Scots to come to the West Indies believing they were 'very good servants'. Beggars could not be choosers. Many youths and children were also kidnapped from west and north Scotland and sold into servitude – one incident being recorded as recently as 1805 to Barbados.

When the Act of Union opened trade with the American colonies, Glasgow merchants were quick to exploit the growing demand for tobacco – throughout Europe, not just in Scotland. Raw tobacco and cotton were imported – particularly from Virginia – in exchange for basic manufactures, either direct or by a three-cornered trade: manufactured goods and indentured servants to the West Indies, sugar and rum to the American colonies, tobacco and raw cotton back to Glasgow. Huge fortunes were made and much of the wealth was invested in the city. As a result the infrastructure of a great port began to take shape and the 'tobacco lords' became the middlemen of the European tobacco industry. Sadly, as tobacco was generating wealth, the long-established herring fisheries of the Clyde, the Minches and the North Sea were suffering both from a decline in the number of shoals and from increasing competition from northern Europe –

particularly from Holland. With the American Declaration of Independence, however, the tobacco trade collapsed almost overnight. The city turned to the manufacture of textiles and then to engineering and shipbuilding in the nineteenth century.

Union had been sold to the Scots on promises of wealth from free trade with England. The Royal Bank of Scotland was established in 1727 specifically to provide the Bank of Scotland with competition, to administer the tail-end of the financial settlement under the Act of Union, and also to act as treasurer to the newly established board of trustees for fisheries and manufactures. In practice, although the export of Scottish cattle for finishing in English pastures and sale in English markets yielded profits to some, the trade in coal, salt, wool and textiles, which had previously been protected from English competition, was suffering badly. In September 1736 riots broke out in Edinburgh as an indirect outcome of the introduction of heavy taxes on imported tea, wine and brandy, which in turn gave impetus to smuggling.

⚓ ⚓ ⚓

Smuggling developed a well-organised, undercover, second-tier trading structure in Scotland, complete with agents and shipping. Smugglers often worked hand in glove with the customs and excise officers. A wide range of commodities was smuggled into ports and harbours, lochs and bays from the Solway Firth to the Moray Firth and from Berwickshire to Ross-shire. Whisky was the main commodity smuggled internally and exported, because a heavy duty was imposed after the Act of Union. The main commodities smuggled into Scotland were tea from the Baltic, Geneva gin from the Low Countries, wine and brandy from France and tobacco. In fact, any goods subject to import duty were smuggled, provided the ratio of value to weight and bulk made it profitable.

Smuggling was so widely approved by the general public that it was virtually impossible to obtain evidence or witnesses to testify against anybody taken to court. Sometimes smuggling involved whole communities such as Kippford on the estuary of the River Urr, which flows into the Solway, or Collieston under the cliffs facing the North Sea, 15 miles north-east of Aberdeen. The tiny island of Cara, which lies to the west of the Kintyre peninsula and a mile south of Gigha, has two claims to fame: the attic of Cara House is said to be inhabited by the ghost of a MacDonald murdered by the Campbells; and the island was used by smugglers from Gigha, Jura and Islay in the eighteenth century. Perhaps the stories of a ghost were a ruse to deter the inquisitive.

Ordinary work might come to a halt in a coastal village when a familiar smuggler's lugger was sighted and a 'run' was in the offing. Clandestine signals would inform the vessel if the coast was clear and the smuggler would indicate where he intended to land his contraband, invariably after dark. The community would organise the transport – packhorses if necessary, or creels to be carried on the back. If time was short or excisemen were in the vicinity, the contraband might be temporarily buried in the sand or hidden in a cave.

The government became increasingly concerned about smuggling and the consequent loss of revenue. Revenue-cutters were deployed to patrol the coasts where the illicit trade was most prevalent. Look-out stations were set up along the coast, and teams of 'riding officers' were engaged to cooperate with them inland. There were many encounters between smugglers and excisemen both at sea and on the beaches. It was not until customs duties were reduced towards the end of the nineteenth century that the smuggling trade became unprofitable and was brought under a degree of control.

Regrettably, the government appears to be losing that control in the twenty-first century. The very length and complexity of Scotland's rugged coastline invites the illegal importation of drugs, which pose a serious threat to the health of the nation. While governments spend millions on combating the menace of terrorism and weapons of mass destruction, an insidious tide of poisonous drugs is infiltrating the British Isles. It *must* be more economic to prevent them from entering the country than to attempt to prevent their distribution and counteract their disastrous effects. It is far too easy for some old rust-tub of a foreign-registered steamer to anchor between one of the international shipping lanes and a remote point or inlet, to off-load the illegal element of the cargo onto a flat-bottomed raft or inflatable dinghy, run it ashore and arrange for it to be uplifted later and driven away in an innocent-looking vehicle. The gathering of intelligence may be the key to detection, but there must be sufficient support in terms of fast patrol boats to board and investigate every suspect vessel. A single modern cutter off the whole length of Scotland's west coast is no deterrent. Many more of the 'flexible and mobile brigades of customs officers' advocated by Customs and Excise are also essential. This is not an area for economy. To put emphasis on health and education while turning a blind eye to the smuggling of illegal drugs is at best illogical, at worst crazy.

⚓ ⚓ ⚓

During the eighteenth century the size of the Royal Navy increased and quality eventually improved, although morale continued to be undermined by poor and irregular pay, by inefficiency and graft at the Admiralty and in royal dockyards, and by the misappropriation of prize money which should have been divided amongst ships' crews but went instead into the pockets of shore-based officers and officials.

Many Scots entered the Royal Navy. John Campbell, for example, born in Kirkcudbright, was a master navigator who rose to the rank of admiral. In 1739 he was serving in a squadron of six ships in the Caribbean when they attacked and captured the Spanish port and treasure-house of Porto Bello. He was Captain George Anson's navigator when Anson was sent around Cape Horn to attack Spanish shipping on the coasts of Chile and Peru, and, if possible, circumnavigate the globe. Anson returned some four years later with just one ship from his original squadron of six, loaded with Spanish treasure, but only 130 of the 510 men who had started the voyage with him. Among them was John Campbell. Scurvy had wrought havoc with the crew, although it was already known that fresh fruit and vegetables could provide the antidote. By the time the celebrated navigator, James Cook, undertook his voyages of exploration to Australia, New Zealand, the Pacific and the Antarctic between 1768 and 1779, the efficacy of fresh fruit and vegetables in combating this deficiency disease had been widely recognised.

James Cook was born in 1725 in North Yorkshire, well away from the coast. He was the son of a Scottish farm worker who had migrated there, married a local girl and rose to be a farm bailiff. James was apprenticed to a haberdasher at the age of 12 but following a dispute with his employer he boarded a ship as a collier's apprentice and by sheer ability rose eventually to the rank of captain in the Royal Navy, becoming one of the greatest navigators of all time.

The skilled botanist who assisted Sir Joseph Banks, the naturalist who accompanied Cook's expedition, was Robert Brown from Montrose, who was responsible for collecting 4,000 specimens.

Captain James Cook's return from his second voyage of discovery in the southern hemisphere coincided with the outbreak of the American War of Independence in 1775. Two years later the Carron Ironworks near Falkirk started production of the latest weapon for the Royal Navy – the Carronade – which would soon become familiar to naval captains. It was a short, cast-iron muzzle-loader, particularly effective at short range.

An incident occurred at sea in 1776 which raised tensions between politicians of the right and left in Scotland. A prominent Scottish lawyer, Thomas Muir, who had devoted his life to parliamentary reform and championing the cause of the working classes, was found guilty of sedition.

Although the government case for the prosecution had been very weak, Muir was sentenced to 14 years' transportation to Botany Bay in Australia. However he was rescued at sea from a British transport by a ship commissioned by American supporters. He was taken to France and was able to continue his radical campaign.

France, hoping to strengthen its hold on colonial possessions in America and eastern Canada, signed a treaty with the United States of America in February 1778 and declared war on Britain four months later. The USA had declared independence in 1776. The threat of attack by Scottish-born John Paul Jones of the American Continental Navy obliged the government to build a new fort at Leith as a defensive measure. In September of the following year, the American commodore's squadron of three ships won a famous victory off Flamborough Head against two ships of the Royal Navy. In September 1783, however, peace was signed with an independent United States of America, while in Canada and India the British gained ascendancy over France.

It would be wrong to assume that the eighteenth century was a succession of wars with little progress in peaceful activity. The Scottish banks were established. The Carron Iron Works was founded. Merchant ships were being built and James Watt patented his steam engine. Important advances were made in agriculture, manufacturing and navigation. The completion of the Forth–Clyde Canal in 1790 was an important event for Scottish trade, linking the North Sea with the Irish Sea and allowing vessels to avoid the long and frequently stormy voyage around Cape Wrath and through the Pentland Firth. The canal could not take large vessels but was an asset for the transport of raw materials such as coal, slate, stone, iron and timber. The linen industry was thriving, based partly on home-grown flax but to a greater extent on raw materials imported from eastern Europe through the ports of Aberdeen, Dundee and Leith.

Improved facilities for trade in the central belt had, however, done nothing to assuage poverty in the Highlands and rural uplands, or to assist the distribution of agricultural produce. Here, emigration became the safety valve. An estimated 20,000 people left Scotland for the colonies between 1763 and 1780. In 1791 some 1,300 Scottish emigrants, most of them extremely poor, arrived in Pictou, Nova Scotia, in four ships. Conditions on board would have horrified any modern traveller. This trickle became a flood in the early nineteenth century – Scots seeking new homelands 'divided by mountains and a waste of seas' from poverty and oppression in the land of their birth.

Emigration may occasionally have been the outcome of adventurous spirit or a reasoned economic decision, but more often than not it was the only solution to desperate need, arising from the selfishness and inhumanity shown by those in power towards the poor and powerless. Those looking for proof should read John Prebble's *The Highland Clearances*.

It was the Duke of Cumberland, nicknamed 'the butcher', who kick-started the emigration flow by his ethnic cleansing operations after Culloden, a catalogue of war crimes and actions intended to achieve virtual extinction of the clan system. The greed of those who ceased to be fathers of their clans and became hard-nosed landowners accelerated it, though there were, of course, honourable exceptions. The replacement of cattle by a shepherd economy, leading to desertion of the glens and overcrowding of infertile coasts, fuelled and swelled the flow west. Recruitment of Highland regiments to fight in the colonial wars, following which many soldiers settled in America and Canada, set a pattern which relatives and clansmen were encouraged to follow. The tide of emigration, exacerbated by poor harvests, potato famines and brutal clearances, continued until the close of the nineteenth century.

The American Revolution temporarily checked emigration but in 1783 the combination of famine and an invasion by sheep – which resulted in one man occupying land previously providing subsistence for 50 – had an effect like thaw on a Highland river. The stream of emigrants became a spate. Starving families walked to any port where agents advertised sailings to the New World. Thousands took ship for Nova Scotia and Upper Canada from Greenock, Fort William, Ullapool, Thurso and Wick. In Fort William a Major Simon Fraser made a profitable business out of selling shares in emigrant ships to those with capital to spare, and simultaneously selling passages to emigrants who could barely scrape together the exorbitant fare. The advertisements for sailings were often criminally misleading in terms of the space and food provided and the time the passage would take. In some ships each passenger had fractionally over two square feet of deck space on which to spend up to eleven weeks at sea. When lying down, they were packed like sardines in a stinking tin. A Fort William contractor profiteered by overcrowding his ships to Nova Scotia so badly that in one ship alone 50 passengers, packed cheek by jowl, died of cholera.

In 1807 a Bill was passed by parliament to make slave trading illegal but conditions in the emigrant ships were often worse than in slave ships. Efforts by parliament to regulate the minimum amount of space per head were ignored by those profiteering from the trade and little attempt was made to enforce the regulations. Ships sailing from Dublin and Belfast were the worst because steerage passage in them cost only a quarter of what it cost from Greenock. Many from the Highlands crossed the Irish Sea to sail from Ireland but passages from Scotland's west coast were almost as deplorable. A Leith shipowner, William Allen, had the temerity to petition the Treasury, ridiculing even the minimal conditions imposed. A governor-general of British North America reported on one such ship to the colonial secretary in London 'so disgusting a picture [that the] . . . vessel admitted no comparison between her and a French slaver brig captured . . . four years ago'. The slaves, of course, had to be in good condition for sale on arrival, whereas nobody had any interest in the welfare of the emigrants. Conditions apart, the emigrants were fleeced at every turn. Disgracefully misled, more often than not they arrived on the far side of the Atlantic sick, half-starved and destitute.

In 1807 also, clearances began from the Countess of Sutherland's estates to make way for extensive sheep farming. By the 1820s Highlanders were leaving for Canada and America at a rate of 30,000 a year. Would-be emigrants needed 30 shillings to buy minimal deck-space for a transatlantic passage and they often had to wait for weeks, penniless, until the ship was full and ready to sail. Their plight in this confined space, seasick and half-starved in the stormy wilderness of the Atlantic, beggars description.

Some attempts were made to organise emigration humanely. For example, Thomas Douglas, fifth Earl of Selkirk, organised the emigration of 800 Highland tenants to form a balanced community on Prince Edward Island in 1803. In 1812 he organised a second settlement in the Red River area of Manitoba.

In 1831 some 58,000 left for Canada; the following year the number was 66,000. In 1848 the Duke of Argyll 'assisted' 500 from Mull and the Inner Hebrides to leave for Canada by paying their passage. By the 1850s, emigration to Canada was exceeded by emigration to the Antipodes, in particular to New South Wales and to New Zealand. The potato famine of the 1840s, first in Ireland, then in the Highlands, had swelled the flood.

Five ships sailed from the Clyde in 1853 under the auspices of the Highlands & Islands Emigration Society, which was backed by prominent clan chiefs and landowners. They were packed with emigrants of both sexes en route to an Australia desperate for shepherds, flockmasters and unskilled workers inured to hardship and low wages. The journey took three months or more.

The only alternatives to emigration for a starving or displaced Highlander were limited opportunities for industrial employment or joining the Army or the Navy. Poverty and semi-starvation had become endemic among those who were landless and not employed by the government or by one of the large estates. In 1874 those faced with starvation were infuriated to see vessels loaded with grain about to depart for the south. Ships were prevented by the local populace from leaving half a dozen ports in north-east Scotland. The long-term effects of the clearances are indelibly branded on the Highlands.

⚓ ⚓ ⚓

All was not well with morale in the Royal Navy at this time. Simmering dissatisfaction over pay and conditions boiled over in April 1797. Pay had not been increased for more than a century, discipline was tyrannical and food vile. There was a mutiny of the Channel Fleet at Spithead and their example was followed in May at the Nore. Before the end of the year the naval mutinies in home waters were resolved by promises of action to improve conditions and pardons for some of the mutineers. In October of the same year Admiral Duncan, who had played a creditable role in persuading the sailors of the North Sea Fleet to return to duty, achieved a decisive victory at Camperdown over a Dutch fleet which was attempting to launch an invasion of Ireland. In 1798 Nelson annihilated the French Mediterranean fleet at Aboukir Bay at the mouth of the Nile, stranding their army in Egypt. Minorca was captured in November. The writing was on the wall for Napoleon Bonaparte. He may have begun to doubt his invincibility.

What were the sailors like who won these victories over the Dutch and French? If asked today to visualise a typical sailor of the Royal Navy in the century between Union in 1707 and Trafalgar in 1805, British subjects might imagine a muscular John Bull, stripped to the waist, with a coloured kerchief round his forehead to stop the sweat from running into his eyes as he manhandled a gun carriage between the timber decks of a man-of-war. In reality, he had a roughly 50:50 chance of being English. The other half of the crew of a typical British warship in the time of Nelson comprised a polyglot bunch of men – and some women – with skins of various shades from dead-white to coal-black. An interesting insight was provided by Captain Martin of HMS *Implacable* shortly after Trafalgar, who wrote to his brother:

> . . . in ascertaining the diversity of human beings which compose the
> crew of a British ship of war, and as I think you will be entertained with
> a statement of the ridiculous medley, it shall follow precisely as their
> place of nativity is inserted in the ship's book . . .

He went on to list them: of a crew of 563 only 285 were English. The remainder comprised 130 from Ireland, 34 from Scotland, 25 from Wales (all higher percentages of native population than the English), 28 Americans,

45 from all parts of Western Europe with the exception of France, 11 from the West Indies and the rest from places as diverse as Brazil, Bengal and Canada! The crew of a privateer would not have been very different, depending upon where the captain recruited them.

The following was written in the ship's paper of HMS *Goliath* by a sailor who served in this 74-gun ship-of-the-line at the Battle of the Nile in 1798 when Nelson's fleet of fifteen warships, less two which had run aground, either sank, burned or captured all but four of the seventeen more heavily gunned French warships which were caught at anchor and ill-prepared:

> . . . any information we got was from the boys and women who carried the powder. In the heat of action a shot came right into the magazine, but the carpenters plugged it and stopped the water running in. I was much indebted to the gunner's wife who gave her husband and me a drink of wine every now and then which lessened our fatigue much. There were some of the women wounded and one woman belonging to Leith died of her wounds. One woman bore a son in the heat of the action; she belonged to Edinburgh.

It was *Goliath* that had led the British line of ships into the attack, five ahead of Nelson's ship, *Vanguard*.

⚓ ⚓ ⚓

Britain's wars in alliance with the Austrians and later with Russia, against the French, Spanish, Dutch and then the Americans, disrupted the high seas from the Caribbean and American coasts to the English Channel and Mediterranean. It is reasonable to speculate exactly how Scotland would have been involved if the Act of Union had not been signed in 1707. Patterns of trade and employment would have been different; possibly Scots would have found themselves fighting on land and at sea on the side of the French and American colonists. Who can say whether it was more advantageous to be cannon fodder for one colonial power than for another? Either way, the Scots would have been pawns in the hands of one of their more powerful neighbours. What is beyond argument is that the Act of Union opened up some areas of overseas trade to Scottish merchants whilst increasing competition in others. At the same time it allowed Scots to enter a much wider range of government, commercial, naval and military employment. It is, however, arguable that England gained more by the Act of Union than Scotland did.

⚓ CHAPTER 8 ⚓

John Paul Jones

John Paul Jones is considered by many to be the 'father of the United States Navy' but the highest rank he attained in the Continental Navy of the United States was commodore. He was, however, made rear-admiral of Imperial Russia's Black Sea Fleet by Empress Catherine the Great.

Born John Paul on 6 July 1747, his father and mother were respectively gardener and housekeeper to the laird of the Arbigland estate situated on the north coast of the Solway Firth near the Kirkcudbrightshire village of Kirkbean. Ships and fishing boats worked from harbours on both sides of the Firth and it was a nursery for seamen. After leaving school at the age of 13, John Paul was apprenticed to a Scottish shipowner based in Whitehaven on the Cumbrian coast – a much busier port then than it is today. He made half a dozen triangular voyages in the brigantine *Friendship* from Whitehaven to the West Indies with general cargo, then on to the American colonies with rum and sugar and back to Whitehaven with cargoes that included tobacco and cotton. He received an excellent training in seamanship, navigation and trading practices, but in 1763, during the recession that followed the end of the Seven Years' War against France, his employer was obliged to sell *Friendship* and John Paul became unemployed. Desperate for work, he accepted appointment as third mate, then chief mate, of two 'blackbirders' or slaveships operating between England, West Africa and Jamaica. He loathed the trade, which he described as 'this degrading insult to humanity'.

On the island of Tobago he met an acquaintance from Kirkcudbright, Sam McAdam, who offered him a passage home in the brigantine *John*, which was engaged in legitimate trade between the island and his home town. Both McAdam and his first mate died of fever during the voyage and John Paul, aged just 21, was the only man on board with experience as a watch-keeping officer. He brought the ship safely back to Kirkcudbright and was rewarded by being made captain. He apparently looked older than his years – stocky, sandy-haired and well built.

John Paul completed more than one successful voyage as captain of the brigantine before fate disrupted his career. The owners had engaged a ship's carpenter, Mungo Maxwell, son of a well-known Kirkcudbright property owner, who proved to be both incompetent and insubordinate. He was brought before John Paul by the first mate and found guilty on both counts. Captains were all-powerful at sea and John Paul sentenced the carpenter to be flogged – six lashes, which was relatively lenient in that era. When the ship reached Tobago, the man lodged a complaint of victimisation with the office of the Court of Admiralty. It was investigated; John Paul and the first mate were cleared and the man was sent home in another ship. He died of fever on passage, a common-enough fate. When John Paul got back to Kirkcudbright, however, he found himself charged with murder by the man's family. He was able to get the necessary evidence to clear himself but his reputation was damaged and he decided to distance himself from his home port. The owners of *John* gave him an honourable discharge and he was offered the post of captain of a London-based brig, *Betsy*, also engaged in the West Indies trade.

Early in 1773, outward bound, the brig was found to be unseaworthy. They put into Cork for repairs and were delayed many weeks, missing the trade winds so that they did not reach Tobago until October. John Paul had no money to pay the crew until his cargo was sold. The purchase and sale of cargo was one of the captain's responsibilities. The crew mutinied and in the ensuing fracas John Paul, defending himself, killed the ringleader with a sword thrust. The victim had powerful friends on the island and John Paul became a marked man. He took the surname Jones and managed to escape to Virginia.

The young ship's captain was in Philadelphia in 1773 on the eve of the American War of Independence. The Marine Committee of Congress, incensed at the imposition of taxation when the colonists were not represented in the Westminster parliament, was organising a navy to disrupt shipping between Britain and North America. With the help of Scottish friends and fellow-Freemasons, John Paul Jones was offered a commission in the fledgling Continental Navy, the nucleus of the future United States Navy. He was appointed first lieutenant of the 30-gun frigate *Alfred*, flagship of Commodore Hopkins.

Commodore Hopkins' squadron of two frigates and four smaller warships was returning from a successful attack on the poorly defended Bahamas when it was challenged by the single 20-gun frigate, HMS *Glasgow*. The British warship was caught between the two American frigates, outnumbered and outgunned. A grenade was thrown from *Alfred* and exploded on her deck. *Glasgow* retaliated with a double broadside, causing several casualties and damaging both American ships. In danger of being boarded, *Glasgow* extricated herself and escaped, keeping her pursuers at bay with her stern chasers. Commodore Hopkins called off the chase and went to the aid of his crippled consort.

Initially, Congress and the local newspapers hailed this brief action as a great victory. In fact, American casualties were nine killed and fourteen wounded against *Glasgow*'s one killed and three wounded. Commodore Hopkins' career progressed no further; two of the American captains were court-martialled and one was dismissed from his ship, the sloop *Providence*. This benefited Lieutenant Paul Jones who was appointed to her command and in August 1776 was promoted to captain. For the remainder of that year, initially in *Providence* and then as captain of *Alfred* with *Providence* in company, Captain Paul Jones preyed on British shipping off the east coast of North America. They took more than a dozen prizes, including three colliers and an armed schooner, burned nine ships, virtually decimated the British fisheries off Newfoundland and Nova Scotia, destroyed an oil warehouse and also captured a 10-gun privateer. Chased by the 28-gun frigate HMS *Milton*, Captain Paul Jones got away but had to abandon the privateer and prize crew, which *Milton* re-took.

At a time when the war was not going well for Congress, the activities of Paul Jones were considered highly successful and did much to bolster the colonists' morale. In June 1777 he was given command of a new 26-gun frigate *Ranger*, with a complement of 200, and ordered to sail for France under a general directive to harass British merchant shipping. He was to act under the overall direction of the American Commissioner to France, Dr Benjamin Franklin. On the Atlantic crossing it was found that twenty-six guns made *Ranger* top-heavy. Her armament had to be reduced to sixteen 9-pounders.

A Franco-American treaty was signed in February 1778. After completing her fitting out, *Ranger* left the coast of France on 10 April and was escorted through the British blockade by a French frigate. Although *Ranger*'s cruise only lasted a month, Captain Paul Jones created consternation in the British Isles out of all proportion to the material damage done. Off the Mull of Kintyre he captured the crew of a coaster and sank the ship with its cargo of grain. He captured some fishermen off the Irish coast and then made a dawn raid on the harbour of Whitehaven, spiking the guns of a battery manned by a few rather surprised pensioners and attempting – with only limited success – to burn some of the 300 ships aground in the shallow harbour at low tide. John Paul was recognised by somebody who knew him from his apprenticeship days. The raid was later reported in the London newspapers with gratifying propaganda effect.

The same afternoon Captain Paul Jones took the frigate across the Solway Firth and anchored in Kirkcudbright Bay. His objective was to take the Earl of Selkirk hostage and exchange him for American prisoners held in English gaols as pirates. The earl's home was on St Mary's Isle, a promontory jutting into the shallow estuary which is the harbour of Kirkcudbright. A party was landed on the shore below the house, which was surrounded and entered. The earl was not at home. Only the young countess, her children and servants were in residence. They were alarmed but not molested. Paul Jones could not prevent his men, hungry for prize money, from taking the family silver before returning to their ship, but to his credit he purchased the Selkirk silver back from his crew and eventually returned it to the countess with a letter of apology.

Before returning to France the frigate was involved in one further action. Paul Jones knew from the captured fishermen that a British sloop, HMS *Drake*, was in Carrickfergus harbour in Belfast Lough. *Ranger* patrolled off Carrickfergus, challenging the little sloop to come out. Although *Drake* was smaller and less heavily armed and had no gunner on board and no ammunition prepared, she had a bigger ship's company than *Ranger*. She emerged, determined to board the interloper. Captain Paul Jones wisely lay off and concentrated musket and cannon fire on *Drake*'s crew and rigging. The little sloop fought bravely but her masts and rigging were shattered and torn and her captain and first lieutenant were killed by musket balls, leaving her with only one officer. After an hour he surrendered. *Ranger* had lost three killed and had five wounded. *Drake* had four killed and nineteen wounded. Her 133 surviving crew were taken prisoner.

At the entrance to Belfast Lough the captured fishermen were released. Paul Jones gave them a boat with a new sail and some ready cash. They cheered as they left for home. *Ranger* avoided the British warships searching for her by sailing down the west coast of Ireland and entered Brest on 8 May with her prizes and 200 prisoners, whom Paul Jones intended to exchange for Americans.

Appointed captain of a larger ship being built for the American Continental Navy in Holland, Paul Jones became impatient at continual delays. With the support of Dr Benjamin Franklin, he found an old East Indiaman and had her converted and fitted out as a 40-gun frigate, naming her *Le Bonhomme Richard* in Dr Franklin's honour, 'Poor Richard' being the doctor's regular nom de plume. An assortment of modern French ordnance was acquired, ranging from 9- to 18-pounders, and a motley crew, less than half of whom were Americans. The majority were French and Portuguese with a few English, Irish and just four Scots, apart from Paul Jones himself. He had to exercise command by a blend of extremes: severity towards the recalcitrant, indulgence and humanity to the obedient. On the eve of departure he had the whole of his barge crew triced to the rigging and flogged because they had left the barge unattended while they were drinking in a tavern, leaving him to be rowed out to the ship by a local fisherman.

The Marine Committee of Congress promoted Paul Jones to commodore and, with French agreement, put him in command of a squadron of five warships: *Le Bonhomme Richard*, the American built 36-gun frigate *Alliance* commanded by Captain Landais – an American-naturalised Frenchman – and three French frigates which operated under French Naval instructions while under the American flag: a recipe for disaster. The squadron sailed from Lorient on 4 August 1779, heading for the west coast of Ireland.

Off the Irish coast a group of Irishmen took a boat and deserted from *Le Bonhomme Richard*. Another boat, sent in pursuit, was never seen again. One of the French ships abandoned the squadron after taking a prize and never rejoined. Captain Landais in *Alliance* went off alone to look for prizes. When off Cape Wrath, the remnants of the squadron took one valuable prize bound for Quebec and later a few small prizes off the east coast of Scotland. On 14 September Commodore Paul Jones entered the Firth of Forth, intending to threaten Leith and Edinburgh. *Alliance* was not in sight and the two remaining French ships failed to follow him in. The three ships beat up and down, causing some apprehension ashore, but eventually a gale-force wind from the west drove them out of the Firth. They ran south-east past Berwick and down the Northumbrian coast.

On 23 September Captain Landais in *Alliance* fortuitously rejoined the squadron. The same evening, when off Flamborough Head, they sighted a convoy of 41 British merchantmen returning from the Baltic escorted by two warships. Potentially it was a magnificent prize. The sea was calm with a light breeze and a full moon was rising. The enemy warships were outnumbered and conditions were perfect. Commodore Jones gave the order to prepare for action, flying British colours to retain an element of surprise.

The two British warships, the 54-gun frigate HMS *Serapis* and the 20-gun sloop *Countess of Scarborough*, placed themselves between the convoy and the American squadron. When *Le Bonhomme Richard* came within hailing distance, Captain Pearson of *Serapis* asked for identification. Commodore Jones appreciated that he was outgunned, if not outnumbered, and could only prevail by grappling and boarding. Immediately he lowered the Union Jack, hoisted the Stars and Stripes, fired a broadside and closed on *Serapis*. The British frigate returned fire with a devastating broadside from her 18-pounders. The two French frigates engaged the little *Countess of Scarborough*, but *Alliance* lay off, firing wildly at nothing in particular.

The British sloop was soon overwhelmed, but *Le Bonhomme Richard* and *Serapis* became embroiled in a bloody duel. French marines in the American frigate's rigging raked the decks of *Serapis* with musket fire and lobbed grenades onto her. One went down a hatchway and exploded, causing a secondary explosion and a fire, but *Serapis* continued to discharge lethal broadsides into *Le Bonhomme Richard*, inflicting heavy casualties, putting most of her guns out of action and piercing her hull so that she began to take in water. Meanwhile the American frigate persistently tried to grapple her opponent.

The duel between the two frigates continued through the night. Broadsides from *Serapis* were deadly. *Le Bonhomme Richard* was soon in a sinking condition. When Captain Pearson called on Paul Jones to surrender, he gave his famous reply: 'I have not yet begun to fight!' The sharpshooters only spared Captain Pearson because Paul Jones wanted him alive as a prisoner.

At last *Le Bonhomme Richard* got alongside as *Serapis*'s anchor became snarled in the American ship's shrouds. The commodore gave the order to board – just in time. It was only by grappling and lashing his ship to *Serapis* that he contrived to keep *Le Bonhomme Richard* afloat. *Serapis* tried unsuccessfully to break clear. One by one her officers were picked off by the marine sharpshooters. At one stage William Hamilton, one of *Le Bonhomme Richard*'s other Scots, crawled out along a yardarm and dropped a grenade onto the pile of cartridges left in readiness for loading the cannon on *Serapis*'s deck. The detonation caused havoc. The English gunner of *Le Bonhomme Richard*, knowing his ship was sinking, shouted for quarter. Paul Jones instantly knocked him unconscious with the butt of his pistol.

It was Captain Pearson who finally struck his colours. He cannot have realised that the American ship was sinking and had suffered heavier casualties: 150 as against *Serapis*'s 117. Nevertheless, although defeated by a more determined opponent, Pearson had succeeded in his primary role and Jones had failed in his: the convoy escaped unscathed.

A hundred prisoners were released to man the stricken frigate's pumps but to no avail. At 10 a.m. on the morning of 24 September, after everybody had been transferred to *Serapis*, now a prize, the American frigate sank. Commodore Jones took his prizes to the Dutch island of Texel, where he transferred his pennant to the undamaged *Alliance* and sailed to Lorient, evading the ships of the Royal Navy which were searching for him.

To Jones's disgust, Captain Landais was permitted to sail *Alliance* back to America. The commodore stayed in France, relishing the delights of the doomed French Court. He was made a Chevalier of France and presented with a golden-hilted sword by Louis XVI. Returning to America months later, his ship, a sloop captured by the French from the British, nearly foundered off Brittany and was only saved by Jones's outstanding seamanship. Back in Philadelphia he submitted a full report of the action off Flamborough Head to Congress and was formally thanked, while Captain Landais was court-martialled and dismissed from the Navy. For a year Paul Jones served as flag captain to the French admiral, Le Marquis de Vendreuil. Then he spent four years attempting, with only partial success, to reclaim the value of the prizes which he had taken and left in Europe.

In 1787 Paul Jones was invited by Catherine the Great, Empress of Russia, to become rear-admiral of the Black Sea Fleet under the overall command of Field Marshal Potemkin. He was charged with expelling the Turks from the Liman, the shallow waters near the estuary of the Dnieper, east of Odessa. He found himself trapped in a morass of incompetence, surrounded by officers who were more concerned with status than with duty. When consulted by Potemkin, he pointed out that the Russian ships drew less water than those of the Turks. He proposed that they should take advantage of this by challenging the enemy in the shallowest part of the estuary and suggested a plan of action that was accepted. In practice, it was defeated by a combination of jealousy and inept signalling. A subordinate commander concentrated his whole flotilla on the Turkish ships that had run aground, allowing all the others to escape. Rear-Admiral Paul Jones's signals were ignored.

John Paul Jones took the blame for the failures of others and was sent back to St Petersburg. He was allowed to retire to Amsterdam. His attempts to enter the service of Sweden or to return to the Imperial Russian Navy failed; his naval career was finished. He moved to Paris, intending to return in due course to America, but his health was failing. He died on 18 July 1792 in a Paris torn by revolution, 45 years after his birth in a peaceful rural corner of south-west Scotland.

Americans revere John Paul Jones less for his exploits than for his advanced thinking on the qualities of leadership. More than a century after his death President Theodore Roosevelt had his body brought back from France to the United States and re-interred within the precincts of the United States Naval Academy at Annapolis where, paradoxically in a republic, the golden-hilted sword presented to him by Louis XVI lies in a glass case above the sarcophagus.

♪ CHAPTER 9 ♪

Fighting Admirals

In the eighteenth century, Scotland produced admirals who distinguished themselves not only in the Royal Navy of Great Britain but also in the navies of several other nations. The following brief accounts of a few of their careers are offered in chronological order of birth.

Admiral Sir James Douglas (1703–87) was born at Friarshaw, Roxburgh. He was present at the capture of Quebec in 1759. In the following year he became Commodore Commanding the Leeward Islands station and captured Dominica. He was promoted to flag rank and became Commander-in-Chief (C-in-C) West Indies in 1770. He was C-in-C Portsmouth in 1778 and later became MP for Orkney.

Vice-Admiral John Campbell (1720–90), who has already been mentioned, was apprenticed at an early age to the master of a coasting vessel. He entered the Royal Navy by an unusual route, offering himself in exchange for a mate who had been press-ganged into service. In 1740 he sailed in *Centurion* with Captain George Anson on his voyage round the world, as master responsible for navigation. John Campbell subsequently captained two frigates, then a ship-of-the-line before being posted captain of another, the 64-gun *Essex* patrolling in the Bay of Biscay to blockade Brest in 1759. He was Admiral Hawke's flag captain at the battle of Quiberon Bay on 20 November of that year when the French fleet was heavily defeated. George Anson, now Admiral Lord Anson, recommended Captain John Campbell for a knighthood to which he reacted in character: 'Troth, my Lord, I ken nae use that will be tae me!'

'But,' said Anson, 'your lady may like it!'

'Ah weel, His Majesty may knight her if he pleases,' was the reply.
Campbell was not knighted.

John Campbell was appointed captain of the fleet under Admiral
Viscount Keppel, to whom he remained intensely loyal when Keppel was
court-martialled for failing to prevent the French fleet escaping from
Ushant. Evidence was given that his second-in-command, Admiral Sir
Hugh Palliser, was at fault. This view was supported by John Campbell and
others and Keppel was acquitted. Campbell was appointed vice-admiral,
governor of Newfoundland and C-in-C of that station in 1782. After
holding the appointment for four years and proclaiming religious freedom
for all the inhabitants, he died in 1790.

Admiral Sir Samuel Greig (1735–88) was C-in-C of Russia's Baltic Fleet
and considered by many as the founder of its navy. He was born at
Inverkeithing, where his father was a shipowner. He learned his navigation
and seamanship serving in his father's merchant ships before entering the
Royal Navy as a master's mate and first seeing action in *Firedrake* – a 'bomb'
or eighteenth-century equivalent of a torpedo boat – then under Admiral
Hawke during the blockade of Brest and at the Battle of Quiberon Bay. He
was present at the capture of Havana.

When the Seven Years' War ended in 1763, he found himself unemployed
and entered the Russian service as a lieutenant. He was soon promoted to
captain and by 1769 was in command of a division in the Mediterranean.
He distinguished himself at the defeat of the Turkish fleet in 1770 and was
promoted to rear-admiral. Three years later he commanded a small force
which defeated a superior squadron of ten Turkish warships and was soon
afterwards promoted to vice-admiral.

In the years of peace between 1774 and 1788 Admiral Greig devoted
himself to the improvement of the Russian Navy, concentrating on
discipline, training and organisation. Catherine the Great appointed him
grand admiral and governor of Kronstadt, the naval base for St Petersburg.
He was much decorated and highly regarded, recruiting many British and
particularly Scottish officers into the Imperial Navy.

When war broke out against Sweden in 1788, he was in command of the
Russian Baltic Fleet at an indecisive naval action off Gotland. Poorly
supported by senior Russian officers, he sent no less than 17 of them back
to St Petersburg, charged with failing in their duties. Nevertheless, he
succeeded in blockading the Swedish Navy in Sveaborg, Helsinki's naval
base. He died on board his ship in October 1788 and was accorded the
honour of a state funeral.

Rear-Admiral Sir John Lindsay (1737–88) was born at Evelick in
Perthshire. He served under Admiral Hawke in 1757 as captain of a fireship

on an abortive expedition to Rochefort. Later in the year he was given command of a frigate which took part in an expedition against Havana, and there 'gave many proofs of his valour'. He was knighted for gallantry in 1764 and was promoted to commodore and appointed C-in-C East Indies from 1769 to 1772. In the action off Ushant in 1779, he was captain of the 90-gun *Prince George* under Admiral Keppel. At the subsequent court martial he gave evidence against Palliser, resigned his command in support of Keppel and refused employment while Lord Sandwich remained as First Lord, eventually returning to service as commodore in command of a Mediterranean squadron. He was promoted to rear-admiral in September 1787 but died the following year.

Admiral Sir James Athol Wood (1756–1829) claimed descent from Sir Andrew Wood. He was born at Burncroft near Perth and went to sea as an apprentice in a ship of the East India Company in 1772. He became an able seaman in the sloop HMS *Hunter* in 1774, operating off the coast of Ireland and on the North American Station, probably protecting convoys against privateers. In July 1776 he became master's mate – assistant navigator – in *Barfleur*, flagship of Admiral Sir James Douglas. The Merchant Navy was considered a nursery for navigators since many masters and master's mates in the Royal Navy were recruited or pressed from merchant ships.

Promoted to lieutenant in 1778, Wood served in the 50-gun *Renown* in the attack on Charlestown in 1780. Over the next 14 years he accumulated vast experience while employed in small ships of the Channel Fleet, in the 64-gun *Anson* and in merchant ships trading between the British Isles, the East Indies and West Indies. He was in Barbados in January 1794 when the fleet arrived under Admiral Sir John Jervis. He offered his services and took part in the capture of Martinique. In July 1795, while blockading the French and Spanish-held Caribbean Islands, he discovered that Trinidad was under-garrisoned and suggested that it could be captured by an unexpected attack. He was sent to reconnoitre the island and, on the basis of his report, the island was taken unopposed.

In 1798 Captain Wood was in command of the frigate *Garland* en route to Mauritius via the Cape of Good Hope. He sighted a large French ship in the uncharted waters off Madagascar and stood in towards her. *Garland* struck a reef and sank, but not before Wood had her boats lowered and disembarked all her crew. He captured the French ship, built another small ship with the timbers of the wrecked *Garland* and then took both ships, all the men and most of the stores back to the Cape.

In 1798 Wood commanded the 40-gun frigate *Acasta*, blockading Brest. In 1804 he escorted a convoy to the West Indies, where the admiral-in-command, Sir John Duckworth, arrogantly commandeered *Acasta* and appointed one of his own captains to take the ship home with himself on board. Captain Wood was allocated a berth in his own ship as a passenger. On arrival in England, he bravely applied for a court martial of Admiral Duckworth, charging him with tyranny, oppression and using one of HM ships to carry home private merchandise. The court martial cleared Duckworth, but James Wood's brother, a Member of Parliament, moved in the House of Commons that the minutes of the court martial should be 'laid on the table' to make it clear that Duckworth, not his brother, was at fault. The affair attracted publicity and public opinion was strongly on Wood's side. He was immediately given command of another ship and escorted a convoy out to the West Indies, where he remained as second-in-command, assisting in the capture of Curaçao in 1807.

By March 1810 he had been knighted and was captain of *Pompée* in the Channel Fleet, engaged in the familiar occupation of blockading Brest. After two years of tedium, while cruising off Ushant accompanied only by frigates, he sighted a French squadron at a distance of 12 miles. He then saw two line-of-battle ships appear to join them, then wear and stand towards him. The night being exceptionally dark, he tacked and stood away from them, intending to re-establish contact in the morning. Unfortunately the French squadron disappeared during the night and the two line-of-battle ships turned out to be British. Strangely, he was blamed for the French ships' escape and then court martialled. The verdict was that he had been too hasty in tacking from the enemy and that he should have first established the identity of the two strange line-of-battle ships, although they were every bit as guilty. He was unofficially 'admonished' but remained in command of *Pompée* and was sent to the Mediterranean for the next three and a half years. Eventually he was made a Companion of the Order of the Bath and promoted to rear-admiral in 1821, eight years before his death.

Admiral Sir Alexander Forrester Inglis Cochrane (1758–1832) was the first of the Cochrane naval dynasty. He was accused of 'gross jobbery' when he managed to get his son *Thomas John Cochrane* posted captain of HMS *Jason* at the age of just 17. The boy had been entered on the books of his father's ship *Thetis* at the age of seven and was a lieutenant by the time he was sixteen. Although nepotism was rife, this is a particularly clear case of it. To be fair, however, young Thomas John seems to have been well able to cope with his responsibilities. Eventually, in 1841, he was promoted to rear-admiral. He was successively second-in-command, then C-in-C China station; vice-admiral in 1850; C-in-C Portsmouth; admiral in 1856 and admiral of the fleet in 1865, seven years before his death.

Alexander's career was less orderly than his son's and punctuated with active service. He did not reach the rank of lieutenant until he was 20 years old. He was wounded in action off Martinique two years later but continued to serve on the West Indies station. He was posted captain in 1782 but was unemployed on half-pay until 1790, when he was appointed to command the frigate *Hind*, cruising against French privateers. In May 1795 he was appointed captain of the 42-gun *Thetis* on the North American station and, in company with *Hussar*, attacked five armed French storeships, capturing two of them while the other three escaped.

In 1799 Alexander Cochrane was captain of the 80-gun *Ajax*, engaged in detached squadrons on expeditions to Quiberon Bay and against Ferrol. He was then sent to the Mediterranean under Admiral Lord Keith, where he distinguished himself in combined operations against the French, landing troops and supporting them with gunboats. After the Peace of Amiens in 1802, Captain Alexander Cochrane became MP for Stirling Burghs, but when war against France broke out again he was appointed captain of the 74-gun ship-of-the-line *Northumberland* and in April 1804 was promoted to rear-admiral, commanding a squadron off Ferrol. He was responsible for obtaining intelligence which led to the capture of valuable Spanish treasure ships off Cape Santa Maria in October of 1804.

Rear-Admiral Alexander Cochrane was then appointed C-in-C Leeward Islands. He was engaged in the battle of San Domingo on 6 February 1806 when his flagship lost nearly one-third of her ship's company in action. He was knighted for his conduct in this battle and given the freedom of the City of London and a sword of honour. After the capture of Guadeloupe in January 1810, he was made governor of the island until 1814. He was then appointed C-in-C, North American station, flying his flag in the 80-gun *Tonnant*, and finally became C-in-C Plymouth in 1821.

Admiral Sir Richard John Strachan (1760–1828), whose family hailed from Aberdeen, entered the Royal Navy as a midshipman in 1772. His early service took him to the East Indies, North America, Africa and the West Indies. He was present at the indecisive action in Porto Praia in 1781 and in action in the East Indies. While in command of the frigate *Phoenix* he was ordered to search for the French frigate *Resolue*, which he captured after a fierce action in which the French lost 65 killed and wounded before striking their colours. In 1794 he captained the frigate *Concorde* in an action against four French frigates, during which three of the four were captured. He was then appointed in command of a small frigate squadron which cruised successfully off Normandy and Brittany, capturing and destroying many armed coastal craft carrying military stores for Napoleon's armies.

From 1803 to 1804 he was Senior Officer Gibraltar. At the time of Trafalgar he was captain of HMS *Caesar* in command of a squadron of three line-of-battle ships and four frigates detached to the Bay of Biscay to prevent any French ships from northern French ports joining up with the main combined French and Spanish fleets. On 2 November 1805 he intercepted four French ships-of-the-line under Admiral Dumanoir, which had escaped after the Battle of Trafalgar on 21 October. Captain Strachan engaged them in action and captured all four, thus completing the destruction of the French fleet.

On 9 November he was promoted to rear-admiral, formally congratulated by parliament, made Knight of the Bath, awarded a special pension and given the freedom of the City of London and a sword of honour. He was given command of the naval force sent to land troops on Walcheren Island and to destroy French arsenals on the River Scheldt. The force captured Flushing but failed in its main purpose. There were recriminations in the House of Commons but Strachan argued that his ships had fulfilled all their objectives and that the failure was one of military planning. He was promoted to vice-admiral in 1810 but given no further employment.

Admiral Sir Pulteney Malcolm (1768–1838) was born in Langholm, Dumfriesshire, his mother being a sister of Captain, later Admiral, Sir Thomas Paisley. His name was entered in the books of HMS *Sybil*, commanded by his uncle, when he was only ten years old. He served as a midshipman in the South Atlantic and West Indies, later becoming first lieutenant of the frigate *Penelope* on the Jamaican station. *Penelope*, in company with *Iphigia*, captured the French frigate *Inconstante* off the coast of San Domingo in November 1793 and in ensuing months captured or cut out many privateers and merchant ships. Lieutenant Malcolm commanded boats with distinction in many of these hand-to-hand actions.

Posted as captain of the frigate *Fox*, he sailed many thousands of miles, first taking a convoy to the Mediterranean, then crossing the Atlantic to Quebec, back to the North Sea, then to the East Indies and China seas. On 14 January 1798, *Fox* approached the Philippines and entered Manila Bay under Spanish colours, then raised the Union Jack before capturing three Spanish gunboats. In June of that year he was appointed captain of the East Indies flagship, HMS *Suffolk*.

Captain Malcolm served under Nelson off Toulon and was sent to Naples to take command of *Renown*. In 1805 he was captain of *Donegal* and took part in Nelson's celebrated chase of the French fleet to the West Indies. On return to home waters he was sent to reinforce Admiral Collingwood off Cadiz, and in October *Donegal* was sent to Gibraltar for a much-needed refit. While *Donegal* was refitting, the battle of Trafalgar was about to be fought 40 miles to the west and Captain Malcolm learned on 20

October that the combined French and Spanish fleets were coming out of Cadiz. Frantic to join Nelson's fleet, Malcolm did everything possible to get *Donegal* to sea, although her refit was unfinished. She arrived a day too late, on 22 October, but in time to help with disabled ships and prizes. He captured the *Rayo*, and two nights later *Donegal*'s boats saved hundreds of lives when a French ship ran aground. Admiral Collingwood commented on Captain Malcolm's absence from Trafalgar:

> Everybody was sorry Malcolm was not there because everybody knows his spirit and his skill would have acquired him honour. He got out of the Gut [Gibraltar dockyard] when nobody else could and was of infinite service to us after the action.

Donegal continued to blockade Cadiz, where the survivors of Trafalgar had taken refuge, until ordered to sail for the West Indies. There Malcolm played an important role in the battle off San Domingo in February 1806, for which he was awarded a gold medal. He was sent home in charge of a convoy of prizes and on passage rescued the crew of *Bravo*, which was in danger of foundering in a heavy gale. For two or three years he was mainly employed convoying troops to reinforce Wellington's army in the Peninsular War; then, in 1809, *Donegal* was attached to the Channel Fleet commanded by Admiral Gambier. He was present at the action in Aix Roads later that year, when the dithering Gambier failed to support Captain Thomas Cochrane at a crucial juncture and lost the opportunity of achieving a second naval victory as decisive as Trafalgar.

In 1811 Captain Malcolm was appointed to *Royal Oak* and in the following year became captain of the fleet under Admiral Lord Keith, who, perhaps not by coincidence, was his uncle by marriage. He was promoted to rear-admiral in December 1813 and was employed convoying army detachments to North America, where he was third-in-command under Admiral Sir Alexander Cochrane. He then commanded the North Sea squadron, which worked along the coast of mainland Europe in combined operations with the Duke of Wellington's army. From 1816 to 1817 Rear-Admiral Sir Pulteney Malcolm was C-in-C of the St Helena Station – an important transatlantic staging post – and was responsible for ensuring that Napoleon Bonaparte did not escape. He was promoted to vice-admiral in July 1821 and was C-in-C Mediterranean from 1828 to 1831 and then C-in-C in the North Sea in 1832. Much decorated, he became C-in-C Mediterranean once again from 1833 to 1834. He died in 1836, two years after retiring.

Vice-Admiral Sir Patrick Campbell (1773–1841) was born at Melfort on the west coast of Argyll. He joined the Royal Navy as a midshipman in around 1787. On 25 September 1794 he was promoted to lieutenant and to commander in 1797. In 1799 he was in command of the sloop *Dart*, which boasted the experimental armament of thirty-two 32-pounder carronades, cast in the Carron Iron Works near Falkirk. These were light mortars which compensated for shortness of range by their light weight and heaviness of shot. On 7 July 1800 *Dart*, accompanied by two gun-brigs and four fireships, raided Dunkirk and succeeded in destroying four large French frigates. One, the 38-gun *Désirée*, was captured and brought out over the shoals. *Dart* had run alongside her, fired a double-shotted broadside into her and then boarded her to bring her out.

Campbell was promoted to captain in July 1800 and given command of a frigate. In 1805 his ship *Doris*, while on a mission to sound the French anchorage of Quiberon Bay, struck a rock and had to be burned and abandoned. He and his ship's company were captured and taken on board the French flagship *Tonnant* for passage to Brest. While boarding *Tonnant*, their boat was swamped. Campbell was rescued but the captain of the *Tonnant* was drowned. Captain Campbell was later exchanged for a Frenchman of equivalent rank and by 1811 he was captain of the 74-gun *Leviathan* in the Mediterranean. He was promoted to rear-admiral in 1830 and was C-in-C Cape of Good Hope from 1834 to 1837. He was knighted and promoted to vice-admiral in 1838 and died three years later. His son, Colin, who followed him into the Navy, died at sea in 1869.

Admiral Sir Charles Napier (1786–1860) was a colourful and controversial character. He has been described as arrogant, boastful and inclined to drink too much whisky, but he was also highly competent and possessed courage and initiative. Charles Napier was born at Merchiston Hall in Stirlingshire, not far from Falkirk, the son of a Royal Navy captain. He joined his first ship, the sloop *Martin*, at the age of 13 and was employed in patrolling the Scottish coast at a time when Napoleon threatened invasion. He then served with distinction as a lieutenant and commander in home waters, the Mediterranean and Caribbean.

The Admiralty was notorious for being a corrupt organisation and for its failure to refit and maintain ships in a seaworthy condition. On one occasion Napier wrote a note to the Admiralty, in case of his capture or death, informing their lordships that if his frigate were lost it would be due to the state of her equipment and not the fault of her ship's company.

Napier was unemployed on half-pay from 1809 to 1810. He attended Edinburgh University and during the summer vacation went out to Oporto to fight with the British Army engaged in the Peninsular War. It was no holiday. He was wounded at the Battle of Bussaco, took part in the retreat to Torres Vedras, but stayed on until November and took the opportunity to learn Portuguese and Spanish.

In 1811 Napier was appointed captain of the frigate *Thames*. He took a leaf from Lord Cochrane's book and for the next three years wrought havoc up and down the coasts of Spain and France in aid of the Army. He destroyed more than 80 gunboats and coastal craft, razed fortifications and destroyed batteries. As captain of the frigate *Euryalus*, he drove coastal trade from Toulon into Cavalaria Bay, where he helped the 74-gun *Berwick* destroy the batteries and bring out 22 merchant ships and a small warship.

Following the United States' declaration of war in 1812 because their trade with France was being blockaded by the Royal Navy, *Euryalus* was employed escorting troop transports to North America. The ship took part in expeditions against Baltimore and the Maryland coast.

Charles Napier showed increasing interest in the possibilities of steam for ship propulsion. He inherited a fortune in 1818 and went to Paris to experiment with iron steamers on the Seine. After ten years his venture ended in failure. He lost his fortune, returned to the Royal Navy and was appointed in command of the frigate *Galatea* in 1829. She was an experimental vessel with both sails and paddles worked by winches. It took a quarter of an hour to ship or unship the paddles. With them, she could attain a speed of three knots and tow a ship-of-the-line at one to two knots. *Galatea* was first sent to the West Indies, then to Lisbon to repossess British merchant ships seized by Portugal.

Sent to watch over British interests in the Azores, Napier took an interest in Portuguese affairs and when *Galatea* was paid off in 1832 he was offered the command of a Portuguese fleet opposed to Dom Miguel, who had usurped the throne. To avoid the penalties of the British parliament's Foreign Enlistment Act, which forbade British nationals to join foreign armed forces, he changed his name to Carlos de Ponza before accepting the offer.

As admiral he had under his command three frigates, two corvettes and several smaller ships with a total complement of about 1,000 – most of them British – and the support of a small army under Count Villa Flor, which he landed near Cape St Vincent. The troops marched north, securing the ports en route, and captured Lisbon. On 3 July 1833 Napier's squadron sighted Dom Miguel's ships off Cape St Vincent. In an action between the two squadrons on 5 July, Dom Miguel's ships, though superior in both numbers and armament, were conclusively defeated and the four largest were captured. Napier returned to Lagos and reorganised his augmented fleet. He was promoted to full admiral and raised to the Portuguese peerage. He put to sea again on 13 July but unluckily cholera broke out in the fleet.

Fifty died in his flagship and two hundred were on the sick list. He took the fleet out into the Atlantic to blow away the infection, then sailed for Lisbon. He was received as the liberator of Portugal and personally decorated by Dom Pedro. He proceeded to raise the siege of Oporto, secure the coastline, sever supply lines and in a few weeks force Dom Miguel's remaining strongholds to surrender. The civil war was over. In November Napier sailed for the United Kingdom as a count in the Portuguese peerage and admiral of the Portuguese navy.

On his return Napier re-entered the Royal Navy, was appointed captain of the 84-gun *Powerful* and sent out to the Mediterranean to reinforce the fleet commanded by Admiral Sir Robert Stopford. There was trouble in the Levant, where Britain and her allies were supporting the Turks against the Egyptians, who had captured and held Beirut with a force of 15,000. Napier, now a commodore, was directed by Stopford to take command of the allied force on shore. He personally intervened with the irresolute Turkish troops, whom he 'stirred up with his stick', and then directed the capture of Sidon and Beirut.

The fleet moved south to bombard Acre, still held by the Egyptians. Napier disobeyed orders, anchoring independently in a way which constricted the movements of the fleet. Stopford chose to overlook his insubordination and ordered him to take command of a squadron off Alexandria. There he exceeded his authority by concluding an agreement with the Egyptians. Despite this he was knighted, decorated by Britain's allies and received an ecstatic public welcome on returning home. He asked to be put on half-pay and entered parliament as MP for Marylebone, concentrating on improving conditions for seamen and on measures to strengthen the Navy.

In 1846 Sir Charles Napier was promoted to rear-admiral and hoisted his flag in the 120-gun *St Vincent* as C-in-C Channel Fleet. He patrolled the coasts of Portugal and Ireland, and then, based on Gibraltar, fought the Rif pirates operating from Spanish Morocco. Sir Charles was promoted to vice-admiral in May 1853 and given command of a fleet sent to the Baltic to confront the Russians. The Crimean War was imminent. Unable to win an expected victory over the Russian Baltic Fleet, he achieved no more than a blockade of Kronstadt and St Petersburg. He was criticised by the British public and by the Admiralty. Aggrieved, he refused a decoration, but entered parliament as member for Southwark and specialised in criticism of the Admiralty's shortcomings. Nevertheless, he was promoted to admiral in 1858, eventually retiring to Merchiston, where he pursued an interest in practical farming and died in 1860.

Admiral Sir George Cockburn (1772–1853) served under Nelson in the

Mediterranean in the frigate *Minerve* from 1796 to 1802. He was left in command at Leghorn when Nelson was sent by Admiral Sir John Jervis to supervise the evacuation of Corsica, but he missed Trafalgar, having been posted to command the frigate *Phaeton* in the East Indies. When Napoleon surrendered after the Battle of Waterloo, Admiral Cockburn was given the interesting assignment of conveying him to St Helena and was subsequently made C-in-C of that station.

These short accounts give an indication of the involvement of Scottish officers in naval operations over the century following the Act of Union, but it should be remembered that a large number of the seamen would also have been Scots, many of them impressed from merchant ships or captured privateers.

⚓ CHAPTER 10 ⚓

Admiral Duncan and Admiral Keith

Three Scottish admirals whose careers overlapped Lord Nelson's made outstanding contributions to maintaining Britain's naval superiority and freedom to use the high seas for trade. Their names are Adam Duncan, George Keith Elphinstone and Thomas Cochrane.

Admiral Adam Duncan of Camperdown, first Viscount, was a big man in every way. He was over 6 ft 4 in. tall, handsome, massively built and endowed with great physical strength. He was born at Lundie, some seven miles north-west of Dundee, in 1731.

Adam Duncan joined George II's Royal Navy in 1746 under the care of his maternal uncle Robert Haldane, who was captain of the sloop HMS *Trial* and served in the frigate *Shoreham* until 1748. He was appointed to the *Centurion* in 1749, which was then commissioning for Mediterranean service under the command of Captain the Hon. Augustus Keppel. He served under Keppel, first on the North American coast then transferred with him to *Swiftsure* and in January 1756 to *Torbay*. He was in action in 1757 against the French in the Basque Roads, off the island of Aix near Rochefort, and the following year he took part in the capture of a French-occupied island off the coast of West Africa. In 1759 *Torbay* was among the British ships that mounted a blockade of Brest to prevent the French fleet from putting to sea.

On 15 February 1761 he was posted as captain of *Valiant*, flagship of Admiral Keppel. *Valiant* played an important role in the capture of Belle Ile, off the Atlantic coast of France south of Quiberon Point, and took part in the capture of Havana.

When the Seven Years' War came to an end in 1763, Adam Duncan returned home. This was the start of a 15-year period of unemployment on half-pay, despite his repeated requests for a posting. He was obliged to lead the life of a minor laird at Lundie. He married Henrietta Dundas, daughter of Robert Dundas of Armiston, Lord President of the Court of Session.

When war with France broke out again in 1778, Captain Duncan was posted to HMS *Monarch* and later attached to Rodney's command for the relief of Gibraltar, then besieged by the Spaniards. On 8 January 1780, before reaching Gibraltar, Rodney's squadron fell in with a valuable Spanish convoy laden with vital stores for the Spanish fleets at Cadiz and Cartagena. The convoy was protected by seven armed vessels of the Caracas Company. In a short, sharp action Rodney's squadron captured all the ships. Eight days later a Spanish fleet of eleven sail-of-the-line were intercepted south-east of Cape St Vincent. The Spanish admiral, seeing that he was outnumbered, turned and ran for Cadiz. Rodney made the signal for a general chase, the ships to engage as they came up on the leeward side to prevent the Spaniards from escaping. A running battle ensued and continued in heavy seas from 4 p.m. to 2 a.m. on 17 January. Captain Duncan in *Monarch* played a prominent part. One of the Spanish ships was blown up and six were captured, although two were later wrecked on a lee shore. Gibraltar and Minorca were relieved and their food supplies and ammunition replenished before the squadron sailed for Barbados.

Duncan was posted captain of the 90-gun *Blenheim* in 1782 and served under Admiral Lord Howe, who had been given command of a mixed fleet of 183 sail, escorted by 34 ships-of-the-line, for the relief of Gibraltar. The rock was again under attack by the French and Spanish. They managed to land all the troops and stores to reinforce Gibraltar's defence. Duncan was promoted to rear-admiral on 24 September 1787, vice-admiral on 1 February 1793 and made C-in-C North Sea, flying his flag in HMS *Venerable*, in 1795.

For the next two years the ships under his command were employed in a rigid blockade of the Dutch coast. The Dutch had joined the French when France had been invaded by Austria and Prussia after revolution had overthrown the French monarchy. Duncan's task was to prevent the emergence of the Dutch fleet from the Texel.

When he learned in the spring of 1797 that the Dutch were preparing for sea, he faced a predicament. Morale in the British ships was low due to poor and intermittent pay, harsh discipline and revolting food. Mutiny at the Nore — the adjoining command to the south — had spread to some of Duncan's ships and reinforced their inactivity. Only admiration for Duncan personally and 'some happy displays of his vast personal strength' kept his ship's company to their duty. *Venerable* and *Adamant* were the only ships to obey his orders to weigh anchor and leave Yarmouth in order to keep watch on the Dutch. For many months Duncan only maintained the blockade by the ruse of showing his one or two loyal ships off the Dutch coast and making signals to an imaginary fleet just over the horizon.

Finally, in October, the Dutch government ordered Admiral de Winter, with 30,000 troops embarked for the invasion of Ireland, to weigh anchor. They had heard of the mutinies in the British fleet and thought it a propitious moment to put to sea, but by the time they did so the mutinies had been more or less resolved. Duncan's ships stood over to the Dutch coast. The enemy fleet was sighted on 11 October, close to the coastal villages of Camperdown and Egmont. The opposing fleets were roughly equal: Duncan's fleet comprised fourteen ships-of-the-line, seven of 74 guns and seven of 64 guns with a few frigates and cutters. Admiral de Winter had sixteen ships-of-the-line including four of 74 guns, seven of 64 guns and five less heavily armed, accompanied by several smaller ships. The Dutch, however, had a reputation for bravery and skilful ship-handling. When sighted Admiral de Winter formed his ships in line ahead, steering north towards shoal water where the Dutch ships, designed with shallower draught, would have the advantage. To prevent their escape, Duncan had to act very quickly. He had no time to form a single line in the customary manner for the purpose of ship-to-ship engagement. Instead, he gave a tradition-breaking signal, 'pass through the enemy's line and engage to leeward'. Then he approached downwind from the west in two loose columns – one led by himself and the other by his subordinate, Vice-Admiral Onslow, in *Monarch*.

It has been suggested by historians and naval tacticians that this approach set the pattern for Nelson's brilliantly successful tactics at Trafalgar eight years later. Duncan had to engage the Dutch ships before they reached shoal water where he could not have followed. His tactics were risky because the enemy was sailing across his bows in line ahead, so the Dutch ships could rake his with their broadsides before he could bring his guns to bear. A long and bloody engagement ensued. The British ships bore up to leeward of the enemy. Duncan's superior gunnery won the battle. Nine of the sixteen Dutch ships-of-the-line and two frigates were captured. The carnage was appalling. No ships were sunk, although one captured Dutch man-of-war foundered on its voyage to England as a prize. None of the prizes taken proved capable of repair and the lists of British casualties were nearly as long as the Dutch. However, Dutch sea power was irreparably damaged and plans for invading Ireland were relegated to the back of a politician's desk.

Admiral de Winter was taken prisoner and treated with courtesy. The

Dutch had fought courageously. He was a big man physically, almost as big as Admiral Duncan. Standing on the quarterdeck of *Venerable*, he commented incredulously to another officer: 'It is a matter of marvel that two such gigantic objects as Admiral Duncan and myself should have escaped the general carnage of this day!'

Duncan deserved great credit for maintaining morale and discipline in his own fleet, by personal example and inspiration, and for using unorthodox tactics to prevent the escape of a comparable Dutch force. He was raised to the peerage on 21 October as Baron Duncan of Lundie and Viscount Duncan of Camperdown.

There were no major naval actions in the North Sea during his remaining years as commander-in-chief. He died suddenly on 4 August 1804 at Cornhill on the border between Scotland and England, on his way to Edinburgh. His statue stands in St Paul's Cathedral. Nelson wrote to Duncan's son Henry, then a junior captain,

> There is no man who more sincerely laments the loss you have sustained than myself, but the name Duncan will never be forgot in Britain, and in particular by its Navy, in which the remembrance of your worthy father will, I am sure, grow in you.

⚓ ⚓ ⚓

Admiral George Keith Elphinstone, Viscount Keith (1746–1823) came close to immortality on more than one occasion, but fate decreed that he was more often involved in preparing the way for the fame of others than in achieving it himself. He suffered from comparison with Nelson and a prejudice against Scots which was evident amongst the captains who hero-worshipped the victor of Copenhagen and the Nile and resented the appointment of Keith over Nelson's head as C-in-C Mediterranean, in succession to Admiral Lord St Vincent.

George Elphinstone was born at Elphinstone Tower near Stirling on 7 January 1746 and entered the Royal Navy at the early age of 15. He served in the 44-gun frigate *Gosport* commanded by Captain John Jervis, later to become Admiral Lord St Vincent. Whether St Vincent's reported prejudice against Scots was already ingrained is not known and Elphinstone served in *Gosport* until she was paid off in 1763 at the end of the Seven Years' War. After service in three frigates, he joined an East India Company ship commanded by his brother William for a voyage to China, which was highly successful commercially. In those days it was permissible for serving officers and men to make money during their careers by legitimate private trading or by prize money and many gained experience in merchant ships between periods of service in the Royal Navy.

Promoted to lieutenant in 1770, he served in the Mediterranean and on the American Station and was then appointed to command the sloop *Scorpion*, cruising off the coasts of the Balearic Islands and Italy. He was promoted to the command of HMS *Romney* in 1774, convoying merchant and supply ships to Newfoundland, where Britain had established an important fishery. When the American War of Independence broke out in 1775 he was given command of HMS *Perseus* on the American Station and the following year he was promoted to captain. For the next four years he continued cruising to protect merchant shipping against privateers and in support of British troops ashore.

On 12 May 1780 Captain Elphinstone was ashore, in command of a unit of the Naval Brigade, when the city of Charleston, South Carolina, was seized by British forces. Five thousand Americans led by General Benjamin Lincoln surrendered, four American warships were sunk and large quantities of munitions captured.

The following January Captain Elphinstone, in command of the 50-gun *Warwick*, captured the 50-gun Dutch frigate *Rotterdam*. While *Warwick* was engaged in convoying merchant shipping across the Atlantic, the royal prince, Midshipman Prince William Henry, was placed under her captain's care, witness to the high regard in which he was held. On 15 September 1782 *Warwick*, supported by three sloops, captured the 40-gun French frigate *Aigle* and two other vessels in the mouth of the Delaware River.

After the Treaty of Versailles, Captain Elphinstone suffered the fate of many officers between wars, as the Navy failed to offer him any posts for ten years. He became a Member of Parliament, first for Dunbartonshire and then for Stirlingshire. On the outbreak of war with France's revolutionary government, Elphinstone was posted captain of the 74-gun ship-of-the-line *Robust*, which joined the fleet sent out to the Mediterranean under Admiral Lord Hood. Toulon had declared for the monarchy and sent a deputation to Hood asking for his support. On 27 August 1793 Captain Elphinstone was landed with 1,700 men and took the Toulon fort of La Malgue. Three days later he attacked and routed a body of French troops attempting to retake the fort. His experience with the Naval Brigade at Charleston and knowledge of military tactics, unusual in a naval officer, gained him many compliments.

The British fleet entered the outer roads of Toulon harbour on 29 August. Hood's second-in-command, Admiral Sir Sydney Smith, ably assisted by Elphinstone, destroyed the arsenal, most of the stores and ten ships-of-the-line. Three more ships-of-the-line, some frigates, corvettes and a large number of merchant ships were prepared for sea and escaped with the British fleet while the republican troops ran amok in the city. *Robust* played a distinguished role throughout the campaign that followed: the blockade and capture of Bastia, the siege of Calvi and eventual submission of Corsica.

When the Dutch declared war on Great Britain, the newly promoted rear-admiral was put in command of an expedition to the Cape of Good Hope to counter the threat posed by Dutch colonists and troops to Cape Town. He was also given command of HM ships in Indian waters. On 1 June he was promoted to vice-admiral, making him senior to Nelson in the Navy List. This would prove significant in the Mediterranean three years later. He hoisted his flag in *Monarch* ten days before arriving at the Cape and landing troops at Simon's Bay – today the South African naval base of Simonstown.

The Dutch colonists were spreading out and occupying both native and British-occupied territory and had declared the areas they had taken a 'revolutionary republic'. The admiral landed at Simon's Bay with the troops he had brought, then advanced and held positions under attack by a larger force of Dutch troops. British reinforcements did not arrive until 14 September when they defeated the Dutch at Wynberg and reoccupied Cape Town on 17 September.

After this successful operation, Vice-Admiral Elphinstone moved on to reinforce operations against the French off the Indian coast. Returning to South Africa in August of 1796 and finding a Dutch squadron at anchor in Saldanha Bay, he demanded their surrender. All the Dutch ships gave themselves up without a fight. The Admiral returned home to be raised to the peerage as Baron Keith of Stonehaven Marischal – the title being a recognition of his family's links with the Keiths, hereditary Earls Marischal of Scotland. He became known as Admiral Lord Keith.

While Keith was in the South Atlantic, naval mutinies had erupted, first in the Channel Fleet anchored off Spithead, leading to another at the Nore, where the mutineers appeared to be politically motivated. Keith had an excellent reputation for maintaining good relations with the men under his command and was appointed to the Nore as C-in-C, based at Sheerness, in May 1797. He persuaded the ships that had mutinied to come in and surrender their ringleaders. Within a fortnight of his appointment the mutiny was over. He performed the same role at Plymouth for the Channel Fleet.

In the late autumn of 1798, Vice-Admiral Lord Keith was appointed Commander-in-Chief of the Mediterranean Fleet in succession to Admiral Lord St Vincent. He arrived in Gibraltar on 14 December, four months after the Battle of the Nile. Keith hoisted his flag initially in HMS *Foudroyant* before shifting it to *Barfleur*. A relative, Captain Elphinstone, was his flag captain and Thomas, Lord Cochrane, his flag lieutenant.

St Vincent seemed reluctant to relinquish his command and stayed on at Gibraltar, still flying his flag in a hulk, but living ashore. He gave orders to Keith to blockade the Spanish fleet in Cadiz. Although appointed as C-in-C by the Admiralty, Keith was bound to obey the orders of his irascible senior.

Keith duly blockaded Cadiz for more than four months with a squadron that varied between 11 and 15 sail-of-the-line, while St Vincent clung on to his command of the Mediterranean. Keith eventually had to take his whole fleet across the Straits of Gibraltar to the Moroccan port of Tetuan to replenish with water, leaving the single frigate at his disposal to watch the exit from Cadiz.

As Keith's squadron was returning from Tetuan, they were met by two British frigates from whom they learned that five Spanish sail-of-the-line had emerged from Ferrol 650 miles by sea from Cadiz and that the French fleet had been sighted off Oporto. Keith immediately dispatched the first frigate to Gibraltar to report the situation. In response to this news, St Vincent sent three additional ships-of-the-line and one more frigate to reinforce Keith's squadron. Keith formed his fleet of 16 ships in line of battle off Cadiz to await the French. The enemy fleet, which appeared on the western horizon at about 8 a.m. on 6 May, consisted of 33 sail-of-the-line. With the 22 Spanish vessels within Cadiz harbour, Keith's squadron found itself between enemy forces which outnumbered him by more than three to one. Nevertheless, he formed his ships on the same tack as the French and waited to receive them. To his surprise, the French ships wore to the opposite tack and stood away to the south-west.

Keith's squadron had been deployed to prevent the Spanish ships from escaping from Cadiz and at the same time to prevent the French and Spanish from joining forces. At daylight on 7 May, when four French ships were seen to windward, Keith's squadron gave chase but the Frenchmen had more than a head start and the British ships had to return to their blockade, expecting orders from St Vincent to join him in pursuit of the main French fleet – now thought to be heading for Toulon. Receiving no orders, Keith decided to sail for Gibraltar, which lay only 50 miles to the east, leaving some of his ships off Cadiz. When they reached Gibraltar they found, to their astonishment, that instead of acting upon the intelligence conveyed by the frigate, St Vincent had ordered his ships to anchor and take on water and provisions which took three days. When at last St Vincent hoisted his flag in HMS *Ville de Paris* and shaped course east, in company with Keith's squadron and other available ships, instead of pursuing the French on their presumed route to Toulon, he parted company and sailed for Minorca. He left Keith to pursue the enemy, who by now had had time to embark stores at Toulon and continue east before Keith could catch up with them. The British ships crowded all sail in pursuit and at length came in sight of their enemy's look-out frigates between Corsica and Genoa. Before the British squadron could contact the main French fleet, a fast-sailing transport from St Vincent arrived with orders to return to Port Mahon in Minorca. Keith, knowing the enemy's position – which St Vincent did not – ignored the order and continued in pursuit until a second fast-sailing transport hove in sight and fired guns, signalling Keith to bring to. Very reluctantly he did so and received an uncompromising order from St Vincent to return to Minorca. St Vincent was apparently under the misapprehension that the French were making for Port Mahon. Lieutenant Thomas Cochrane was an eyewitness to Keith's chagrin on receipt of this order. In his autobiography he says:

> On Lord Keith receiving this order, I never saw a man more irritated. When annoyed, his lordship had a habit of talking aloud to himself. On this occasion, as officer of the watch, I happened to be in close proximity, and thereby became an involuntary listener to some very strong expressions, imputing jealousy on the part of Lord St Vincent as constituting the motive for recalling him. The above facts are stated as coming within my own personal knowledge, and are here introduced in consequence of blame being cast on Lord Keith to this day by naval historians who could only derive their authority from data which are certainly untrue, even if official. Had the command been surrendered to Lord Keith on his arrival in the Mediterranean, or had his lordship been permitted promptly to pursue the enemy, they could not have escaped.

It is grossly unjust that Keith should ever have been blamed for the escape of the French fleet. Without a shadow of doubt, it was St Vincent's inaction and misjudgement that allowed the enemy fleets to escape at this juncture. A sentence in a letter sent from Port Mahon by Captain Troubridge, one of Nelson's 'band of brothers', throws light on their attitude towards the man who had – through no fault of his own – been appointed over the head of their hero: 'This undetermined method of acting convinces me he is no great thing and a true Scot.'

On 14 May Keith shifted his flag from *Barfleur* to *Queen Charlotte*, taking Lieutenant Cochrane with him, and set sail to find the French fleet. After five days at sea they encountered and captured three French frigates and two brigs of war on passage from Egypt to Toulon. Meanwhile Lord St Vincent at long last decided to relinquish the Mediterranean command and sailed for England. Lord Keith was obliged to return to Port Mahon to complete the essential arrangements relating to transfer of the command.

Almost immediately on arrival, Lord Keith received intelligence that the French fleet had passed on a westerly course, steering for Cartagena to join the Spanish fleet. He sailed immediately in pursuit but was unable to find them and made contact with Gibraltar to ascertain whether the combined fleets had sailed through the straits. They had not been seen, but Keith deduced correctly that they had passed through in the dark and continued the chase. He altered course north-west, confirmed that the combined enemy fleet was not in Cadiz, then rounded Cape St Vincent and proceeded on a northerly course up the Portuguese coast and across the Bay of Biscay in search of it. When the squadron reached Brest, they found to Keith's disgust that the enemy had arrived the day before and were all safely moored within the harbour. In view of their immense predominance over the British squadron, it is surprising that they made no attempt to come out and bring it to action.

The enemy's combined fleets were now in the theatre of operations of Admiral Sir Alan Gardner, C-in-C of the Channel Fleet. This meant Keith was under the command of Gardner, who now had a force of nearly 50 ships-of-the-line at his disposal. Gardner nevertheless allowed the combined French and Spanish fleets to escape from Brest and head back to the Mediterranean. Keith and his squadron immediately set off in pursuit but were unable to catch them. He then resumed the Mediterranean command, which he had delegated to Nelson in his absence.

Keith now made dispositions to intercept supplies destined for the French army under the brilliant General Massena, who had occupied Genoa. Keith blockaded and bombarded the town, forcing Massena to sign a treaty by which he surrendered his person and allowed Britain's allies, the Austrians, to occupy the town while the British squadron took possession of the harbour.

On 17 July 1799, seven months after he had taken command of the Mediterranean Fleet, Admiral Lord Keith commanded the naval expedition which successfully landed Turkish troops to capture Aboukir from the French. Unfortunately the French soon recaptured it from the Turks.

Nelson, complaining of ill-health, made it clear that he did not wish to remain in the Mediterranean under Keith's command. Keith wrote to him: 'My dear Nelson. . . . Strictly speaking I ought to write to the Admiralty before I let a flag officer go off the station . . . but when a man's health is concerned, there is an end to it all, and I will send you the first frigate I can lay hold of.' In the event, Nelson arrived at Leghorn with two ships-of-the-line which, against Keith's orders, he had taken from the blockade of Naples to bring the Queen of Naples and her entourage to Vienna. A month later, accompanied by the queen, and Sir William and Lady Hamilton, Nelson set out for home by an overland route.

Following the successful defence of Acre, Rear-Admiral Sir Sydney Smith had concluded a convention with the French, allowing their army free passage from Egypt to France. Keith, appreciating the folly of letting the French thus reinforce their armies in Europe, asked the British government to countermand this convention. They agreed, then retracted. Keith was unjustly blamed when Napoleon himself successfully got back to France in October of 1799.

In August 1800 Keith received orders from London to prepare to take Cadiz with troops commanded by a fellow-Scot, the distinguished General Sir Ralph Abercromby, who 'by skilful administration and humanity had gained the affection of the whole army'. The order to attack was an example of an order issued by senior officers unaware of prevailing conditions. In October the British force anchored off the Spanish port with an armada of 130 ships. Not only was the anchorage exposed and swept by strong currents, but a virulent form of plague was also raging in Cadiz. The transfer of troops from the transports into landing craft was taking so long, due to the adverse conditions, that the two senior commanders had second thoughts. They informed the Spanish authorities that if the ships in Cadiz harbour were surrendered, the attack would be called off. The Spaniards, appreciating the British commanders' reluctance to put troops ashore into a plague-ridden city, naturally refused, whereupon the British force returned to Gibraltar. Keith and Abercromby were criticised for taking an eminently sensible decision.

Less than three weeks later, the same British force was ordered to invade Egypt. Keith immediately proceeded to Malta, which had surrendered to the British in the previous month, and thence in stages – beset by frequent storms which can be surprisingly severe in the Mediterranean winter – to the Egyptian coast. On 1 January 1801 Keith was gazetted admiral. By the beginning of March, the armada was anchored in Aboukir Bay. In a model combined operation, all Abercromby's troops were landed in a single day. The French troops were decisively defeated, but General Abercromby was severely wounded and brought back to Keith's flagship *Foudroyant*, where he later died – wrapped, according to legend, in a blanket that one of his soldiers had insisted on giving him. On 2 September the French in Egypt capitulated and Alexandria surrendered, together with all the shipping in the harbour. Keith and the Mediterranean Fleet were accorded a vote of thanks by parliament – a vote which was seconded by Nelson. Keith was also decorated by the Sultan of Egypt, with whom the British had been allied against the French.

On his return to Britain from Alexandria in July 1802, Admiral Lord Keith was given the freedom of the City of London and presented with a sword of honour. In May 1803 he was appointed C-in-C of the North Sea Fleet. He was closely involved in preparing Britain's home defences against French invasion. He remained in command until two years after the Battle of Trafalgar and his role in devising the strategy which prevented Napoleon from invading England and from escaping after the Battle of Waterloo has not been adequately recognised.

From 1812 to 1815 Admiral Lord Keith was C-in-C of the Channel Fleet. It was he who sent HMS *Bellerophon* to Rochefort to intercept the French dictator. Napoleon's surrender was accepted on board on 15 July 1815. Keith then acted as the intermediary between Napoleon and the British government and sent him on his final journey to St Helena.

In retirement at Tullyallan on the north bank of the River Forth, Lord Keith reclaimed land and constructed an embankment and piers. The house he built there is now the Scottish Police Training College. The Admiral himself is buried in a mausoleum in Tullyallan kirkyard, a man whose contribution to the defeat of Napoleon has been greatly undervalued.

⚓ CHAPTER 11 ⚓

Thomas Cochrane

SEAMAN AND SEA WOLF

If Horatio, Admiral Lord Nelson (1758–1805), was the greatest admiral ever born in the British Isles, then Thomas, Admiral Lord Cochrane (1775–1860), was the most able seaman ever to reach the rank of admiral. Yet he is largely unknown to the vast majority of the British public.

Both men were brilliant professional naval officers. Both were men of limitless courage and resource. Both were regarded with love and respect by those who served under them. Both were accorded the ultimate accolade of success in the eyes of the British establishment – the burial of Nelson in St Paul's Cathedral and of Cochrane in Westminster Abbey. Why, then, the huge difference between the levels of public and historic recognition of the two men?

Lord Nelson was the son of an English country parson, Lord Cochrane the son of an impoverished Scottish aristocrat who had spent all his substance on scientific experiments and inventions, but lacked the commercial acumen to profit from them. The former was small, slight, charismatic, politically conventional, with a gift for one-liners and a fair share of vanity. The latter was tall, powerfully built, robust, radical, outspoken, but personally modest. Both were wounded in action more than once in the course of their naval service but Cochrane lost nothing visible whereas Nelson lost an arm, an eye – and his life at the climax of what is perceived as the greatest victory in British naval history. Nelson was given command of great fleets whereas Cochrane achieved astonishing success with minimal resources. Nelson's victory at Trafalgar may have prevented

Napoleon from invading England. Cochrane, named the 'Sea Wolf' by Napoleon, did as much as anybody in the period between Trafalgar and Waterloo to prevent the French dictator from annexing Spain and dominating the Mediterranean by cutting his supply lines and severing his coastal communications. He also played a leading role in winning independence for Chile, Peru, Brazil and Greece.

Nelson was unquestionably front-page material. His naval victories were given banner headlines in every newspaper. His affair with Lady Hamilton, wife of the British Ambassador to Naples, would have featured in the *News of the World* – had it then existed. Cochrane might have made the front page of the same paper because he was framed by political enemies and convicted on circumstantial evidence of a crime he did not commit; but an article featuring his faithful, loving, lifelong commitment to a wife 21 years younger than himself could have graced the pages of a respectable women's magazine or been the plot of a romantic novel. As it was, his exploits at sea provided the inspiration for three novels by the famous naval author, Captain Marryat, who served under him in HMS *Imperieuse*.

Although Cochrane was 17 years younger than Nelson, the two did meet once and Cochrane had great respect for the older man. He describes their meeting briefly when he was serving as a lieutenant under Admiral Lord Keith in HMS *Queen Charlotte*:

> It was never my good fortune to serve under his lordship, either at that or any other subsequent period. During our stay at Palermo I had, however, opportunities of personal conversation with him, and from one of his frequent injunctions, 'Never mind manoeuvres, always go at them', I subsequently had reason to consider myself indebted for successful attacks under apparently difficult circumstances. The impression left on my mind during these opportunities of association with Nelson was that of his being an embodiment of dashing courage, which would not take much trouble to circumvent an enemy, but being confronted with one would regard victory as so much a matter of course as hardly to deem the chance of defeat worth consideration.

Cochrane's radical sense of justice and outspoken candour made him enemies in high places and created obstacles to his promotion that only his tenacity, courage, toughness and longevity were finally able to overcome. A lesser – or perhaps a shrewder – man would have tholed the injustices, kept his counsel and smoothed his own path to promotion, to the ultimate benefit of the Royal Navy – but that was not Cochrane's way. Cochrane has been accused of pecuniary greed, but this does not tally with the character of a man who deliberately turned his back on a fortune in order to marry the impecunious girl he had fallen in love with, in preference to the wealthy heiress recommended to him by an equally wealthy uncle who had promised him half his own fortune if he married her. In Cochrane's own words, 'I did not inherit a shilling of my uncle's wealth, for which loss, however, I had a rich equivalent in the acquisition of a wife whom no amount of wealth could have purchased.'

It is important to disperse the cloud which cast a shadow over Cochrane's astonishing career – the result of a flawed verdict in an English law court which two of the most eminent judges and Lord High Chancellors of the nineteenth century subsequently confirmed as a glaring miscarriage of justice.

False news was conveyed to London in 1814 that Napoleon Bonaparte had been killed and that the allied armies were marching on Paris, resulting in a steep rise in the market value of government stocks. Cochrane's stockbroker had a standing order to sell such stocks when their value rose by 1 per cent on the stock market. Cochrane made a relatively small gain, but, because he was acquainted with the perpetrators of the fraud, he was unjustly charged with 'conspiracy' and found guilty by a politically prejudiced judge on the flimsiest of circumstantial evidence. He was refused a re-hearing, imprisoned, expunged from the Navy List and humiliated.

Subsequently he escaped; passed through hell and various adventures; refused a Spanish invitation to command their navy because he disliked their reactionary government, but accepted a similar invitation from the rebel government of Chile. Eighteen years later, after successively commanding the naval forces of Chile, Brazil and Greece in their wars for independence, he was granted a 'free pardon' by William IV in 1832. This never satisfied him. He wanted to have the 'conspiracy' verdict overturned. Eventually he was accepted back into the Royal Navy, his honours were restored and augmented, and in 1848 at the age of 73 he was appointed commander-in-chief of the American Station with the rank of rear-admiral.

Thomas Cochrane was born on 14 December 1775 in Eddlewood House on the farm of Annsfield, now in a suburb on the south side of Hamilton in Lanarkshire. Eddlewood House was a modest two-storey mansion house built in about 1732 by Thomas's maternal grandfather, Captain James Gilchrist, Royal Navy.

Captain Gilchrist had commanded the 32-gun *Southampton* in March 1758 when she engaged the 40-gun French frigate *Danae*. The duel lasted for six hours until *Southampton*, despite being outgunned, closed and boarded the French ship, which finally surrendered. *Danae* lost a quarter of her crew of 340. *Southampton* had only one killed and ten wounded. Among the wounded was Captain Gilchrist, whose shoulder had been shattered by grapeshot.

There were naval connections on Thomas's paternal side too: a captain in the Royal Navy, Ochter Cochrane, appears in his ancestry. His father Archibald, the ninth Earl, served in the Navy for a few years and reached the rank of acting lieutenant, but he did not enjoy it and, after briefly trying the Army, decided to pursue his overriding interest in chemistry and scientific experimentation. A few of his experiments, although financially disastrous, were scientifically successful. They included a new process for extracting tar from coal (abundant beneath the Forth adjoining the family seat at Culross), which was then used as an effective agent to protect submerged timber from decay. This was the perfect answer to depredations by worms, at least until copper-bottoming was introduced half a century later, but when he offered the invention to the Admiralty they turned it down. In contrast, the Dutch and other northern navies immediately adopted the idea with complete success. When Archibald offered it to a commercial shipbuilder in London, the man replied (in the presence of Thomas, who had accompanied his father), 'My Lord, we live by repairing ships as well as by building them. The worm is our best friend. Rather than use your preparation I would cover ships' bottoms with honey to attract the worms!'

On 27 June 1793 Thomas joined his uncle's frigate HMS *Hind* at Sheerness as a midshipman. In that ship he came under the direct supervision of a man who had an enormous influence on his naval career: Lieutenant Jack Larmour, one of those rare individuals who had been promoted from the fo'c'sle to officer rank due to his superb seamanship and ability. When Larmour discovered that the midshipman wanted nothing more than to learn as much as possible, as quickly as he could, about everything pertaining to the ship, and was willing to dirty his hands at any sort of work at all hours, the two soon became fast friends.

Thomas's first cruise in *Hind* was to Norway, with the aim of discovering any French privateers that might be lurking in the fjords and to watch out for an enemy convoy from the West Indies which was expected to approach by the northern route round the Orkneys. Although every inlet was searched, no privateers were found, nor was the convoy sighted. The young Lord Cochrane was greatly impressed by Norwegian hospitality, simplicity and scenic grandeur. There were opportunities to enjoy sledging, fishing and shooting. He commented:

the principal charm was . . . a people apparently sprung from the same stock as ourselves, and presenting much the same appearance as our ancestors . . . without any symptoms of that feudal attachment which then prevailed in Britain. I have never seen a people more contented and happy . . .

Thomas's uncle was appointed captain of HMS *Thetis* – taking both his nephew and Jack Larmour, his first lieutenant, with him. The responsibility for fitting her out was the first lieutenant's. Thomas offered to help – an offer that Larmour accepted only on condition that the young midshipman would discard his uniform and dress as a seaman. Thomas willingly agreed and was given skilled and practical instruction in the arts of knotting, splicing and rigging. He came to regard this as essential training and rejected the view that such skills were unnecessary for any officer except the boatswain.

When *Thetis* arrived at Halifax, Nova Scotia, they found many American vessels that had been detained and Thomas's sympathy for those seeking freedom from colonial oppression was aroused. He took the view that '. . . a little more forbearance and common sense on the part of the home authorities might have averted the final separation of these fine provinces from the mother country'. He gained unusually rapid promotion to the rank of lieutenant and joined Admiral Lord Keith's flagship in the Mediterranean.

Early in 1800 Cochrane was given his own command: the 158-ton *Speedy*, a brig given the courtesy title of sloop. Into this little ship, perhaps 75 feet in length, were packed eighty-four men, six officers and fourteen 4-pounders, described by Thomas as 'a species of gun little larger than a blunderbuss'. To increase the sloop's speed, he contrived to get the foretopgallant-yard of a second-rate ship-of-the-line as the mainyard. He was ordered to cut it down in size but evaded the order by planing the ends to make it look as if it had been cut, thereby achieving at some risk, both to his own career and the vessel's stability, a greater spread of canvas.

Thomas's cabin in this tiny warship did not even have room for a chair, the table being surrounded by lockers for the dual purpose of storage and seating. When shaving, he had to remove the skylight, his head and shoulders projecting above the upper deck on which he had to arrange his gear. Within a week or two, *Speedy* was actively engaged in boarding and searching numerous vessels, to ensure that they were not carrying supplies or dispatches, and convoying merchantmen of friendly nations. On 10 May 1800 he took his first prize while convoying 14 merchantmen to Leghorn: a 6-gun French privateer. Over the course of the next eight months, *Speedy* was constantly in action, convoying merchantmen, fighting off French and Spanish privateers and gunboats, rescuing prisoners from the ships boarded and engaging shore fortifications. Her astonishing tally over this period was one French gunboat sunk, one driven ashore on the rocks, nine ships captured – including the 10-gun Spanish privateer *Assuncion* from under the guns of Bastia, another Spanish ship cut out from beneath the fortifications of Cape Sebastian and a 10-gun Spanish gunboat bound from Alicante to Marseilles taken. As a result of this remarkable success rate, *Speedy* had made herself the prime target of the Spanish naval authorities. She continued her activities until the end of January 1801, capturing another Spanish merchantman and three armed privateers.

In February a French 4-gun brig carrying guns, ammunition and wine for the French army in Egypt was captured. Soon afterwards, *Speedy* was chased by a large Spanish frigate which began to overhaul her. After dark, Cochrane had a tub with a light in it lowered from *Speedy*'s stern. She then altered course, leaving only the tub to be captured by the Spaniards. In April Cochrane took four more vessels, one of them being cut out from under the guns of a fort. In May the capture of a Spanish 4-gun sloop and the 7-gun privateer *San Carlos* was followed by a battle with a swarm of gunboats which emerged from Barcelona. On 6 May 1801, as *Speedy* ran in towards Barcelona, a large Spanish frigate, later identified as the 32-gun *El Gamo*, was sighted close to the land.

The ensuing action is the supreme example of a victory by David over Goliath in terms of ship-to-ship naval warfare. The Spanish frigate had 32 heavy guns and a crew of 319. *Speedy*'s crew was reduced to 54, because some 36 officers and men had been detached to man her prizes, while her 14 guns were puny by comparison with *El Gamo*'s. This is best illustrated by the comparative weight of shot in each ship's single broadside: *El Gamo* – 190 lb, *Speedy* – 28 lb.

Cochrane made straight for the Spanish frigate, which fired a warning gun and hoisted Spanish colours. To confuse her, *Speedy* hoisted American colours and went about onto the opposite tack, so that she was bows on to the Spaniard's broadside; then she hoisted her true colours. The Spanish frigate unleashed two broadsides in succession without effect. Cochrane deliberately ran under the frigate's lee, locking *Speedy*'s yards amongst *El Gamo*'s rigging and then – having treble-shotted and elevated his little guns – returned the enemy's broadside, effectively raking her main deck and killing her captain and boatswain. Cochrane's tactics ensured that *El Gamo*'s broadsides, due to her height out of the water, flew over the top of *Speedy*, while the little sloop's elevated guns wrought havoc above and below the frigate's upper deck.

The Spaniards were ordered to board the sloop. Cochrane heard the order and sheered off to widen the gap between the two ships, just far enough to make boarding impossible; then closed again and gave them a volley of musketry followed by another broadside. Twice this manoeuvre was repeated with devastating effect, Cochrane demonstrating superb ship-handling skills. The Spaniards abandoned their attempts to board *Speedy* and stood to their main armament which, though doing little damage to *Speedy*'s hull, was cutting up her sails and rigging from stem to stern. In the first hour of the battle *Speedy* lost only six men, two killed and four wounded, but Cochrane knew that combat against such heavy odds could not continue. He told his men that they would either have to take the Spanish frigate or be taken. The sloop's Scots doctor, Mr Guthrie, volunteered to take the helm. Cochrane, having first made some of his crew blacken their faces to appear more ferocious, gave the order to board. He himself then scrambled onto the Spanish frigate's deck. Those with blackened faces boarded over the frigate's bow, causing fear and consternation. The boarders, outnumbered by nearly six to one, made a rush for the frigate's waist, where a hand-to-hand fight with cutlass, sword and pistol continued until Cochrane ordered one of his men to haul down the Spanish colours, whereupon the Spanish crew immediately surrendered. *Speedy*'s casualties were three seamen killed, one officer and seventeen men wounded, whereas *El Gamo*'s captain, boatswain and thirteen seamen had been killed and forty-one men wounded – her casualties thus exceeding the whole complement of the British sloop. Cochrane was left with only forty-two men to sail two ships to Port Mahon – both with their rigging in ribbons – and simultaneously to guard 263 prisoners. The Spanish gunboats made no attempt to leave the safety of Barcelona to rescue the frigate.

It would have been customary after such an action for the senior officer to be promoted, but Cochrane was not and his recommendation of his first lieutenant for an award for gallantry was ignored. Cochrane's sense of grievance against the Admiralty began to build up, reinforced by 'the peculations of the Mediterranean Admiralty Courts by which the greater portion of our captures [prize money] was absorbed'.

Following another successful action when ten merchantmen lying in the Spanish port of Oropesa – protected by a fort, a 20-gun frigate and three gunboats – were either destroyed or captured, Cochrane was disgusted to find on his return to Port Mahon that his prize *El Gamo* had been sold to the Algerians while he had to continue his operations in the vastly inferior *Speedy*.

When he set fire to some supply ships on the Spanish coast between Port

Mahon and Gibraltar, the blaze, reflected in the night sky, attracted the attention of three French line-of-battle ships. At daybreak on 3 July 1801 the three French warships gave chase. The wind was light and the enemy's great spread of sail enabled them to overtake the tiny British sloop, although Cochrane ordered his crew to throw the guns overboard and ran before the wind, crowding on every available square inch of canvas. The French ships were deployed in line abreast, to cover any manoeuvre *Speedy* might make, firing at her with their bow chasers and discharging broadsides whenever a change of tack made that possible. The chase continued for more than three hours. *Speedy*'s rigging was badly cut up, reducing her speed. Like a disabled mouse cornered by three large cats, her plight was desperate. Cochrane ordered all stores to be thrown overboard and when the closest French battleship came ahead of *Speedy*'s beam, the sloop bore up, set studding sails and ran between the two nearest French ships, both of which discharged their broadsides harmlessly. The leading French warship, *Dessaix*, tacked in pursuit, taking less than an hour to come within musket-shot of her prey. She let fly a full broadside of round shot and grape. Fortunately for the little sloop, the broadside missed, the shot plunging into the water ahead of her. Had she been hit by that great weight of round shot she would have been sunk, but the grape made rags, tatters and matchwood of her sails, rigging, masts and yards. Astonishingly no man had yet been killed or wounded.

Cochrane realised that to delay for another broadside would mean certain destruction of his ship and crew and that escape was impossible. With reluctance, he ordered *Speedy*'s colours to be hauled down. He repaired on board the *Dessaix* and presented his sword to Captain Pallière, who politely refused to take it, saying he 'would not accept the sword of an officer who had for so many hours struggled against impossibility' and that he was glad to have terminated *Speedy*'s operations as they were under special instructions to take her. In the 13 months of Cochrane's command the little sloop had taken upwards of 50 vessels, 122 guns and 534 prisoners.

Cochrane was treated with great kindness by his captors and given the freedom of the ship. He admired the sailing qualities of the French man-of-war, particularly noting the superior cut of her sails and the flat surface they exposed to the wind. He was eventually released as part of an exchange of prisoners.

TACTICIAN AND STRATEGIST

Following his return from the Mediterranean, Cochrane applied repeatedly to the Admiralty for a ship, but for two years he was unemployed. To use the time profitably, he entered Edinburgh University, where he studied moral philosophy.

At last, towards the end of 1803, Cochrane outfaced the First Lord of the Admiralty, Admiral Lord St Vincent. 'Well,' said St Vincent, 'you shall have a ship. Go down to Plymouth and there await the orders of the Admiralty.' Thus he found himself appointed to HMS *Arab*, an old semi-derelict collier, an example of Admiralty graft and inefficiency in the use of public funds for the purchase of ships. 'A single glance at the naked timbers showed me that, to use a seaman's phrase, she would sail like a haystack,' was Cochrane's verdict. Nevertheless he waited patiently until her conversion was completed – for the most part with old timber from broken-up vessels. Then he received orders to cruise round Land's End into St George's Channel, before being sent to patrol off Boulogne. Napoleon was making preparations for a cross-Channel invasion of England.

Cochrane found that HMS *Arab* would not work to windward. She could get off Boulogne with the prevailing wind but found it almost impossible to return. The only way to do so was to watch the tidal streams and drift. Cochrane reported to the C-in-C that his ship was incapable of performing the task to which she had been assigned. Shortly afterwards, *Arab* was sent to convoy ships from Shetland to Greenland and then to cruise north-east of the Orkneys to protect the fisheries. However, there were no fisheries there to protect! 'Not so much as a single whaler was seen from the mast-head during the whole of that lonely cruise, though it was as light by night as by day,' Cochrane reported.

When Lord St Vincent was replaced by Lord Melville in December 1804, Cochrane was promptly transferred from HMS *Arab* to command a new fir-built frigate, HMS *Pallas* of 32 guns, with orders to cruise off the Azores with a view to disrupting transatlantic trade between France and Spain on one side, and America or the West Indies on the other. In four days he captured four Spanish merchantmen carrying diamonds, gold and silver ingots and dollars. One of the ships carried an extraordinary item: bales of 'papal bulls' – dispensations for eating meat on Fridays and other indulgences, all with sale prices affixed. Cochrane called them 'a venture from Spain to the Mexican sin market, supply exceeding demand'.

On the way home, *Pallas* was chased by three French line-of-battle ships. It had begun to blow a gale with a heavy sea. Cochrane escaped by executing a manoeuvre requiring extreme skill and daring. With every sail spread, the frigate heeling so that the lee main-deck guns were under water, all the hawsers secured to the mast-heads and hove taut to support the straining masts, and the bows plunging fo'c'sle under, Cochrane watched as his pursuers frequently flashed the priming of their guns but were unable to fire them. Two of them came up on either side, within half a mile of *Pallas*, and one astern. Unable to escape by superior speed, he had to exercise superior seamanship – at considerable risk to his masts. Having warned the crew, he gave the order to clew up and haul down every sail simultaneously, and at the same instant put the helm hard up. *Pallas* wore and was brought up suddenly, shuddering from stem to stern. The pursuers, unprepared for the manoeuvre, shot past at full speed and ran on for several miles before they could come about. *Pallas* spread all sail on the opposite tack and increased the distance between herself and her enemies 'at a rate of 13 knots and upwards'. After dark a ballasted cask with a lantern attached was lowered overboard to simulate her lights and *Pallas* altered course. When dawn broke there were no ships on the horizon. The frigate returned safely to Plymouth. With substantial prize money due, Cochrane was philosophical about half of his share going to the port admiral, Sir William Young, who had blatantly intercepted Cochrane's orders and recopied them over his own signature, exploiting the established system which allowed port admirals to claim a major share of any prize money won by ships based in their port.

Pallas sailed from Portsmouth on 28 May 1805, convoying merchantmen to Quebec. On making the American coast, they were many miles out in their dead reckoning, although their latitude had been corrected whenever weather conditions, notably the fogs on the Newfoundland Banks, permitted celestial observations. They soon discovered the cause. The binnacle of the magnetic compass was secured with iron instead of copper bolts. This dockyard 'economy' could have been disastrous for the frigate and the convoy. Cochrane took the convoy into Halifax, Nova Scotia, and refused to leave until the iron bolts were replaced by some made of copper.

Cochrane's fertile mind was never at rest. Noticing that the stern cabins of some merchant ships outshone the convoy lights, making station-keeping difficult, he devised a lamp more powerful than any other ships' lights, to be carried by the protecting frigate, enabling the merchantmen to follow her and to keep in touch. The Admiralty ignored the design he submitted, but a few years later they offered a substantial prize for the best design of a convoy light. Cochrane resubmitted his design in his agent's name. After repeated trials against others, it was awarded the prize, but when it became known at the Admiralty that the design was Cochrane's, the lamp was never ordered or brought into service. Another of his inventions met with similar treatment: an enormous kite that could be used to increase a vessel's speed without requiring extra masts or spars.

Pallas was in mid-Atlantic when the Battle of Trafalgar was fought but in the early weeks of 1806 Cochrane cut out a French merchantman protected by a battery at the mouth of the Somme, and captured a lugger carrying dispatches. *Pallas* then captured seven French fishing smacks. After eliciting some useful information from them, Cochrane pleased the skippers by buying their fish and letting them go. As a result of the information obtained, *Pallas* took five prizes over the next few days. Cochrane had designed and had built a galley, rowed double-banked with 18 oars, which he now shipped on board *Pallas* and used for cutting out expeditions. 'Her beautiful build rendered her perhaps the fastest boat afloat,' he claimed.

During 1806 Cochrane carried out many daring attacks. At one point he ran for the mouth of the Garonne, where he had learned that several French corvettes were sheltering and decided to cut one out under cover of darkness. Cochrane anchored off the lighthouse at the river's mouth and sent all but a skeleton crew away in the boats to capture the 14-gun *Tapageuse*. Two other corvettes which came to assist her were beaten off by her own guns. *Pallas* was still lying at anchor off the lighthouse, with only a sixth of her crew on board, when three more French corvettes appeared off the river mouth. Being dangerously undermanned and outnumbered, Cochrane needed another ruse to fool the enemy and so his few remaining hands furled the sails with rope yarns; all the yarns were then released simultaneously, giving the impression that a highly trained crew was on board. Seeing the cloud of canvas, the three enemy corvettes ran before the wind, just off shore, with *Pallas* in pursuit. One by one their captains deliberately ran their ships aground. Had they known that *Pallas* only had enough men on board to man the single bow chaser, they could easily have turned the tables. *Pallas* beat back to the river mouth to pick up her boats and their crews and to take charge of her prize, *Tapageuse*. On 14 April *Pallas* returned to the Garonne and, in the face of batteries which the French had placed to protect the three grounded corvettes, made certain they would not be re-floated by blasting holes in their hulls.

Towards the end of the month, *Pallas* carried out two daring reconnaissances, first off Isle de Ré and then in the Basque Roads. Cochrane made a meticulous report to the C-in-C, giving precise details of the 12 ships in the Basque Roads. He reported that they could easily be taken or burned and suggested exactly how.

On 14 May *Pallas* again entered Aix Roads to reconnoitre the French squadron. She deliberately ran within range of the French batteries to challenge the frigates sheltering beneath them. The frigate *Minerve* – 44 guns as against *Pallas*'s 32 guns – weighed anchor and came out to meet the challenge, supported by three brigs of 18 guns each. Simultaneously the shore batteries opened fire on *Pallas*. After an hour *Pallas* got to windward of *Minerve* and, after discharging three broadsides into her, Cochrane ordered his master, Mr Sutherland, to lay her alongside the French frigate, which was driven aground, seriously disabled. Two more French frigates came to *Minerve*'s assistance. *Pallas* was damaged but fortunately the sloop HMS *Kingfisher* came to take her in tow and the French frigates and brigs made no attempt to follow. *Pallas* had taken a number of French prisoners. Considering the ferocity of the action, her own casualties were extraordinarily light: one killed and five wounded.

While *Pallas* was refitting, Cochrane won a seat in parliament for the Honiton division, unusually without employing any form of bribery. He made himself unpopular in parliament by drawing attention to Admiralty abuses, so on 3 August 1806 he was appointed in command of the frigate *Imperieuse*, which was commissioned a month later with the crew of *Pallas*. So eager was the Admiralty to get their awkward critic to sea that *Imperieuse* was ordered out before she was anywhere near ready. She had lighters alongside, the guns were not secured, the ballast had not been put below and the rigging was not set-up. Had the ship encountered a storm – or an enemy – she would have been helpless. They had to heave to in mid-Channel to finish their basic preparations. In fact they drifted, struck a shelf off Ushant and only saved the ship by dropping three anchors in deep water and warping her off. Cochrane was so angry at his treatment by the dockyard and by the port admiral that he afterwards demanded a court martial but, knowing they were to blame, the authorities refused.

On 29 November *Imperieuse* joined the blockading squadron in the Basque Roads. In the second half of December she captured three vessels and on 4 January 1807 chased several others which ran inshore. Giving chase, her own boats were nearly swamped by the surf; the enemy ships escaped and ran ashore beneath a battery. When boats from *Imperieuse* tried to warp them off two days later, the battery protected them. Cochrane's solution was to destroy the battery. He led the landing party at dawn on 7 January, stormed the battery, spiked or destroyed four 36-pounders, two field pieces and a 13-inch mortar, set fire to the fort and burned several gunboats.

In April 1807 parliament was dissolved. By now Cochrane was disillusioned with Honiton, a 'rotten borough' where he was constantly expected to keep his supporters sweet with financial inducements. Instead, he decided to stand for the prestigious City of Westminster seat as an independent – a liberal 'reformer' beholden to neither Whigs nor Tories. Out of five candidates, Cochrane topped the poll. On 10 July he brought forward a motion on naval abuses. It was a long speech which met with many interruptions and much embarrassed and ill-informed opposition. The issues raised affected all those who were serving in the Royal Navy:

ships kept at sea in a dangerous state of disrepair and without a break for eight months or more; surveys of ships at sea substituted for proper examination in harbour; men forbidden to go ashore when storm-bound for 12 days in harbour; lime juice used as a substitute for fresh provisions; no man sent to hospital unless first examined by the C-in-C's surgeon, who might not be available; a man with a rupture refused admission to hospital because 'everything possible' had not been done in his own ship; the quantity of lint available for dressing wounds in ships and hospitals reduced for the sake of economy; the Boards of Admiralty paying no attention to those under their command; lack of continuity on these Boards, which changed with every change of government. His speech had one immediate effect: *Imperieuse* was ordered to rejoin the fleet of Admiral Lord Collingwood in the Mediterranean. She sailed on 12 September 1807, in charge of a convoy of 38 merchantmen.

When off the coast of Corsica, after leaving part of the convoy at Gibraltar, *Imperieuse* challenged two vessels, which answered by opening fire. In the action that followed, *Imperieuse* lost two men and had thirteen wounded, two severely, before forcing the surrender of the vessels. They turned out to be Maltese pirates and for the capture of one a reward of five hundred pounds had been offered, but this reward was never received. It was not paid because Admiralty officials in Malta had shares in the ships.

Over the next six months, Cochrane lived up to the soubriquet awarded by the French: the 'Sea Wolf'. He captured or destroyed twenty-eight vessels, including four gunboats and a Turkish vessel from under the guns of a battery, and destroyed another shore battery, two armed towers and a barracks. Then in June 1808 Napoleon made his brother, Joseph, King of Spain and the Indies; Spain revolted, declared war against France and proclaimed peace with Great Britain. Almost immediately, Cochrane received orders to render every possible assistance to the Spaniards.

Cochrane had his most recent prize refitted as a gunboat for use as a tender to *Imperieuse* and on 25 June, flying British and Spanish colours, they anchored off Cartagena and were warmly welcomed. Cochrane, having received intelligence that a French army was advancing along the coast to reinforce the garrison in Barcelona, landed with a party of seamen, blew up overhanging rocks to block the road and destroyed bridges, thereby preventing the passage of artillery, stores and cavalry. Anchoring near Mataro, he destroyed a French battery. Several French brass guns from another cliff battery were captured and transferred by carrying a hawser to the cliff top, securing the other end to the ship's mainmast then – using tackles and the capstan – hauling the guns on board. Cochrane spent two days ashore instructing the local residents in guerilla tactics and demolition, making (to quote his own words) 'as throughout life I have ever done, common cause with the oppressed'.

Having learned that the French had occupied Fort Mongat, he personally reconnoitred the fort. *Imperieuse* then stood in and anchored within range. After she had delivered a couple of well-directed broadsides, the French hung out flags of truce.

Imperieuse continued to carry out disruptive operations along the French-occupied coast almost without respite. Vessels were cut out; forts, batteries, barracks, signal towers and telegraph stations were destroyed – invariably under fire; signal books were captured and half-burnt papers were scattered around to persuade the French that the books had been destroyed. These books and codes forwarded by Cochrane enabled the Admiralty to forecast all movements of French ships 'from the promontory of Italy northward'.

Cochrane's chief problem at the time, however, was not the enemy but shortage of water. On one occasion they were so desperate that, having sewn up sails as semi-watertight bags, Cochrane sailed into the mouth of the Rhone, sent boats upstream until the water was pure, filled the bags, towed them alongside the ship, and pumped the fresh water into their hold using their fire-engine pump.

Fort Trinidad stood on a hill dominating the town of Rosas, situated about 12 miles from the French border at the eastern end of the Pyrenees. The town was under attack by the French army but the citadel in the town centre and the fort on the hill above had been held by the Spaniards with the help of the Royal Navy. *Imperieuse* joined two other British frigates in the Bay of Rosas on 19 November 1808. The senior British captain had decided that the fort was indefensible and had withdrawn his marines. Spanish morale had collapsed and the commandant of the fort was about to surrender. Cochrane landed in a gig, persuaded the commandant to continue resistance, reinforced the garrison with marines from *Imperieuse*, reorganised the defences of the battered fort, designing ingenious mantraps to prevent a French assault through a breach they had created by bombardment, and engaged the French batteries with accurate gunfire from *Imperieuse*. His aim was to hold the fort until promised Spanish reinforcements could relieve the town.

During the action Cochrane was wounded in the face by a splinter, which caused him 'intolerable agony', flattening his nose and penetrating his mouth. He commented, 'by the skill of our excellent doctor Guthrie my nose was after a time rendered serviceable'. Meanwhile, he carried on directing the defences of the fort. A French assault in overwhelming numbers was confronted by Cochrane's mantrap – a slippery drop of 50 feet baited with fishhooks on chains – and repelled. The French sustained heavy casualties.

Nevertheless, the citadel fell before Spanish reinforcements could reach it. Cochrane, his sailors, marines and the Spanish garrison – massively outnumbered and under continuous bombardment – had defended it for two weeks. It was now pointless to continue and Cochrane organised an orderly withdrawal. He invariably took the greatest care to ensure the least possible loss of life. Sir Walter Scott wrote a eulogy of Cochrane referring to his 'consummate prudence'. The effectiveness of Cochrane's operations was recognised by the French and grudgingly praised by Napoleon himself. Collingwood reported:

> Nothing can exceed the zeal and activity with which Lord Cochrane pursues the enemy. The success which attends his enterprises clearly indicates with what skill and ability they are conducted, besides keeping the coast in constant alarm – causing a general suspension of the trade, and harassing a body of troops employed in opposing him. He has probably prevented these troops . . . from advancing into Spain by giving them employment in the defence of their own coasts.

From the Admiralty, however, there was no official gesture of thanks or recognition.

Cochrane did not rest on his laurels. He found a convoy of 11 merchantmen in the Bay of Caldaques, loaded with supplies for the French troops, escorted by two small warships and sheltering under a battery supported by troops on the hill above the bay. *Imperieuse* anchored and then opened fire on the warships, successfully sinking them. Cochrane then warped *Imperieuse* inshore to get within range of the batteries, which, with the extra height of the hill, had been able to straddle the frigate. He landed marines near the town to distract attention, then landed blue jackets on the beach opposite the battery. The French abandoned it and fled to the hill to join their comrades. The sailors took five brass cannon and threw the rest over a cliff. Later the two sunken brigs were raised and thirteen ships were captured.

Captain Lord Cochrane now asked to be allowed to return home. He wanted to lay before the Admiralty proposals which, if accepted, he later claimed, 'neither the Peninsular War, nor its enormous cost to the nation from 1809 onwards, would ever have been heard of'. His own experiences had convinced him that if a single frigate could paralyse the movements and supplies of the French armies in the Mediterranean theatre, then 'with three or four ships it would not be difficult so to spread terror on their Atlantic shores as to render it impossible for them to send an army into western Spain'. However, those in power in the Admiralty ignored what he had achieved and failed to give intelligent consideration to his proposals. Instead, he was officially reproached for having expended more on gunpowder, shot, stores and sails than any other captain in the service.

One individual who recognised Cochrane's merits was the Second Lord of the Board of the Admiralty, the Hon. Johnstone Hope – a Scot. When *Imperieuse* arrived at Plymouth, Cochrane received a friendly letter from this individual, congratulating him on his safe arrival and on his 'exertions' in the Mediterranean. Unfortunately Johnstone Hope was on the verge of retiring and returning to Scotland when he wrote.

⚓ ⚓ ⚓

The Battle of Aix Roads was fought on the night of 11 April 1809 and on the following day. Admiral Lord Gambier had the opportunity of a victory as significant as Trafalgar, but he failed to grasp it through dithering incompetence. That Cochrane later felt compelled to oppose a vote of thanks to Lord Gambier in the House of Commons, because he knew the scale of the missed opportunity, was characteristic of the man.

The French fleet was blockaded in the anchorage in Aix Roads, sheltered by Isle d'Oleron to the west, guarded by shoals to the south and with a safe retreat into the mouth of the River Charente to the east. With batteries on Isle d'Oleron and on Isle d'Aix to the north, the French admiral thought his ships were in an impregnable position. There were ten line-of-battle ships there, four frigates, an armed storeship and seventy or more boats and small craft. Gambier's fleet was anchored in the Basque Roads some 15 miles away to the north-west.

The Admiralty ordered Cochrane to carry out his own plan to attack the French fleet with fireships, bottled up as it was in a confined anchorage. He had previously reconnoitred the anchorage and taken soundings. He now demurred, because he was junior to most of the captains in Gambier's fleet. He feared that his lack of seniority would excite jealousy and antagonism. Gambier himself was opposed to the idea but people at home were dissatisfied with the inactivity of the Channel Fleet. The Admiralty and the government needed some sort of victory. Cochrane was the answer: he was more likely to succeed than anybody else and they did not care if success or failure made him unpopular. He was ordered to prepare a plan and go.

Imperieuse arrived in the Basque Roads on 3 April 1809 and Cochrane's fears were vindicated. The captains of the fleet were furious. Many of them had volunteered for such duty and were insulted that its execution had been entrusted to a junior officer from outside the fleet.

Cochrane reported to the C-in-C on board his flagship. He was astonished when a hero of Trafalgar, Admiral Harvey, informed Gambier, in Cochrane's presence, that 'if he were passed by, and Lord Cochrane or any other junior officer was appointed in preference, he would immediately strike his flag and resign his commission'! Harvey proceeded to tell Gambier that he 'never saw a man so unfit for the command of the fleet as Lord Gambier . . .' Afterwards, in the flag captain's cabin, Admiral Harvey shook hands with Cochrane and assured him that his outburst had been nothing personal to himself.

Cochrane soon discovered that the fleet was dangerously divided, morale was low and no dispositions for attack had been made. He decided to carry out his own close reconnaissance and to supervise the preparation of the fireships and explosion vessels himself. The French admiral had erected a massive boom to protect his line-of-battle ships from the north and west and deployed frigates outside the boom to intercept and tow away any fireships that the British might send down on his fleet with the prevailing wind and flood tide. Cochrane knew that there was enough sea-room to approach the French anchorage outwith the range of the guns on the islands, which were in any case in a poor state of repair and readiness. This was not accepted by Gambier, who continued to be given inaccurate information by his own staff about the width and depth of the channel.

Cochrane's plan was to float the fireships down at night and force the French fleet either into action or to run aground. The two leading 'fireships' would be packed with high explosives. Cochrane calculated that when the first of these went off it would not only breach the boom but would cause panic because the French would conclude that all the other 22 'fireships' were also explosive vessels.

Gambier, indecisive, refused to allow Cochrane to make the attack on 10 April when conditions were perfect. The following night Cochrane sought permission again. It was blowing half a gale but wind and tide were still in the right direction, although the strength of the wind would make it much harder for the volunteers to return in their boats after setting the explosive ship and fireships on course. This time Gambier reluctantly assented.

Cochrane anchored *Imperieuse* within three miles of the boom and embarked with four volunteers in the first explosive vessel to lead the attack, followed by the fireships. Judging their distance as well as they could in the dark, they lit the fuses on the explosive vessel then pulled for their lives into the wind, against the tide and away from the boom. The wind caused the fuses to burn at twice the intended rate. The vessel struck the boom and exploded only eight minutes after they had left it. In Cochrane's own words:

> . . . the rockets and shells from the exploded vessel went over us . . . for a moment the sky was red with the lurid glare . . . The sea was convulsed . . . rising in a huge wave, on whose crest our boat was lifted like a cork and as suddenly dropped into a vast trough, out of which, as it closed upon us with a rush of a whirlpool, none expected to emerge . . . in a few minutes nothing but a heavy rolling sea had to be encountered, all having again become silence and darkness.

They watched two fireships pass through the gap in the boom which the explosion had created. The French warships began firing in the dark towards their own frigates. Only four of the fireships actually got through the boom, but the panic created in the French fleet surpassed all expectations.

At dawn on 12 April Cochrane saw that the boom had completely disintegrated and all of the French ships except two line-of-battle ships were helplessly aground, lying on their bilges, their bottoms exposed to gunfire, unable to retaliate. At 6 a.m. Cochrane reported the situation by signal to Gambier's flagship. Never had a commander-in-chief been presented with a better opportunity to overwhelm an enemy fleet, but, despite repeated signals from Cochrane, Gambier did not move. Again and again – at least six times – Cochrane signalled to the admiral that the enemy fleet was at his mercy. The only response was the answering pennant. The fleet remained motionless. By 9 a.m. the tide was rising fast. Cochrane, desperate, resorted to a deliberately provocative signal: 'The frigates alone could destroy the enemy.' Again, just the answering pennant. Soon the ships aground would be able to float off and escape. Already they were heaving guns and stores overboard to this end. Cochrane signalled, 'The enemy is preparing to heave off.'

Imperieuse's position, out of range of shore batteries, but with sea-room, was proof that Gambier's fleet could have attacked with absolute impunity. At last, at 11 a.m., the British fleet weighed and stood towards Aix Roads, only to come to anchor again three and a half miles away, just out of range. By now several of the French line-of-battle ships had got afloat. The opportunity to destroy them without retaliation had been missed. In despair, Cochrane weighed anchor and allowed *Imperieuse* to drift stern first towards the enemy, intending to engage them and force Gambier to send ships to his assistance. If he had not done this, not a single enemy ship would have been destroyed. At 1.30 p.m. Cochrane made for the nearest enemy ship and ran up a signal, its wording somewhat restricted by the shortcomings of the signal book: 'Enemy superior to chasing ship but inferior to the fleet.' Gambier took no notice. At 1.45 p.m. Cochrane signalled, 'In want of assistance', and with that his 44-gun frigate began to engage simultaneously three enemy ships of 80, 74 and 56 guns respectively, eventually capturing the 56-gun *Calcutta*. At long last seven British ships, ignoring their admiral, came to the assistance of *Imperieuse* – five frigates and two line-of-battle ships. Gambier's never came within range. At 5.30 p.m. two French '74s' surrendered to the ships that had come to Cochrane's assistance. At 7 p.m. another blew up.

Before daybreak the following morning Gambier hoisted the recall. Cochrane ignored it. There were still two French ships-of-the-line aground, at the mercy of their attackers, and he was determined to force their surrender. All but one of the seven ships that had come to assist him returned to the fleet. The exception was Captain George Seymour (later the distinguished Admiral Sir George Seymour) in Cochrane's old ship *Pallas*. Again the flagship signalled the recall. Cochrane, with the support of Seymour, continued the action, signalling 'The enemy can be destroyed.' Gambier finally resorted to sending Cochrane a letter by boat demanding his return. Cochrane sent a letter back which read: 'We CAN destroy the ships which are on shore, which I hope your lordship will approve of.'

At daylight on 14 April Cochrane received a final letter from Gambier, which he could not ignore, demanding his return to the fleet in order to convey the flag captain back to England with dispatches. Cochrane pleaded with Gambier to send sufficient ships to finish off the French fleet but Gambier cut the matter short by handing Cochrane a written order. Had Gambier followed up and attacked the panic-stricken and disorganised enemy fleet, it could have been annihilated. That he was subsequently cleared by a court martial is an absolute indictment of that court, of those who gave evidence in favour of the admiral and of the establishment which did not wish to see one of its favoured placemen publicly destroyed.

FREEDOM FIGHTER

Between the Gambier court martial in 1809 – which paradoxically was more damaging to Cochrane's naval career than it was to Gambier's – and his appointment as vice-admiral of Chile in 1817, Thomas Cochrane's life was a continuous battle against misrepresentation, naval abuses, waste of public money, inept military strategy, maltreatment of prisoners, flogging and any of the other numerous evils which blighted Britain in the first half of the nineteenth century and which happened to engage his attention. This battle was fought in the courts and in the House of Commons. He was sustained by his faithful Westminster constituents, who elected and re-elected him as an independent, by a few staunch friends and by a marriage from heaven. He put forward projects which were successively rejected by Admiralty and government. Despite this, he consistently refused to disclose his plans or inventions to any other country or faction which might have acted against the interests of his native land.

In the spring of 1817 Don José Antonio Alvarez, a Chilean patriot, visited Great Britain looking for financial support, ships and a naval commander who could assist Chile's struggle for independence from Spain, which at this time still claimed Mexico, Central America, Colombia, Venezuela, Ecuador, Peru, Bolivia and the Argentine, as well as Chile. He was introduced to Cochrane, who readily agreed to undertake the organisation and command of a naval force to protect the young republic from the tyranny of a reactionary Spanish government. Ironically, while he was preparing for departure that very government approached him and offered him the command of the Spanish navy to suppress the independence movement he had just contracted to support. He declined the offer out of hand and ignored a warning that the Foreign Enlistment Act, drafted by the Tory government at the instigation of the Spanish authorities, could have serious consequences for him.

Spain refused her American territories the opportunity for foreign trade except through the port of Cadiz. Due to the dearth of roads and railways, it was evident that their independence movements would not succeed unless the Spaniards could be defeated at sea and Spanish strongholds on the coast wrested from them.

The Chilean struggle for independence had begun in 1810 with the deposition of the Spanish governor. The Chileans were assisted by the Argentinian General, San Martin, who had already helped to achieve independence for his own country. Bernardo O'Higgins, the republican son of an Irishman who had been viceroy of Peru under the Spaniards, had taken over as the supreme director of the Republic of Chile. The Spaniards were, however, still in possession of the country between Concepçion and the island of Chiloe in the south.

Cochrane embarked for Santiago in August 1818 as vice-admiral of Chile. He sailed in the old 300-ton merchantman *Rose*, together with Lady Cochrane and their two infant sons. They were royally entertained on arrival in November and he had to remind their hosts that he had come to fight, not to feast.

Cochrane's first task was to attack Callao, the port for the Peruvian capital, Lima. The 14 Spanish vessels anchored there and the port's batteries vastly outgunned Cochrane's little fleet. As Cochrane sailed out of Valparaiso, flying his flag in the 50-gun frigate *O'Higgins*, the last boat pulled alongside carrying his flag lieutenant – and the elder of his two infant sons! The child had persuaded the young officer to take him out to his father. Drawn to an upper-storey window by the sound of shouting and hurrahs, to her horror Lady Cochrane saw her five-year-old son Thomas sitting on the lieutenant's shoulders in the middle of a crowd, waving his cap and shouting 'Viva la patria!' It was too late to get him back.

O'Higgins, accompanied by two old armed merchantmen, approached Callao while a carnival was being held. They captured a Spanish gunboat but in the ensuing action *O'Higgins* was subjected to heavy fire from shore batteries. She succeeded in silencing one of the batteries before withdrawing to the island of San Lorenzo three miles away. During this action Cochrane's small son escaped from the after cabin where he had been locked and, wearing a miniature midshipman's uniform which the sailors had made for him, was found handing gunpowder to the gunners, spattered with the blood of a marine who had been decapitated by a round shot. Cochrane was, in his own words, 'spellbound with agony', thinking the blood was his son's.

Cochrane occupied the island of San Lorenzo and from it succeeded in blockading Callao for five weeks. He released 37 Chilean soldiers whom the Spaniards had captured eight years before and kept in chains ever since.

In April, Cochrane's little squadron embarked on a two-month cruise, routing the Spanish garrison in Huacha, capturing their stores and a huge sum of money destined for payment of Spanish troops, which he later presented to the Chilean exchequer. Everywhere, he insisted on paying generously for any food or stores taken. The admiral returned to Valparaiso on 16 June, where they were received enthusiastically by General O'Higgins and the inhabitants – and no doubt by Lady Cochrane, who must have been more than a little relieved to see her husband and son safely back.

Cochrane decided to attack the major port of Valdivia, the heavily defended base for Spanish operations in the south of Chile. There being no accurate charts, the port and its approaches had first to be thoroughly reconnoitred. Under Spanish colours, *O'Higgins* arrived off Valdivia on 18 January 1820, hoping to be mistaken for the Spanish frigate *Prueba*. They signalled for a pilot, who promptly came off, accompanied by an officer and four soldiers who were at once taken prisoner. The prisoners provided Cochrane with all the intelligence he required, including news of the imminent arrival of the brig *Potrillo* with money for payment of the garrison. While *O'Higgins* was sounding the channels, the commandant of the garrison, suspicious because the officer and four soldiers had not returned, opened fire. *O'Higgins* did not reply but, having completed the necessary reconnaissance, withdrew. The following day *Potrillo* was captured without a shot.

Cochrane returned to Concepçion and obtained from the governor 250 soldiers to enable him to carry out his plan to capture Valdivia. He augmented his squadron by conscripting the Chilean schooner *Montezuma* and accepting an offer of assistance from a Brazilian brig, *Intrepido*. On 25 January they set sail again for Valdivia. The voyage to Callao proved eventful due to the inefficiency of the only two naval officers in *O'Higgins*'s crew: one was put under arrest for disobedience to orders; the other was incompetent. As a result, Cochrane himself had to remain constantly on watch. Becalmed on the night of 29 January, Cochrane thought it safe to take some badly needed rest, leaving the ship in charge of the incompetent lieutenant. The lieutenant took advantage of the vice-admiral's absence to retire also, leaving command of the flagship to a midshipman who then fell asleep. A breeze sprang up and the frigate ran aground on a rock. They were 40 miles from the mainland, their two consorts were out of sight, there were 600 men on board – nearly half of them soldiers – with only sufficient boats to hold 150; the hold was flooded, the pumps were out of order and the ship's carpenter had no idea how to repair them. Some of the men were all for abandoning ship, but Cochrane put them to work baling out with buckets and, taking off his coat, descended into five feet of water to repair the pumps himself. By midnight he had them in working order and the water was not gaining on them. The admiral himself then laid out the stream-anchor by boat and they commenced heaving the ship off the rock. With the leak now under control, Cochrane estimated that the ship could reach Valdivia without sinking. He reasoned that once they had captured the fortress they could repair the ship at their leisure. Unfortunately the powder magazine had been under water, so they would have to capture the forts, 15 of them, at bayonet-point.

On 3 February the two smaller ships, with the troops on board, anchored off the outermost fort on the west bank where there was a landing place. The Spaniards opened fire and mustered troops at the jetty. Cochrane landed, using the only three boats available, personally directing operations from one of them. The first boat landed 44 marines, who drove the Spaniards at bayonet-point up the beach and back into their fortifications. Thereafter the boats shuttled back and forth, landing 300 men under fire in less than an hour.

By subterfuge and daring, Cochrane attacked the main fort from the front and the side, forcing the defendants to retreat to the next fort along.

In this manner, all the forts on the western shore were overrun, more than 100 Spaniards were bayoneted, another 100 or more taken prisoner, while the rest escaped into the forest or by boat up river. The total losses of Cochrane's force – marines, soldiers and sailors – were seven killed and nineteen wounded.

On 5 February *Intrepido* and *Montezuma* entered the river, under fire from the forts on the eastern bank. When *O'Higgins* appeared at the harbour entrance, the Spaniards abandoned the eastern forts, which were then occupied by Cochrane's Chilean troops. The following day they received a flag of truce and occupied the town. With a force of three small ships and a total of 600 men, Vice-Admiral Cochrane had neutralised 15 forts, defeated the Cantabria Regiment of the Line consisting of 800 men supported by 1,000 militia, freed the major town of Valdivia from Spanish occupation, and captured a huge amount of military stores. The victory persuaded all the indigenous tribes in the region, previously subjugated by the Spaniards, to declare in favour of the Chilean republicans. The Spaniards lost their main southern base and suffered a blow to their morale from which the remnants of their administration in Chile never recovered. No wonder they had nicknamed Cochrane 'el diablo'.

When the little squadron dropped anchor off the island of Chiloe on 17 February, they found a body of Spanish cavalry and upwards of 1,000 infantry with a heavy gun ready to dispute their landing. Undeterred, Cochrane organised a diversionary landing at a distant point, effected a landing against the divided force, captured their gun and left Fort Corona with all its guns spiked and military stores destroyed. The praise Cochrane received in Valparaiso caused jealousy and at one point Cochrane offered his resignation but retracted after a public appeal by the officers of the fleet.

While he was away, Lady Cochrane had been attacked by a man who threatened to kill her if she did not divulge the orders given to the vice-admiral. She had refused and been wounded by the man's stiletto before servants came to her rescue. Her attacker was condemned to death without the last rites of the Catholic Church, but the man's wife pleaded with Lady Cochrane, who intervened to have his sentence commuted to banishment.

Cochrane spent three days in August carefully preparing a secret plan: to cut out the *Esmeralda*, the biggest and best Spanish warship in the Pacific, together with a vessel she was escorting with a million dollars on board, which he intended to use for long-overdue payment of his men. She was lying in Callao harbour under the protection of 300 pieces of shore artillery, a strong boom with chain moorings, 27 gunboats and several armed block ships.

Every man volunteered to accompany Cochrane, but he took only 160 seamen and 80 marines in 14 boats to make the attack. After dark the boats were moored alongside the flagship outside the harbour. Each man was armed with a cutlass and pistol and wore a white sleeve with a blue band for distinction.

At 10 p.m. all was ready. The fourteen boats were in two divisions, Cochrane himself in the first boat of the leading division. The orders were strict silence, muffled oars, and cutlasses; pistols to be used only as a last resort. The flotilla entered the harbour by a small gap in the boom, which was protected by a guard-boat. When challenged, Cochrane hissed a threat of instant death to the occupants of the boat if they made a sound. Within minutes the boats were alongside *Esmeralda*, the sailors and marines boarding her simultaneously at several points. During the action Cochrane was severely injured. Boarding by the main-chains, he was struck by the butt-end of a sentry's musket and fell back on a tholepin projecting from the boat's gunwale. The pin entered his back near the spine, inflicting an injury that troubled him for the rest of his life. He regained his footing, again climbed on board *Esmeralda* and was promptly shot through the thigh. He bound a handkerchief round the wound and managed, with difficulty and in acute pain, to direct the contest to its close.

A Spanish frigate of 40 guns and 370 men had been taken in an action lasting a quarter of an hour. The Chileans lost 11 killed and 30 wounded but 160 of the Spaniards were dead. The operation had been brilliantly successful. Among other prisoners from *Esmeralda* was the Spanish admiral. Cochrane exchanged the captured Spaniards for a large number of patriot prisoners, which made him highly popular.

Captain Basil Hall, Scottish captain of a British warship then in the Pacific, later commented:

> The loss of the *Esmeralda* was a death blow to the Spanish naval force in that quarter of the world; for although there were still two Spanish frigates and some smaller vessels in the Pacific, they never afterwards ventured to show themselves, but left Lord Cochrane undisputed master of the coast.

Cochrane became increasingly aware that his aim of winning independence and self-determination for Chile differed from San Martin's, which was to establish a form of military despotism headed by himself. When San Martin refused to provide funds to pay the fleet's sailors and marines, Cochrane decided that desperate situations demanded desperate measures. He sailed to Ançon, where a large amount of treasure had been deposited by San Martin in his private yacht, and took possession of it, returning what could be identified to its lawful owners. He kept only a small part of the residue to meet the squadron's debts and purchase essential stores, distributing the remainder – a sum in the region of 285,000 dollars – to the officers and men of his squadron as arrears of pay. San Martin was furious.

Cochrane realised that there was little more he could do for the Chilean republic and his services had had effects far beyond the west coast of South America. His defeat of Spanish naval power had opened 7,000 miles of Pacific coastline – previously a Spanish monopoly – to international trade and, significantly, the United States now recognised the independence of the South American republics. Cochrane sent O'Higgins a letter of resignation and looked elsewhere for employment. He was offered an embarrassment of choices: command of the navies of Mexico, Brazil or Greece. Before accepting the Brazilian invitation, Cochrane received a formal resolution of thanks from the Chilean president and Assembly. By many there he is still regarded as a national hero.

⚓ ⚓ ⚓

At the time Lord Cochrane entered the service of Dom Pedro, the Regent of Brazil, who had proclaimed the colony's independence from Portugal, the northern provinces, loyal to Portugal, were ruled by the aristocratic Portuguese Party and held by Portuguese troops supported by a formidable fleet. Cochrane arrived in Rio de Janeiro on 13 March 1823 and hoisted his flag in the 74-gun *Pedro Primiero* five days later. His supporting squadron comprised three small ships, the largest of which boasted thirty-two little guns, plus two old vessels for use as fireships and two other warships which were still fitting out. When he attempted to blockade the port of Salvador, the Portuguese fleet of thirteen warships, which included a 74-gun line-of-battle ship and five frigates, emerged to engage him. Cochrane succeeded in breaking their line, but his other ships did not obey the order to follow him. Their crews were poorly trained and disciplined and the action had to be broken off. On return to Rio, Cochrane immediately initiated 'a rigid inquiry'. He transferred all the best men, weapons and fittings to *Pedro Primiero* and the 32-gun frigate, then gave instructions for training the more promising members of the other crews before returning with the two best ships to Salvador.

Having taken careful bearings at the mouth of the bay where the Portuguese fleet was anchored under the shelter of shore fortifications, Cochrane entered the anchorage at night and succeeded in establishing exactly how the ships were deployed, threading his way among them in the darkness. The Portuguese admiral was attending a ball but when he learned, with astonishment, of Cochrane's audacity he decided to vacate the anchorage. On 2 July the fleet of 13 warships accompanying between 60 and 70 troop transports and merchantmen streamed out of the bay and sailed north-east up the coast, making for Maranham.

Cochrane's two ships attacked them with the assistance of some of his other ships which had now come up from Rio. He gave orders that all troopships should be boarded, then have their masts cut away to oblige them to comply with written instructions to return to Bahia. Their water-casks were to be broken, leaving them with only sufficient water to carry out this order.

Many prizes were taken. Cochrane in his flagship took no prizes but got among the escorting Portuguese warships – one against thirteen – out-manoeuvring them. They fired broadsides which did no damage, then turned and resumed escorting what was left of the convoy. Cochrane followed and as night fell got among them again, boarding the nearest ships, disarming the officers and forcing them to give parole that they would not serve against Brazil. *Pedro Primiero* continued with these tactics for two weeks; from 2 July until 16 July; from latitude 12° south to 5° north of the equator! A single ship, daringly and expertly handled, drove 13 warships out of the South Atlantic. Of the original convoy of 60 or 70, only a baker's dozen made it back to Lisbon. *Pedro Primiero* finally had to cease her attacks when the inferior sailcloth of her mainsail split as she tacked to fire a second broadside at the Portuguese admiral's flagship. Only then did Cochrane decide it was time to set course for Maranham to ensure that the Portuguese troopships had obeyed instructions and gone back to Bahia.

Cochrane reached Maranham, the wealthiest province of the Portuguese colony of Brazil, on 26 July. He entered the harbour under Portuguese colours. A Portuguese brig-of-war was sent out with dispatches revealing important secrets – and congratulations on the ship's safe arrival from Portugal! The captain of the Portuguese brig, discovering his mistake, was then victim of another trick: he was informed that *Pedro Primiero* was the first of a formidable squadron on its way from Rio to invade the province. He was sent back to the commandant of the garrison with a letter to this effect, well laced with a mixture of promises and threats. The following day leading members of the junta, the commandant and the Bishop of Maranham came on board and tendered their submission to Dom Pedro. Within 24 hours of Cochrane's arrival, the flag of Brazil flew where the Portuguese flag had previously flown.

The liberation of Maranham was publicly celebrated on 28 July and the Portuguese troops embarked for Lisbon four days later – a little suspicious at the non-arrival of the occupying force from Rio.

One remaining province of importance, Para, was still under Portuguese control. Cochrane immediately dispatched a Portuguese brig he had captured to Para, under the command of one of his officers, with orders to carry out an operation that replicated his capture of Maranham. This he achieved successfully. The whole of Brazil was now free of Portuguese domination, but political unrest threw up an opposition group in Pernambuco. Cochrane, with his two warships and with diplomacy backed by the threat of bombardment and the imminent arrival of soldiers, induced the insurgents to capitulate without bloodshed.

The strain of his unremitting activity, combined with the heat and humidity of a climate so different from that of his native Scotland, was now seriously affecting his health. Having made arrangements for a reliable officer to relieve him in Maranham, he took over the frigate *Piranga* and on 18 May 1825 set sail for the Azores, intending to return to Rio after blowing the equatorial air from his lungs. Lady Cochrane and their children had left for home some time before.

During the journey, however, they ran into a gale and discovered that *Piranga*'s maintop mast, and her main and maintop yards, were sprung and her running rigging was rotten. It also transpired that the provisions were bad. There was only enough edible food to last a week and a return to Rio was out of the question. Cochrane decided to set course for the English Channel and dropped anchor off Spithead on 26 June, flying the flag of Brazil. He enquired whether, if he fired a salute, it would be returned. The answer was affirmative. Great Britain was thus the first European state formally to recognise Brazilian independence.

Agreement was reached between Portugal and Brazil on 3 November 1825, making it unnecessary for the admiral to return to South America. When Lord and Lady Cochrane went to the theatre in Edinburgh, the whole audience rose to their feet to give them a prolonged and rapturous welcome that caused Lady Cochrane to burst into tears and Sir Walter Scott to write a six-verse poem of ecstatic praise and questionable quality.

⚓ ⚓ ⚓

The cause of Greek independence had the support of leading politicians in Great Britain and of the renowned poets, Byron and Shelley. Cochrane's adherence to it temporarily silenced those who opposed his rehabilitation and the restoration of his rank and honours. He was eventually commissioned in the service of the Greek government on 21 February 1827 and took the small vessel *Unicorn* and a French-built corvette *Sauveur* to the tiny island of Poros, south of Athens, where the aptly named steamship

Perseverance and American-built frigate *Hellas* awaited him. These were his only ships, poorly officered and manned, with the dubious support of about 250 Greek armed merchant and coastal craft with piratical ambitions. Cochrane's command was only nominal. He had insufficient money to pay his crews and there was no code of discipline. In the background was a plethora of rival factions vying for supremacy.

Cochrane's practical service to the Greek cause was limited to the last nine months of 1827 – nine months of frustration and embarrassment. The Greek sailors would do nothing without payment in advance. They had no concept of discipline and proved almost impossible to train. His primary objective was to attempt to relieve Athens, besieged by the Turks, but the troops with whom he was expected to cooperate liked to stop every few yards and build little fortifications called *tamburias*, which they then garrisoned. Their progress was therefore imperceptible and shrinking, and they were slaughtered by the Turkish cavalry.

Because Egypt was in alliance with Turkey, an expedition against Alexandria was planned. With his flag in *Hellas*, accompanied by *Sauveur*, fourteen Greek brigs and eight fireships, Cochrane sailed from Cape St Angelo, arriving off Alexandria on 15 June. His plan was to enter the harbour, capture as many Egyptian ships as possible, and to release the fireships among the rest to cause them to be abandoned. In the event, the Greek captains were frightened to follow him into the harbour. One ship only and two fireships came in with him. A single Egyptian man-of-war was destroyed, but the attack caused panic. The rest of the Egyptian ships prepared for flight, but the Greeks, thinking they were about to be attacked, fled too and scattered over an area of 20 square miles of sea. Cochrane and his consort spent a night and a day collecting them together again.

On 1 August *Hellas* and *Sauveur* reconnoitered Navarino (Pylos) at the south-west extremity of the Greek mainland, where they discovered a large Turkish corvette, two brigs and two schooners. After an action lasting nearly an hour, the corvette was forced to surrender. This was the only occasion on which Cochrane succeeded in getting Greek sailors to fight. David Urquhart from Inverness, a lieutenant on *Hellas*, went on to become a diplomat and was responsible for the introduction of hot-air Turkish baths into Britain.

The rest of Cochrane's time in the Greek service was spent in conveying Greek troops between islands, taking a few Turkish or Egyptian prizes and attempting to suppress piracy – Greek against Greek. Early in 1828 he visited London and Paris in an attempt to raise funds to pay his crews and to fit out the rest of the naval squadron, but he found that, due to the unreliability of the Greeks, the Greek Committees had lost faith and enthusiasm. Cochrane resigned office on 20 November and on 20 December left Poros for good.

⚓ ⚓ ⚓

Lord Cochrane now began the long process of seeking public acknowledgement that he had never been guilty of 'conspiracy'. In May 1832 he was granted a 'free pardon' but he did not wish to be pardoned for a crime he had never committed. He was restored to the Navy List and in January 1841 awarded a pension for 'good and meritorious service'. In 1847 he was reinstated as a Knight Grand Cross of the Order of the Bath and at the end of the same year appointed C-in-C of the North American and West Indies Station. He used much of his time pursuing his scientific interests in ship propulsion, development of the Newfoundland fisheries and of the great pitch lake at La Brea in Trinidad. According to Cochrane's grandson: 'his great desire was to return to Scotland and the scenes of his early years'.

In a letter to his friend Professor Playfair of Edinburgh University (under whom he had studied), written five days before his death on 29 October 1860, Lord Cochrane said, 'My health was improving so fast a couple of months ago that I had formed the intention of spending the remaining portion of my life in my native land. Since then the progress has not warranted the attempt . . . ' After his death – by unanimous decision of the House of Commons – his heirs and successors were awarded the half-pay due to him for the years between his wrongful conviction and his restitution to the Navy List. Without actually ordering a retrial, this was as close as it was possible to go to acknowledging that there had been an appalling miscarriage of justice. His burial in Westminster Abbey was the final seal on acknowledgement of his innocence and on his close association with the electors of Westminster. It was also posthumous recognition of a career as astonishing as that of any British subject who has ever lived.

Longship with arms of Campbell of Argyll and MacDonald
of Ardnamurchan featuring galleys with sails furled.

HMS *Vanguard*: the last battleship built on the Clyde,
completed in 1945 – too late for the Second World War.

Sir Andrew Wood's *Yellow Carvel* launched about 1475 in the Firth of Forth.
(Picture courtesy of the National Museums of Scotland)

The Great Michael built at Newhaven for King James IV in
1511 – the greatest warship in the world.
(Picture courtesy of the National Museums of Scotland)

Admiral Adam Duncan – 1st Viscount Duncan of Camperdown. (Picture: Henri-Pierre Danloux. Courtesy of the Scottish National Portrait Gallery)

Admiral Lord Keith, George Keith Elphinstone – Viscount Keith – Nelson's Commander-in-Chief. (Picture: William Stavely. Courtesy of the the Scottish National Portrait Gallery)

Thomas Cochrane – Admiral Lord Cochrane – admiral of the navies of Chile, Brazil, Greece and Great Britain.

Admiral B. Cunningham – Admiral of the fleet Lord Cunningham – 'the greatest admiral since Nelson'. (Picture courtesy Mrs S.E. Pratt)

Captain Lord Cochrane in HM sloop *Speedy* (14 guns, 54 men)
takes the Spanish frigate *El Gamo* (32 guns, 319 men), 1801.

Admiral Lord Cochrane in the Brazilian flagship *Pedro Primiero* alone
decimates a Portugese convoy of 13 warships and 70 transports, 1823.

Clipper *Sir Lancelot*, built in Greenock, did the China run in 90 days in the 1860s, averaging 14.75 knots per day.

Lusitania, Clyde-built Cunarder sunk by a German U-boat on 7 May 1915 with the loss of 1,198 lives.
(Picture courtesy of the Mary Evans Picture Library)

Clyde-built Cunarders: *Britannia* (1840); *Queen Mary* (1934), 'blue riband' holder in 1936, crossing the Atlantic at 30.63 knots average.
(Picture courtesy of the NMPFT/Science & Society Picture Library)

The derelict site of John Brown's shipyard, Clydebank, in 2002
– birthplace of some of the world's finest ships.
(Photo by James Davidson)

Container port and refinery at Grangemouth,
linked by pipeline to the oil terminal at Finart.
(Photo by James Davidson)

The BP oil terminal at Finnart on Loch Long which can
accommodate the biggest tankers in the world.
(Picture courtesy of BP Finart)

Star of Scotland – a typical twentieth-century trawler;
backbone of the fishing fleet.
(Picture courtesy of the Picture Library of the National Museums of Scotland)

RNLI Lifeboats at Buckie on the Moray Firth
– one alongside, one on the slipway.
(Photo by James Davidson)

⚓ CHAPTER 12 ⚓

Exploration and Empire

Until the Act of Union in 1707, Scotland had been more concerned to survive within a perimeter of rugged coastline and border hills than to exploit the world beyond. Scots were adventurous and traded where they could but the urge to dominate or exploit foreign peoples or territory was never a prominent aspect of the Scottish psyche. Glasgow's wealth depended largely on the import of tobacco and sugar and later on engineering and shipbuilding, whereas Bristol's and Liverpool's owed much to the slave trade. Certainly, Scots were not above profiting from exploitation by others but Scotland's contribution to the British Empire was mainly made through emigration, exploration and mercenary, technical and administrative activity.

Some skill in the art of navigation was essential for exploration and trading. Most early 'navigation' was coastal pilotage and recognition of landmarks. Early Norse seamen even used captive birds, releasing them to indicate the direction of the nearest land. The Portuguese, Spanish and French were pioneers in producing manuals of navigation or 'rutters'. Early Scottish navigators learned their art in the French school and to some extent depended on translations of French rutters for their knowledge of the coasts of Western Europe.

The year 1614 witnessed an invention by an Edinburgh mathematician which became a boon to navigators and others. John Napier published a book entitled *Descriptio*, which gave logarithms to the world, enabling time-consuming trigonometrical calculations to be made by simple addition and subtraction using his logarithmic tables. A ship's latitude could be worked out from astronomical observations in less than a quarter of the time previously required, although longitude remained a difficulty until accurate chronometers became available more than a century later. Napier also invented, in the year of his death, a primitive submarine – although details of it are not known – and a mechanical calculator.

By the middle of the seventeenth century, Scottish merchants were beginning to make efforts to expand their trade beyond Europe. As early as 1634 the Scottish Guinea Company was formed with the purpose of trading home-made goods for African gold but it faced fierce competition from the East India Company, which had received its original charter from Queen Elizabeth of England in 1600. The Company of Scotland bought gold in 1699 from which the last gold coins from the Scottish mint were struck – pistoles for the ill-fated Darien scheme.

After the Act of Union, a few Scottish merchants, mostly from the Dumfries and Kirkcudbright area, did become involved in the slave trade abroad. One Scottish consortium – Grant, Oswald and Company – bought a ruined fort near Freetown, Sierra Leone, in 1748 and set up a business supplying slaves to the sugar plantations in America. They even built a golf course to pass the time while waiting for local chiefs to bring down captives for sale. The slaves were bartered for goods shipped from Europe, America and India. Grant and Oswald were relatively humane, caring for the health of the slaves whilst they awaited shipment and using beads in preference to branding for identification. In Scotland there were particularly strong feelings against slavery and in 1778 the Court of Session ruled that any slave entering Scotland became free. It was not until 1807, however, that Britain made slave trading illegal and 1833 before an Act of Parliament was passed at Westminster abolishing slavery in Britain.

In the eighteenth century large areas of the world's seas were still uncharted. The world-renowned voyages of Captain James Cook – the Yorkshireman with a Scottish father – took place between 1768 and 1780. He had the advantage of an improved sextant and on his second and third voyages round the world he had an exact copy of John Harrison's No. 4 model chronometer, which was consequently subjected to severe tests of climate and motion. While Captain Cook was exploring the opposite side of the world, Dr Samuel Johnson and his acolyte James Boswell were exploring the Hebridean islands and enduring seasickness on a storm-tossed voyage to Coll.

The East India Company was responsible for compiling many of the early charts of seas and coasts beyond the ambit of Europe. Their hydrographer, Alexander Dalrymple, was born at New Hailes near Edinburgh in 1737. He joined the East India Company as a writer and was sent to the company's offices in Madras in 1752. Two years later he became deputy secretary, a responsible job for a 17-year-old. In 1758 he was given permission to sail in the schooner *Cuddalore* to the 'eastern islands' – the East Indies – to try and negotiate a commercial treaty with the sultan of Sulu. This voyage preceded a series of others to eastern destinations as far away as China, enabling him to learn the basics of seamanship and navigation and to publish a book of his discoveries in 1764. He later published a chart of the Bay of Bengal, followed by pamphlets on Sumatra, the East Indies and the Pacific. In 1795 he became the first hydrographer to the Admiralty, which had become the ultimate authority on maritime charts, a post which he held for 13 years, collecting, collating and publishing a large number of charts and at the same time organising the Admiralty's hydrographic department. In 1830 the first official catalogue of charts – 952 of them – was published.

Dalrymple held advanced views on maritime trade, holding that it should be developed with countries whose sovereignty was not in dispute and which were not subject to any colonial power. He seems to have had no difficulty with subordinates but his superiors found him awkward to deal with.

Pitcairn Island, which lies in the Pacific half way between Australia and America, was discovered in 1767, before Captain Cook embarked on his first voyage or set foot in Australia. It was named after a midshipman of the Royal Navy sloop who first sighted it: Robert Pitcairn, who was born in Edinburgh in 1747 and died in 1770 when his ship *Aurora* was lost in a cyclone off Mauritius. The island became the first British possession in the South Seas but remained uninhabited – despite its fertility and fine climate – until occupied by the mutineers from the *Bounty* in 1790.

Sir Alexander Mackenzie (1759–1820) explored huge areas of Canada on behalf of the North West Fur Company. He followed the Mackenzie River, which was named after him, to the Beaufort Sea and the Arctic – the western end of the long-sought North West Passage. As well as reaching the sea at Mackenzie Bay, he was believed to be the first white man to cross the Rocky Mountains, reaching the Pacific at Cape Menzies. Born in Inverness, Sir Alexander died in Scotland in 1820.

The Arctic explorer, Sir John Ross, who was born at Balsarroch in Wigtownshire in 1777, was first put on the books of HMS *Pearl* when he was only nine years old. He eventually attained the rank of rear-admiral and was uncle of the equally famous Sir James Clark Ross. Between them they were responsible for much of the earliest scientific exploration of the Arctic. John Ross was apprenticed for four years to a shipowner in Greenock, trading with the Baltic and the Caribbean. He went on three voyages to each of those contrasting seas. In 1794 he entered the service of the East India Company and remained in their employment until 1799, when he joined HMS *Vessel* as a midshipman, serving in the North Sea, the Channel and the Baltic. He was promoted to lieutenant in 1805 and in that year was wounded whilst cutting out a Spanish vessel under the batteries of Bilbao. During his naval career he was wounded no less than 13 times and spent some time as a prisoner of the French.

In February 1812 he was promoted commander of a sloop in the North Sea and the Baltic. Then until 1815 he was captain of the sloop *Actaeon*, surveying the White Sea coast and establishing the longitude of Archangel by observing eclipses of Jupiter's satellites. From 1815 to 1817 he surveyed the Scottish coasts in HMS *Driver*. Then in 1818 he was given command of an expedition to attempt to make the North West Passage by way of the Davis Strait between Greenland and Baffin Island. He was given two ships: a whaling schooner *Isabella* and a smaller vessel *Alexander*, commanded by Lieutenant William Parry. They sailed in April 1818 and after passing through the Davis Strait and Baffin Bay attempted to sail west through Lancaster Sound along the north coast of Baffin Island. Had they made it through the Sound, through the Barrow and McClure Straits, they could have entered the Pacific by the Bering Strait, but – apart from ice – the way appeared to be barred by a range of mountains: 'the Croker Mountains'.

Ross was promoted to captain in December 1818 and published a description of his recent voyage the following year. Controversy ensued as to whether the Croker Mountains really existed or had been a mirage produced by the strange Arctic light. They do not, in fact, exist.

In 1829 Ross was given command of *Victory*, to search for a passage south from Regent Inlet which opens into Lancaster Sound. He was accompanied by his nephew, James Clark Ross. They were stopped by ice and forced to spend the winter of 1829–30 in a barren inlet named Felix Harbour. In 1830 they penetrated to Victoria Harbour but were held there by ice until 1832. They made their way to Fury Beach and spent a fourth ice-bound winter in a hut built from the wreck of the *Fury*, a relic of the previous expedition under Lieutenant William Parry accompanied by James Ross. The enormous effort and hardship had not been wasted. The Boothia Peninsula and much of King William Land had been surveyed and in 1831 James Ross established the position of the magnetic pole on Prince of Wales Island, west of the Boothia Peninsula. The expedition also reached the conclusion that no feasible North West Passage existed.

John Ross was knighted and received Gold Medals from the Geographical Societies of London and Paris. He also published descriptions of the winters spent in the Arctic which proved valuable to future expeditions.

In 1845 Sir John Franklin turned down Sir John Ross's application to join his Arctic expedition. Franklin never returned. In 1849 Ross received a grant from the Hudson Bay Company, backed by private subscription, to carry out another expedition, hoping to cast light on the mystery of Franklin's disappearance. He sailed in *Felix* from Stranraer on 25 May 1850. On returning the following year, he published a criticism of the government's previous failure to send out a search and rescue expedition after Franklin's disappearance. Sir John wrote several treatises and pamphlets in addition to his descriptions of his expeditions. Their subjects included navigation by steam, deviation of the mariners' compass and intemperance in the Royal Navy. He died in 1856.

Sir John Ross's nephew, Rear-Admiral Sir James Clark Ross, was a midshipman under Lieutenant William Parry on two voyages of Arctic exploration, first in *Hecla* from 1819 to 1820 and then in *Fury* until 1825. *Fury* was wrecked in the Prince Regent Inlet and had to be abandoned. In 1827 James Ross made an unsuccessful attempt, again with William Parry, to reach the North Pole across the ice from Spitzbergen. Promoted to commander in 1827, he became a Fellow of the Royal Society in 1829. He was with his uncle's expedition when the position of the magnetic pole was established on 1 June 1831. Promoted to captain in 1834, he commanded *Cove* on a successful expedition to Baffin Bay in 1836 to rescue whalers caught in the ice.

Captain James Ross was employed by the Admiralty in a magnetic survey of the British Isles before being appointed to command an expedition to undertake a magnetic and geographical survey and voyage of discovery in the Antarctic. Two ships with specially strengthened hulls, *Erebus* and *Terror*, sailed in September 1839 and crossed the Antarctic Circle on 1 January 1841. They discovered Victoria Land, the range of mountains on longitude 160°, which included the 12,000-foot volcano which they named Mount Erebus, and a range of ice cliffs which appeared to bar the way to the South Pole. The expedition surveyed some 2,000 miles of Antarctic coast and returned to the British Isles in 1843 having lost only one man through illness in four years. Captain James Ross received Gold Medals from the Geographical Societies of London and Paris. He was knighted, and published detailed accounts of his voyages. Five years after his return he was appointed in command of *Enterprise* on an Arctic expedition to relieve Sir John Franklin. They were, of course, too late but found some evidence of his fate. Rear-Admiral Sir James Clark Ross died in 1862.

Sir John Richardson, born in Dumfries in 1787, was a naval surgeon who became involved in Arctic exploration in mid-career. He had seen active service from Copenhagen to Quebec and from the Baltic to Portugal. He joined Sir John Franklin's polar expeditions in 1819 and again in 1821 in the combined role of surgeon and naturalist. In 1826 he went with a party of 11 to explore east of the Mackenzie River in northern Canada. The party travelled 2,000 miles in 10 weeks and was responsible for recording a great volume of scientific observations. In 1847, accompanied by Orkney-born Dr John Rae, he sailed on an unsuccessful search for Sir John Franklin and his missing expedition.

Hugh Clapperton, born in 1788 in Annan, in Dumfriesshire, is best known for his African journey from the Mediterranean to Lake Chad. His career started as a cabin boy in a merchant ship. He became ship's cook, then a midshipman, then drill-master in HMS *Asia* under Admiral Sir Alexander Cochrane. Promoted to lieutenant in 1815, he became involved in an exploration in Labrador where he saved the life of a boy who had fallen through the ice, hunted with the Huron Indians and experienced other adventures before leaving the Navy and embarking on his African journey.

James Weddell, who was born in 1787 in Lanarkshire, gave his name to the Weddell Sea off the coast of Antarctica. He was a navigator by profession, son of a working upholsterer, whose widowed mother apprenticed him in a Clyde coaster and then in a West India merchantman. In that ship he struck the captain, under extreme provocation, and in 1808 was handed over to HMS *Rainbow* in disgrace. He recovered his reputation, took every opportunity to learn the art of navigation and rose to be master. Admiral of the Fleet Sir George Ross described James Weddell as 'one of the most efficient and trustworthy officers I have met with in the course of my professional life'. Between 1814 and 1816 he was master of a sloop and two frigates. When the war with France was over he went on half-pay, then accepted command of the 160-ton brig *Jane* of Leith, owned by a Mr Strachan, for a sealing voyage in the southern seas around the South Shetland Isles. His first voyage took two years: 1819–21. Mr Strachan was sufficiently pleased with the outcome to give James Weddell a share in the brig. On the second voyage *Jane* was accompanied by the 65-ton cutter *Beaufoy*. They explored and surveyed the Falkland Islands, Cape Horn, the South Shetlands, and the South Orkneys, which Weddell had discovered on the previous voyage. The two ships reached a latitude of 74°15' south. Weddell published an account entitled *A Voyage towards the South Pole performed in the years 1822–24*, followed by two further volumes of meticulous observations. He stayed at sea as captain of a merchantman but his skill as a merchant did not equal his skill as a navigator. He died 'in straitened circumstances' in 1834.

Captain Basil Hall RN was born in Haddington in 1788. He entered the Navy at the age of 14 and was promoted to lieutenant in 1808. He was involved in landing reinforcements for Scots general Sir John Moore at Corunna in 1809. He undertook voyages of discovery on behalf of the Admiralty, exploring and surveying the coasts of Korea and adjacent islands, the west coast of South America, the Galapagos Islands and Mexico.

Scots also contributed to exploration of the coasts of Australia. Lachlan Macquarie, from the Hebridean Isle of Ulva, was governor of New South Wales from 1810 to 1820 and encouraged both internal and coastal exploration of the continent.

Admiral Sir James Stirling, born in 1791 in Lanarkshire, entered the Navy in 1803. He served in *Glory*, flagship of his uncle Rear-Admiral Sir Charles Stirling, in the action off Cape Finisterre which preceded Trafalgar; then in operations in the Rio de la Plata. He also commanded the sloop *Brazen*, which operated and surveyed over a wide area from the West Indies to Hudson Bay and from the estuary of the Mississippi to the coast of Ireland and the North Sea. Promoted to captain in 1818, he was sent to Australian waters to establish a settlement in the extreme north of Queensland on the Torres Strait. He explored the coast westwards and in 1828 established a settlement of 1,300 people in west Australia, marking out the future sites of Fremantle and Perth. He was made governor of Western Australia when it became a state and remained there until 1839. The following year he returned to active service in the Royal Navy and first commanded the 78-gun *Indus*, then the 120-gun *Howe* in the Mediterranean, before being promoted to rear-admiral and C-in-C China and East Indies in 1851. He became a full admiral three years before his death in 1865.

Much of New South Wales and central Australia was surveyed by Sir Thomas Mitchell, who was born in Stirlingshire in 1792. Sir Thomas was in the Army, not the Navy, but he published books describing the Australian shores of the Pacific and Indian oceans.

It would be unrealistic to attempt to give credit here to all the Scots who have participated, in various roles, in virtually every important British voyage of exploration in the last three centuries, but doctors have been prominent among them. William Baikie, born in Kirkwall in 1825, was a surgeon in the Royal Navy who died before reaching the age of 40 but performed a vital role as surgeon and naturalist to the 1854 expedition that explored the River Niger in west Africa and opened it to navigation.

John Rae, born in Orkney in 1813, studied medicine in Edinburgh and was appointed surgeon to the Hudson Bay Company in 1845. He had a broad interest in scientific experiment and application. Between 1845 and 1847 he surveyed the coast between Boothia and the Hecla Strait with the Rosses and Parry and then surveyed 700 miles of newly explored coast. In

1847 he joined one of the expeditions searching for Sir John Franklin, covering the thousand miles of coast between the mouths of the Mackenzie and Coppermine rivers in both directions. He crossed part of the Wollaston Peninsula and surveyed its coast, covering 1,100 miles at a rate of 24 miles a day in Arctic conditions, and also surveyed some 90 miles of the Victoria Channel. Much of his exploration, both coastal and internal, was carried out by boat and he travelled 5,350 miles in eight months. In 1853 he led another expedition to explore the coast of Canada's North West Territory, proving amongst other discoveries that King William Land, west of the Boothia Isthmus, was an island. On one occasion, to prove the efficacy of snow shoes, he walked the 40 miles from Toronto to Hamilton in seven hours, apparently with no sign of fatigue. In 1860 John Rae surveyed part of the route of the telegraph line from Scotland to America via the Faeroes, Iceland and Greenland. He died in his 80th year and is buried in Kirkwall. It has been estimated that he walked 23,000 miles in the course of his explorations, but nobody has calculated the total distance he covered by boat.

Sir Charles Wyville Thomson, a naturalist who specialised in oceanography and made a huge contribution to human knowledge of the seas around us, was born in Linlithgow in 1830. He studied at Edinburgh University but had only limited opportunity to pursue his interest in marine life in the sea depths until 1868, when he embarked as a supernumerary in the gunboat HMS *Lightning* to undertake investigations in the deep water between Scotland and the Faeroes. He also carried out investigations off the west coast of Ireland, in the Bay of Biscay and in the Mediterranean. In 1872 the Admiralty equipped the 2,306-ton corvette HMS *Challenger* specifically for oceanographic exploration, with a naval surveying staff under Captain George Nares. Thomson was appointed chief of a civilian scientific staff of six. *Challenger* left Sheerness on 7 December 1872, crossed the Atlantic from the Canary Islands to the West Indies, sailed north to Halifax, Nova Scotia, then by Madeira and the Azores to the Cape Verde Islands. From there, the ship steered west to the coast of Brazil, across the South Atlantic by Tristan da Cunha to the Cape of Good Hope, thence into the Antarctic Ocean until stopped by ice-pack well south of the Antarctic Circle. *Challenger* returned to the United Kingdom by Melbourne, Sydney, Fiji, Japan, the Sandwich Islands, Valparaiso, the Magellan Strait, Montevideo and the Canaries, arriving off Spithead on 24 May 1876. In the course of a voyage of 68,890 nautical miles, observations and soundings had been taken at 362 places. Charles Thomson and George Nares were both knighted, but Thomson's work was far from over. He was appointed director of the project to collate and publish all the results of the voyage at public expense. Before he died at Linlithgow in 1882 he completed this work, published 45 special papers and reports and wrote another book describing the voyage of the *Challenger*. He was the recipient of countless scientific honours and honorary degrees.

The name of McNeish, the highly skilled ship's carpenter on Sir Ernest Shackleton's 1914–17 Antarctic expedition, only appears three times in Shackleton's own book but, according to a more recent account, without McNeish's outstanding manual skills Shackleton's epic boat journey and eventual return would not have been possible.

Later in the nineteenth century, overseas trade was thriving. In 1878 William Mackinnon leased territory from the sultan of Zanzibar and founded the British East Africa Company. Glasgow was developing as a world-renowned shipbuilding and heavy engineering city as well as already being a centre for the import and processing of sugar and tobacco. In 1890 the railway bridge across the Firth of Forth was completed, changing both the commercial outlook and self-assessment of the two great city-ports of north-east Scotland – Aberdeen and Dundee.

The century came to a close with Great Britain in possession of the greatest empire and the largest battle fleet and merchant navy the world had ever seen. The Royal Navy consisted of more than 300 warships and 90,000 men. The 'two-power standard' was the prevailing strategy: to possess a navy of greater power than that of the next two largest navies combined, though it was a strategy that could not survive two world wars in the twentieth century and the coming of age of the greater part of the British Empire. Bolstered by an economy dependent on cheap overseas labour, on artificially cheap raw materials, it also depended heavily on recruitment from Scotland for the ships and regiments of men of whom many – if not most – joined because there were few alternatives on offer.

⚓ CHAPTER 13 ⚓

Ports and Harbours

Some 230 ports, harbours, anchorages, ferry termini and shipyards can be identified around the coast of the Scottish mainland and islands, varying in size and importance from world-renowned ports such as Clydeport, Grangemouth, Leith, Dundee and Aberdeen to tiny fishing harbours like Auchmithie in Angus – the village called Musselcrag in Sir Walter Scott's *The Antiquary* – or Carsethorn in Kirkcudbrightshire, which was the final point of departure for many Scots emigrating to North America and the Antipodes.

In this chapter we take a voyage round the coast of Scotland, starting on the Scottish side of the Solway Firth and finishing in the seaport of Berwick-on-Tweed, which was one of Scotland's first four royal burghs. Berwick changed hands between Scots and English eight times between 1174 and 1406 and was declared neutral territory in 1551. Although now in Northumbria, it gives its name to the adjoining Scottish county – and has a football team in the Scottish League. Berwick is a fishing harbour with shipbuilding yards and an industry netting salmon as they enter or emerge from the Tweed – a Scottish river. There is no more suitable place to terminate this voyage.

Kirkcudbright, a royal burgh and capital of the Stewartry, faces towards the Isle of Man across the waters where the Solway Firth merges into the Irish Sea. It is closely associated with John Paul Jones and has been an active port since the Middle Ages; its harbour is dominated by the ruins of the sixteenth-century McLellan's Castle. A notorious pirate, Leonard Robertson, used Kirkcudbright as a base in the 1570s. Among other acts of piracy, he raided the estuary of the English River Dee, dominated by the historic city of Chester, taking a valuable cargo from a merchant ship and selling it off to landowners around his home port. When Queen Elizabeth of England complained to James VI, the king appointed a commission of enquiry to investigate but as the commission comprised most of the 'receivers of stolen goods' the pirate got away with it.

Portpatrick on the west coast of the Rhins of Galloway first became a burgh of barony in 1620, although its charter was later allowed to lapse. It is still a fishing port but it owed its importance, before the development of Stranraer, to its proximity to Ireland. It is only 22 miles from Donaghadee and traditionally owes its name to St Patrick, who was said to have 'strode' from Donaghadee to Portpatrick. Portpatrick harbour was planned by the famous Edinburgh civil engineer, John Rennie, but unfortunately the harbour was dangerously exposed to southwesterly gales and was allowed to silt up when Stranraer became prominent.

Stranraer, at the head of Loch Ryan, sheltered from the south-west, snug between the northern promontory of the Rhins and the hills of Galloway, is ideally placed for sea trade and communication with Northern Ireland. It is a royal and municipal burgh overlooking a fine natural harbour which is the Scottish terminus of the Larne ferry and is also used by yachts, fishing boats and a variety of small craft. There is a house near the pier built in the form of a ship by the Arctic explorer Sir John Ross, who was born nearby.

Girvan, on the Ayrshire coast 25 miles north by east from Stranraer, has a good harbour that was used regularly by the Clyde herring fleet until Ayr was able to offer better facilities. In the past, Girvan's main industry was the building of ring-net drifters, but tourism is now increasingly important to the town.

Ayr has a royal charter dating back to the beginning of the thirteenth century. The harbour became a major base for the Clyde fishing fleet, which has since declined, but the harbour is still used by inshore fishing boats. It has both wet and dry docks where ship repairs are carried out.

Ardrossan, 15 miles north by west up the coast from Ayr, has a harbour that was constructed in 1805. Small ships are still built there. Trade with Irish ports is important to the town, which also has an oil refinery. It is one of the termini for ferry services to the Isle of Arran and is a component of Clydeport, which embraces 450 square miles of water from Ardrossan to Finnart and Glasgow itself.

Glasgow was one of the greatest ports in the world from the nineteenth to the twentieth century and the Clyde the greatest-ever shipbuilding centre. It is still a busy port and anchorage, and familiarity cannot diminish the beauty of its approaches. Sailing north up the Firth of Clyde at sunset, the jagged silhouette of the Isle of Arran frets the western sky. The clustered lights of Ayr, Troon, Irvine, Saltcoats and Ardrossan glimmer to starboard, and ahead loom the lighthouses on Little Cumbrae. There is a glow over Millport. If you are on a ferry heading for Fairlie or a yacht steering for Largs, you will leave the Cumbraes to port and Hunterston nuclear power station, cooled by the waters of the Clyde, to starboard. The adjoining harbour at Hunterston is to be developed as an international container trans-shipment hub by Clydeport, who have concluded contracts with the world's largest container operators, Maersk Sealand. A £30-million wind farm is also planned there. Other vessels will pass the Cumbraes to starboard, the Isle of Bute and the bright lights of Rothesay to port, before steering north by east and entering the estuary which is less than two miles wide when Cloch Point is on the starboard beam and Dunoon to port.

Sailing upstream towards the great city, past Gourock and Kempock Point, Greenock is the first major harbour to starboard, then Port Glasgow. Greenock is both an industrial and shipbuilding town with a famous anchorage to the north, the Tail of the Bank. Birthplace of Captain William Kidd in 1645 and of the pioneer of steam propulsion, James Watt, in 1736, Greenock was already an established port with a pier by the early seventeenth century, trading with the Baltic, Scandinavia, Germany, the Low Countries, France and Ireland. There was a herring fleet in the Clyde comprising more than 300 boats, half of which sailed from Greenock. A proper harbour and quays were completed in 1710 on the initiative of the Shaw family, who had been prominent in the town for more than a century. The graving dock was completed in 1786.

Greenock harbour and facilities continued to expand over the next century. The East India Harbour, designed by the ubiquitous John Rennie, was started in 1805. The Victoria Harbour was completed in 1850 and twelve years later construction of the Albert Harbour started. The Garvel graving dock followed ten years later, the James Watt dock in 1881 and by the end of the century Greenock Harbour extended to 195 acres. A dry dock, opened in 1964, was one of the largest in the world. The town played a key role during the Second World War, fitting out and refitting many of HM ships, and providing a base for the Free French Navy, commemorated by a monument on Lyle Hill, a prominent landmark. Now Clydeport have established Greenock Ocean Terminal as an international container port.

Moving up river, Port Glasgow is next on the starboard side. Back in the sixteenth century it was a fishing village called Newark but in 1668 the harbour was upgraded to serve as the port for Glasgow, before the Clyde was deepened in the late eighteenth century to allow sea-going vessels to proceed up to the Broomielaw – the city's harbour. The chief customs house for the Clyde was built at Port Glasgow in 1710 and the first graving dock – following James Watt's design – in 1762. When the river was deepened upstream, Port Glasgow's significance as a port declined but its importance as a shipbuilding centre increased with the adaptation of steam for ships' propulsion.

Renfrew, site of Malcolm IV's victory over Somerled, Lord of the Isles, in 1164, is passed to starboard before the city docks are reached. Within the city of Glasgow, there were miles of docks which were once capable of accommodating ships of every description, but offices and homes have replaced the port.

Clydebank, on the north side of the river opposite Renfrew, was farmland until 1871 when the Thomson brothers, James and George, decided to construct a shipyard there. The first ship was launched a year later. By 1886 Clydebank's population had reached the thousands and it achieved burgh status. It would become the greatest shipbuilding riverbank in the world. It is not surprising that it was regarded as a priority target by the Luftwaffe in the Second World War and was almost obliterated in 1941. Although the burgh has since been largely rebuilt, it has not reclaimed its supreme status in the shipbuilding industry.

Eight miles downstream of Clydebank, on the north bank of the river, stands the historic royal burgh of Dumbarton, where ships were being built when Clydebank was still agricultural land. The town is spread at the base of a rock 240-feet high, a volcanic plug of basalt that has been a fortress from prehistoric times. The name of the burgh is a modified form of the Gaelic *Dunbreatan*, meaning fort of the Britons, who dominated Strathclyde until the tenth century. The rock has successively been the site of a fortress, a royal castle, a barracks and a museum, while shipbuilding was developing at water level. William Wallace was imprisoned on the rock by the English in 1305 before being taken to London to be executed. Another interesting fact about the town, though one not widely known, is that the first flight in a heavier-than-air craft in the UK was made by Glasgow naval architect Percy Pilcher at Auchensale near Dumbarton.

Leaving Dumbarton, we emerge into the estuary, then steer north-west past the yachting centres of Helensburgh and Rhu into the Gare Loch. At Faslane, sited on the eastern shore, a deep-water dock was constructed during the Second World War. It was a shipbreaking yard where large vessels such as the Cunard liner *Aquitania* and the Royal Navy's capital ships *Malaya* and *Renown* were converted into scrap metal, but it is now a naval base for nuclear submarines. The loch is also used as a torpedo range and Garelochhead was at one time popular with yachtsmen. In 1853 a 'battle' was fought there when Sir James Colquhoun of Luss and the staff of his estate on Loch Lomondside tried unsuccessfully to prevent passengers landing from an excursion steamer on a Sunday.

The Finnart Ocean Terminal, constructed in the 1950s, is situated close to Coulport on the east shore of Loch Long, the next sea loch west of the Gare Loch. Finnart is a sheltered oil terminus that can take the world's largest ocean-going tankers at any stage of the tide and in any weather. From Finnart, crude oil is pumped 57 miles overland by pipeline to the Grangemouth refinery, thereby substantially reducing the sea passage for tankers from the Atlantic.

By taking a detour through the Kyles of Bute and past Ardlamont Point, a course north-west and then north by west takes us up Loch Fyne to Lochgilphead, the inner terminus of the eight-and-a-half-mile Crinan Canal, which shortens the sea passage for fishing boats and yachts heading for the west coast by 130 miles. Larger vessels must round the Mull of Kintyre.

Campbeltown, at the head of the loch of the same name, is well-sheltered from the prevailing winds. Formerly Lochhead, Campbeltown has been a royal burgh since 1700. The port had a thriving trade exporting Ayrshire-mined coal, whisky and fish and was involved in both the whaling industry and herring fishing. At the close of the nineteenth century its fishing fleet comprised upwards of 650 boats. During the Second World War it became an anti-submarine training centre and it is still an important fishing port.

There is a choice of routes from Campbeltown to Oban but the most direct one bypasses Islay and takes us north-east through the Sound of Jura, then north, leaving the island of Scarba to port, through the Sound of Luing and north-west up the Firth of Lorn and Sound of Kerrera into Oban Bay. At the turn of the tide it is feasible to negotiate Corrievrechan, the constricted channel between Scarba and the north end of Jura, but inadvisable when the tide is ebbing or flowing because of the fierce currents and whirlpools. Oban expanded in the nineteenth and twentieth centuries as the gateway to the Western Isles but it is also an important fishing port. The town was given a royal charter in 1811 and by the 1880s the population had reached 4,000. As well as being a mainland ferry terminus for many of the Western Isles, it is popular as a yachting centre. It is the anchorage where King Haakon of Norway assembled his fleet of longships in 1263 before sailing south to be defeated at the Battle of Largs.

After leaving Oban Bay, we can either head north for the Lynn of Lorn, passing between the island of Lismore and Benderloch, or continue north-west between Duart Point, crowned by Duart Castle, seat of the chiefs of the Macleans, and the lighthouse off Rubha Fiart at the south end of Lismore. Then the choice is between a northeasterly course up Loch Linnhe or continuing north-west through the Sound of Mull. Fishing boats and pleasure craft proceeding up Loch Linnhe can continue past Fort William and enter the Caledonian Canal. For small ships, this 60-mile waterway to Inverness, through 22 miles of engineered canals, 28 locks and 4 fresh-water lochs – Loch Lochy, Loch Oich, Loch Ness and Loch Dochfour – avoids a 360-mile, potentially stormy voyage through the Minches, past Cape Wrath, through the Pentland Firth, past Duncansby Head, Moss Head and through the Moray Firth to the Highland capital.

If we proceed through the Sound of Mull, we pass Tobermory, capital of Mull, to port before we emerge into open waters off Ardnamurchan – the most westerly point and lighthouse on the mainland of the British Isles. It is then less demanding on the navigator to take a northwesterly course, leaving Skye to starboard, than to hug the coast and negotiate the Sound of Sleat, the Kyle of Lochalsh and the Inner Sound between Raasay and Applecross. Neither route takes us close to Skye's capital, Portree.

Stornoway on the east coast of Lewis is the principal port of the Outer Hebrides, 'the long island'. The Macleods of Lewis held Stornoway Castle before the Mackenzies of Seaforth acquired it by marriage. The natural harbour was used for centuries before it became a town. Norsemen rallied there before and after making raids on the coasts of the islands and mainland. In the sixteenth century it was settled by planters from Fife with the government's encouragement, but their settlement did not survive. After occupation by Cromwell's forces it was still just a village at the end of the seventeenth century, although it was made a burgh of barony by James VI. Stornoway developed as a centre of the herring fishing industry in the nineteenth century. The modern harbour, which is well protected from the north and west, is split by a small peninsula with wharves and quays on both sides.

From Stornoway we steer north-north-east for the sheltered harbour of Stromness at the south-west corner of the Mainland of Orkney, making a dog-leg to clear Cape Wrath. Despite its Norse name, Stromness did not become a port of any significance until well after the Orkney Islands had been ceded to Scotland by Norway in 1590. The town then became a trading entrepôt between Scotland, Scandinavia and the Baltic. Although Stromness is only 12 miles west of Orkney's capital, Kirkwall – an easy road journey – the voyage by sea from one harbour to the other is more than 40 miles round Costa Head.

Scapa Flow, the almost landlocked anchorage that covers about 70 square miles of navigable sea water between Orkney Mainland and the islands of Hoy, Flotta, South Ronaldsay and Burray, played a significant role in both world wars because of its strategic position relative to the northern exits into the Atlantic from the Baltic and the North Sea. It became the base of the British Grand Fleet in 1914 but was not secure against German submarines. At the end of the war it was the scene of the scuttling of the German High Seas Fleet following its surrender. In October 1939, at the beginning of the Second World War, a German submarine again succeeded in entering the Flow and torpedoed the old battleship *Royal Oak* while she lay at anchor, inflicting a heavy loss of life. Thereafter the defences were strengthened and several of the entrances to the anchorage were blocked with barriers. Scapa Flow was the base of the British Home Fleet until the end of the war, and has since become an important supply base supporting the North Sea oil industry. Kirkwall is situated on the one-and-a-half-mile-wide isthmus which separates Scapa Flow from Kirkwall harbour. It has ferry links with Thurso, Aberdeen and Leith.

From either Stromness or Kirkwall it is a voyage of about 125 miles to Lerwick, capital of the Shetland Islands. Lerwick is just over 200 miles from Bergen in Norway and roughly the same from Aberdeen. Norse and fishing traditions are strong there, but close association with the oil industry is now of paramount economic importance to the islands. Lerwick has a fine sheltered harbour with a ferry service to the Scottish mainland. Apart from the much-reduced local fishing fleet, the harbour is frequently used by boats from northern Europe and Russia.

Scrabster, the harbour on the north coast of Caithness which serves Thurso, lies about 140 miles south and west of Lerwick, 20 miles by sea from Stromness and 150 from Aberdeen. The mail steamer for Orkney sails from Scrabster, which is sheltered from the north and west and clear of the powerful tidal currents of the Pentland Firth. It is also used by inshore fishing boats.

After clearing Duncansby Head, we steer south for 20 miles or more before altering to a southwesterly course and heading towards Tarbat Ness, which divides the Dornoch Firth from the Moray Firth. Leaving the Tarbat Ness lighthouse to starboard, we hold this course for a further 25 miles before altering some 45° to starboard and passing between the Sutors into the Cromarty Firth. This is another superb natural sheltered anchorage. Nigg Bay to starboard accommodates a yard where oil rigs can be built or repaired. Rigs may be seen in the Firth, waiting either to enter the yard or to be towed out to their allotted positions in the oil fields. As we steer west between the Sutors with the Cromarty lighthouse abeam to port, the wharves and jetties of Invergordon lie directly ahead, seven miles away on the Ross-shire shore.

Invergordon, which was called Inverbreakie until the eighteenth century, was not developed as a harbour until 1828. Early in the twentieth century it became a naval base and dockyard with coaling – and later oiling – facilities that could accommodate the largest ships of the Royal Navy. The base and anchorage were vitally important to the Navy in both world wars and were also used by RAF flying boats in the Second World War. The naval base was closed in 1956, but the facilities are now used by the oil industry and the anchorage is still important for British and NATO naval forces.

Inverness, the Highland capital, situated at the junction of the Moray and Beauly firths, where the River Ness flows into salt water, not only has busy harbour facilities but is also the northern terminus of the Caledonian Canal. The city is the communications centre of the north of Scotland. Sailing east out of the Moray Firth and bypassing the renowned fishing ports, which are mentioned in a later chapter, we clear Kinnaird Head, Rattray Head, Peterhead and Buchan Ness and steer south-west for the granite city.

Arguably, Aberdeen has gained more from the development of the North Sea oil industry than it has lost from the partial decline of its historic fishing and shipbuilding industries. The city is situated between, and now extends north and south beyond, the mouths of the rivers Dee and Don. The area where the Denburn enters the estuary of the Dee has been associated with fishing since prehistoric times and is now part of the harbour. The basis of the modern shipyards was built in 1809 on the site of the ancient fishing village of Fitty – now Footdee – at the mouth of the Dee. The north pier and the south breakwater were constructed to convert the river estuary into a tidal harbour. In the fish market, which was developed beside the Albert Basin, catches from the trawler fleet are auctioned every morning. The harbour trades with Scandinavia and the Baltic, as well as being a mainland terminus for ferry links with Orkney and Shetland. The shipbuilding yards on the north side of the harbour near the river's mouth are connected by quays to the docks and the Albert Basin. The shipyards were once famous for building some of the finest clippers ever launched. Among Aberdeen's research stations are two which emphasise the city's affinity with the sea: the Marine Laboratory, researching fishing techniques and locations; and the Torry Station, researching fish conservation.

Stonehaven is situated 27 miles down the east coast from Aberdeen. Formerly called Stanehyve, it has a natural harbour south of the River Carron, round which the old town and the smaller fishing village of Cowie are grouped. It was named as a royal burgh by King David I, trading with the European continent. Stonehaven itself became prosperous in the early nineteenth century through herring fishing. It is now a base for line fishermen and is popular with yachtsmen and water skiers. The ports and harbours between Stonehaven and the Firth of Tay are of special significance to the fishing industry.

Dundee, Scotland's fourth city, is on a site which has been a village or town since Roman times. The River Tay is navigable as far as Perth, 22 miles to the west, which is still an active small port. In the ninth century, Dundee became Kenneth MacAlpin's capital when he overcame the Picts to become the first king of a more or less united Scotland. Three times the city was sacked by the English and a fourth time by Cromwell and the Covenanters. The Firth of Tay provides a relatively sheltered anchorage but it can suffer fierce storms, as witnessed by the collapse of the first railway bridge across the Firth in a storm between Christmas and Hogmanay 1879. The city, which was at one time Scotland's second port, was a centre of the whaling industry and was involved in shipbuilding, marine engineering, steam boiler-making and the manufacture of sailcloth and cordage. Both *Discovery* and *Terra Nova*, used in polar exploration by Shackleton and Scott, were built in Dundee and *Discovery* is now prominently displayed in a specially constructed dock on the city's waterfront.

Submarine repair and maintenance were important activities in the shipyards during the Second World War. The city became famous for other industries not connected with its maritime role, notably the manufacture of sacking, jute and carpets. But even the manufacture of jute had more than one link with the sea: jute fibre had to be imported from India and the city's experienced flax weavers found difficulty in working the fibre until it was discovered that the addition of whale oil to the batching process solved the problem. Now the city's industries are diversified and a variety of different products are exported from the Tayside docks.

Bypassing the fishing harbours of the Fife coast, including Anstruther, home of the Scottish Fisheries Museum, and heading up the Firth of Forth, we pass the twin ports of Methil and Buckhaven to starboard. There has been a harbour at Methil since 1665. It became important as a coal port and later as a rendezvous for east-coast convoys in both world wars, but like both Kirkcaldy and Burntisland, further up the Firth, activity in the ports has diminished with the decline of the Fife coal-mining industry.

Inverkeithing, just east of the Forth road and rail bridges, was less dependent on coal. Its shipbreaking yard was established in 1922 and has been active ever since. Although Inverkeithing depends on modern industries, there has been a settlement there since Roman times and William the Lion granted the town a royal charter in 1165.

Rosyth Dockyard, just west of the Forth road and rail bridges, was only bought by the government for development as a naval dockyard in 1909. It was completed just after the outbreak of the First World War, when it was used as the main base for the Grand Fleet's cruiser squadrons. In the Second World War it was a base for destroyers of the Home Fleet and smaller ships. Now, less than a century after becoming a Royal Navy dockyard, it has been sold to a commercial firm, Babcock BES. However, the refitting of nuclear submarines can still be undertaken within half a mile of the fifteenth-century ruin of Rosyth Castle on the shore within the dockyard perimeter, and the Royal Navy's two new aircraft carriers will be assembled there.

Directly opposite Rosyth, on the south shore of the Firth, another small harbour, Port Edgar, served as a base for some of the Royal Navy's destroyers, coastal craft and fishery protection vessels, but is now a yachting marina.

Also on the south shore of the Forth, ten miles due west of Rosyth, stands the massive oil refinery and container port of Grangemouth. It is the busiest port on the east coast of Scotland, handling considerably more cargo than Leith, Dundee or Aberdeen, as well as receiving crude oil through the pipeline from Finnart. Indeed, its twentieth-century expansion from an industrial village is due more to the oil refinery and related manufacturing than to the port.

Not only can Grangemouth handle the largest container ships but its docks are equipped with electric cranes capable of discharging and loading every kind of cargo from and into freighters. The Grangemouth shipyard, which is still active, built the first effective steamboat, the *Charlotte Dundas*, in 1801. She operated experimentally on the Forth–Clyde Canal between Grangemouth and Glasgow. The 35-mile canal became uneconomic and was closed to commercial traffic in 1963, but was reopened in 2001 and comprehensively restored. A spectacular boat-lift, open to the public, has been installed at Falkirk to transfer boats between the levels of the Forth and Clyde.

After making a 180° turn and proceeding downstream, we pass Bo'ness just a couple of miles east of Grangemouth. It has a longer history than its neighbour but is now of far less importance. Borrowstounness, to give the port its full name, was still the third seaport in Scotland at the end of the eighteenth century, dominant in the trade with Holland and France, and important in the whaling industry.

South Queensferry, eight miles downstream of Bo'ness adjoining Port Edgar, and North Queensferry on the other side of the Firth, lost their principal raison d'être when the road suspension bridge was completed in 1964. The ferry had 800 years of recorded history. When built, the Forth Road Bridge was the largest suspension bridge in Europe. To quote from the official story published by the Forth Road Bridge Joint Board:

> The construction . . . called for skills not used in this country before. The men at work needed every ounce of brain, dexterity and physical courage they possessed. The majority were Scots, but many came from south of the Border. Modern instruments, new devices and engineering resources saved manpower and lightened labour, but it was still a big job – a dangerous task accomplished, happily, with very few accidents.

The Forth Rail Bridge, completed in 1890, had a less creditable accident record.

We now pass the yachting harbours of Cramond and Granton – formerly important in the fishing industry – to starboard before we reach Leith, the port of Edinburgh. It was formerly independent but has been incorporated with Edinburgh since 1929. Leith is arguably the most historic port in Scotland. It has been in active use since before the fifteenth century. It has seen kings and queens arrive and depart. It has handled trade and troop movements to and from the continent. It has built, repaired and accommodated liners, freighters, tankers, warships and fishing boats.

Until 1998, Leith was home port to an interesting vessel, the MV *Gardyloo*, named for the cry which heralded the disposal of 'night soil' from the windows of upper-floor tenements in the city of Edinburgh. It was captained by Master Mariner R. Leask MBE, who gained his award for 'services to public sanitation'. Captain Leask was a great ambassador for the city, who took parties out into the Forth and around the Isle of May on his regular voyage to deposit treated sewage into areas designated by the Scottish Department of Agriculture and Fisheries off St Abb's Head and the Bell Rock lighthouse. Parties from the city could, for a small fee payable to the local authority, enjoy an odourless and spectacular day at sea, an excellent lunch and the entertaining company of Captain Leask. It has yet to be proved that current methods of sewage disposal from Scotland's coastal settlements are more efficient or environmentally safe than was dumping from the *Gardyloo*.

Leith now berths the former royal yacht *Britannia*, which is open to the public. *Britannia*, like her namesake, the very first Cunarder, was built on the Clyde. She was launched from John Brown's yard in 1953. Areas near the quays that were previously slums are now considered fashionable. With its excellent harbour, dock and warehouse accommodation, Leith looks forward to a prosperous future.

Leaving the Port of Leith and steering north-east by east to clear Fidra and the Bass Rock, we pass Dunbar and Eyemouth and alter course to the south-east, heading for our final port of call, Berwick-on-Tweed.

In a voyage of well over 1,000 miles we have visited ports and harbours of unsurpassed variety, great and small, and bypassed many more of character and interest. Few countries in the world can offer such comprehensive facilities to vessels of every class, tonnage and function: the legacy of a nation with a long and hard-earned maritime tradition.

⚓ CHAPTER 14 ⚓

Fishing the Sea

HUNTING AND GATHERING

Scotland's fishing industry has a historical and cultural significance out of all proportion to the number of men and women it employs or its contribution to the country's gross national product. For millennia, it has shaped the lives of countless thousands in numerous settlements and coastal villages and towns; it has influenced foreign policy – some would say insufficiently – and it has provided an invaluable element of our basic diet. Fish and chips has a better claim to being the national dish than haggis and neeps or oatmeal porridge.

Scots have fished the sea for subsistence, barter or sale from prehistoric times. Fish comprised much of the daily diet of communities who lived on the coasts or by estuaries, rivers or lochs – both sea and inland. They gathered shellfish, hunted in shallow water with spear or hook and trapped fish in creels or woven baskets – or in pools, natural or artificial, left by the ebbing tide. The baited hook – made of bone or horn – has long been the basic method of catching fish, but woven baskets containing bait, similar in design to the creel, partan-cage and eel-trap still used today, were amongst the earliest methods employed. There has always been a plentiful supply of bait along the shores: lugworms, limpets, mussels or other shellfish. Shell middens beside the Forth or on Hebridean islands are proof that these were used in quantity for bait or for human consumption. These middens have also been found to contain fish and seal bones, some of the bones from fish that can only have been caught from boats at sea.

The development of fishing as an industry has depended on the interplay of many factors: boats and their means of propulsion and cost; the types of lines, nets and other equipment available; the movements and prolificacy of the various species of fish; and, of course, the markets and artificial regulations devised by governments to control both catching and selling. Many towns and villages, from Lerwick and Stornoway to Campbeltown and Eyemouth, owe their origins entirely to fishing. Scots fishermen were once members of an industry or fraternity employing a high proportion of the population at subsistence level. Now they are a small minority threatened by decreasing stocks, increasing overheads and international disagreements. Compared with nearly 50,000 Scots employed as fishermen in 1887 – and approximately the same number employed in shore-curing, without taking into account the women who baited lines and mended nets – by 2001 the number of fishermen on Scottish-based boats had fallen to 6,637, of whom 5,353 had regular jobs in the industry, 81 were crofters who relied heavily on fishing for their main subsistence and the rest were irregularly employed. This figure was less than 0.3 per cent of the total Scottish labour force, but it does not take account of the large number with occupations in supporting industries and distribution. The figure represented more than 70 per cent of fishermen in the United Kingdom, crewing 2,595 boats, varying in length from under eight metres to over fifty. The industry is relatively more important to Scotland than it is to England and, as James Miller writes in his fascinating book *Salt in the Blood*, 'there are no fishermen in London'.

⚓ ⚓ ⚓

Four broad categories of fish have been of great importance to Scotland over the centuries – five, if whales are included. The first category is the pelagic fish, which move freely in the upper levels of the sea, usually in shoals. This group includes the 'silver darlings', the herring, of prime importance, and the less significant mackerel. Second are the demersal or 'white fish' such as haddock, cod, whiting, saiths and sole, which are bottom-dwellers, inhabiting the lower levels of the sea. Next are the crustaceans such as lobsters and crabs and the sessile species like mussels and oysters. Finally there are the salmon and sea trout which spend part of their adult lives in the sea and are trapped or netted in river estuaries and sometimes caught out at sea. Several historic cities and towns, such as Aberdeen, Banff, Berwick, Inverness, Montrose and Perth, owe their origins at least in part to important salmon fisheries at the mouths of rivers.

Established fishing communities in Scotland have tended to specialise in one or other of these categories of fish, although objectives may change seasonally, or with the decline or increase of a particular species. The salmon fisheries were owned by the crown and have always been commercially important as a source of food for sale or barter, comparable with the herring. The crown usually granted the rights in salmon fisheries to owners of nearby land – monasteries or individuals who would sub-lease to the men who actually got their feet wet. In the fifteenth century, salmon and herring comprised 90 per cent of the fish exported from Scotland. The men who worked the salmon fisheries under licence were usually the same who fished the nearby coastal waters.

Herring fisheries had been in existence off the Scottish coasts – particularly in the firths of Clyde and Forth and off the west coast – since at least the twelfth century, and the Dutch had been buying salt fish from Scottish fishermen since the ninth century. Techniques for drying, smoking or otherwise preserving fish for winter consumption, or for sale abroad, had been developed since the very earliest times and salted fish had become one of Scotland's limited range of staple exports. 'White herring' were packed in barrels between layers of salt. 'Red herring' were smoked over wood fires for a month or more before being packed in barrels. The right to fish for herring in the Clyde was given in a charter to the Abbey of Holyrood by King David I in 1138, although the Forth appears to have been the main source. There is a record in 1240 of dues being paid on herring from Ayr, Dumbarton, Inverness and Crail, which were traded through the royal burghs, Crail being a centre of the trade. By the fifteenth century, there were fishing communities established all round Scotland. Sites were often selected not just for proximity to good fishing, but also where dwellings could be built on rock foundations and where boats – before the days of artificial harbours – could be readily drawn up on shingle beaches. There was a regular export trade in fish but the amount of cured white fish exported was less than 10 per cent of herring and salmon. James III, by act of parliament, obliged the coastal burghs 'to make ships and bots with nets and other pertinents for fishing . . . according to the substance of each burgh'. The boats were to be at least 'twenty tunn' and all 'idle men' were to be 'compelled by the sheriffs . . . to go on board the same'. In 1491 the Spanish ambassador to the Scottish court noted that herring were being exported from Scotland to England, Flanders, France and Italy. In the sixteenth century, cod exports varied between 20,000 and 80,000 fish a year. Bishop Leslie recorded that in 1578 cod, flounder, plaice and turbot were commonly available for home consumption.

When the Dutch moved into Scottish fisheries during the fifteenth century, with busses equipped with nets, they caused great resentment. Busses were substantial three-masted vessels, sometimes displacing as much as 100 tons, which could salt and store large quantities of fish – predecessors of the modern factory ship – and they were escorted by armed vessels to prevent any interference with their operations. Attempts in the seventeenth century to tax them and to lay national claim to the coastal fisheries could not be enforced. An Association for Fishing formed in 1632 by Charles I, based in the Isle of Lewis, was no more successful and had to be abandoned after five years because French privateers were interfering with the fishing and the subscribers were failing to keep up payments.

Large numbers of 'crears', half-decked fishing boats from the East Neuk of Fife, fished for herring around the Northern and Western Isles. A fleet of a hundred sail is recorded as anchoring off Aberdeen in January 1587 en route from Loch Broom back to the Forth. They were smaller than the three-masted busses used by the Dutch but offered them some competition and also participated in the seasonal fishery in the Forth. Crears were dual-purpose boats and were also used for trading. Inshore herring fisheries with nets attached to posts were sited on both sides of the Forth, involving 16 communities from Dunbar to Pittenweem. There were also 'draves', meaning the hunting of shoals, conducted by boats equipped with drift nets involving more than 100 boats, each manned by an average of seven men, the proceeds being fairly divided between them on an agreed system. It is said that there were 200 large Scottish boats, supplied by some 1,500 small 'catcher' boats, involved in the west-coast herring fishery by 1630. Meanwhile, merchants from northern Europe were active in Shetland, encouraging the local fishermen to take advantage of the rich herring and haddock fisheries around the archipelago and to cure the fish for the European market in exchange for manufactured goods such as linen, muslin and brandy.

To make a broad generalisation, most herring and mackerel were caught in nets by the gills and most white fish by hooks on lines, until the advent of the steam trawler. In the nineteenth century, herring fishing dominated the Scottish industry, reaching a peak of over 9,000 boats in use in 1866, followed by a trend towards fewer and better boats. By the end of the century, an average of well over a million barrels a year – multiplied by 1,270 to get an approximation of the number of fish – were being exported, mostly to Europe. Scottish herring dominated the market until the outbreak of the First World War. The demand for herring was such that the herring drifters developed a pattern of moving south from Shetland to East Anglia as the season progressed and in 1885 inshore waters were closed to trawlers which, with the advent of steam power, were threatening both drifters and line fishermen. Comprehensive statistics were kept from 1887 and for four years to 1891 low-interest loans were offered through the Crofters' Commission for the purchase of boats.

Line fishing involved laying a line along the sea bottom with both ends anchored and marked by floats. 'Sma' lines' had smallish hooks at intervals of three or four feet. Several 'strings', each with a hundred or more hooks, baited on shore by wives and daughters before being placed in layers in baskets, would be shot across the tide in coastal waters and left for about an hour before being hauled in, hopefully with fish such as haddock, sole or codling on the hooks. Haddock vied with herring as the most popular fish on the Scottish kitchen table.

'Great lines', used during the nineteenth century, which were longer and stronger, were intended to catch cod, ling, halibut, skate, hake and turbot and were laid in deeper water, sometimes as far away as Iceland. They were baited at sea as the lines were shot – the fisherman's term for paying out lines at a steady pace to match the boat's speed – and it took skill and experience to avoid getting a hook embedded in the hand. It was usual to shoot great lengths of line at a time, perhaps two or three miles of it, and the long job of hauling in and taking the fish off the hooks would start with the first line soon after the last had been shot. Fish caught in distant waters had to be packed in ice until they could be landed. The same fishermen probably had both great and small lines for use in different seasons but great-line fishing has become rare in the era of the deep-sea trawler.

Ring-nets, which were used principally in confined waters and sea lochs such as Loch Fyne, consisted of a long strip of netting which could be pulled around a shoal, sometimes with one end secured ashore and the other in a boat. Nets of this kind were probably used by Jesus's disciples in the Sea of Galilee. If the bottom of the net was closed it became a bag or purse-net, forerunner of the trawl-net. The ring-net fishermen of the Clyde and its sea lochs found a ready market for fresh and kippered herring in and around Glasgow.

The modern otter trawl-net, which the trawler drags along the bottom on rollers – the mouth kept open by otter boards on the surface – is simply a development of the ring-net that became possible when steam propulsion of fishing vessels, soon to be followed by trawlers with diesel engines, superseded oar and sail. Bag-nets, based on the same principle, may still be used in coastal waters. The drift-net was a more scientific and less indiscriminate method of net fishing because it depended on knowledge of the location and the habits of the fish sought. It was weighted at the bottom, hung from floats and allowed to drift with the tide or current across the direction in which the shoal or school of fish was expected to swim. The depth depended on whether the aim was to catch herring, mackerel, pilchard or something else. Drift-netting for herring had originally been learned from the Dutch as long ago as the fifteenth century but it remained the commonest fishing technique of Scottish boats until the twentieth century. It started on the west coast of Galloway, where herring were plentiful on the Ballantrae Banks, but was soon taken up by fishermen from Macduff and other ports on the south side of the Moray Firth. The drift-net, normally between 40 and 80 metres long, was shot to windward of the drifter, which was then kept head to wind by a small mizzen sail. Net and boat drifted in unison like a pair of ballroom dancers and the fish were caught by the gills in the meshes of the net. The seine-net was normally much longer. It was dragged around a shoal and the ends drawn together to capture the fish, which were then hauled back to the boat.

⚓ ⚓ ⚓

Before the publication of Charles Darwin's *Origin of Species* in 1859, the whale was generally considered to be a large fish, at least by the men who had hunted it for oil, ambergris and baleen since the twelfth century. It was not until the eighteenth century that purpose-designed whaling ships set sail from Scottish ports. The average whaler, which displaced about 200 tons and was under 100-feet long, carried a crew of about 50 and several small pinnaces for chasing and harpooning the unfortunate whales. Harpooning required a high degree of skill.

Until about 1870 Peterhead was the main whaling centre in Scotland but thereafter it was superseded by Dundee, partly because whale oil came to be used in the processing of jute. By 1872 the city had become the principal whaling port of the British Isles, although the crews were drawn from many seafaring communities beyond Dundee. Whalers usually left the Tay estuary in April and hunted in the Arctic Ocean until September. If they stayed in the Arctic any later in the year, they risked being trapped in the ice.

In 1751 only six whalers set sail from Scotland. Five years later the number had increased to sixteen. By 1770, the government was offering a bounty of two pounds for each ton of ship's capacity to hold the blubber, bone and saleable parts of the carcass. The bounty was paid even if no whales were caught, which more or less covered the owner's costs. The largest cargo of blubber ever landed in Scotland was by the *Resolution* at Peterhead in 1814. She had caught 44 whales. One whale was then worth between two hundred and fifty and five hundred pounds, valued in a ratio of 10 to 1, oil to bone: a handsome return when multiplied by the inflation of two centuries. However, whaling was a risky business. Casualties and injuries were frequent. In 1837 the Scottish whaler *Advice* was trapped and crushed in the Arctic ice. When she was found months later, only seven of her crew of forty-nine were still alive.

In 1840 a whaling master from Peterhead, Captain William Penny, with the help of a young Inuk, rediscovered the entrance to Cumberland Sound on the east coast of Baffin Island and it proved to be a rich hunting ground. Whalers began wintering there to get an early start in the spring. The huge catches of the mid-nineteenth century inevitably reduced the population of this slow-breeding mammal and by the 1890s the Arctic whaling industry was shrinking. Nevertheless, a shore whaling station was established by Scots at Albert Harbour, nearly six degrees north of the Arctic Circle on the north shore of Baffin Island, as recently as 1903.

The River Tay, the first iron-hulled, steam-powered whaler, built at Kinghorn in Fife in 1865 for Gilroy Brothers & Co. of Dundee, had a reinforced hull to withstand the pressure of ice. Her range and speed enabled her to make two Arctic voyages in one season but she had only one profitable Arctic season before she became uneconomic due to the scarcity of whales.

Some owners decided to try the Antarctic. Three ships were sent south in 1893 and these voyages continued until the outbreak of the First World War. By 1911 the Leith-based firm of Christian Salvesen had become the largest whaling company in the world, although their whaling operations in the Antarctic had not started until 1909. Because of the time and distance involved, Antarctic whaling by ships from Scotland never approached the profitability of the Arctic industry and whaling continued to decline, although it was still associated with Leith until the 1950s, when international agreements made it non-viable.

⚓ ⚓ ⚓

The British Fisheries Society had been set up in 1786, funded by private subscription, with the purpose of establishing fishing villages and later of improving fishing harbours. The Fishery Board, set up by the government in 1809, took over this function, together with the wider role of promoting the fishing industry as a whole. From the 1880s, the Board offered a bounty on each properly cured barrel of herring, an export bounty and another on the weight of cured white fish which passed a quality inspection. Bounties based on the tonnage capacity of fishing vessels or busses were also offered as a general encouragement to the industry and in 1824 part of the available funds was diverted to improve harbours and help with boat repairs. The Board also commissioned two fishery cruisers to police the fishing grounds. There were sometimes hundreds of British and foreign boats in the same area.

Because of Scotland's dominant position in the British industry, a separate Scottish Fisheries Board was instituted in 1882 and three years later it was given responsibility for regulating shell fisheries, as well as herring and white fish. There were extensive mussel beds in the Firth of Clyde, the Dornoch Firth, the estuary of the Ythan, the Montrose Basin and elsewhere which were a vital source of bait for line fishing. If the mussels had not previously been dredged from the seabed, fishermen's wives and their families would have to start collecting them from the foreshore before dawn. It could take ten hours to put two mussels on each of the 1,300 to 1,400 hooks on an average boat's small line. It was the Scottish Fishery Board's responsibility to ensure that the mussel beds were not over-exploited.

⚓ ⚓ ⚓

The discovery of fertile cod banks off the Shetland coasts led to the formation in the 1820s of the Shetland smack fishery, which continued to thrive throughout the nineteenth century. The smacks were fast sailing boats, about 70 feet in length with a crew of 15. They used 50-fathom lines with double hooks baited with herring. They needed to catch cod by the thousand to be profitable.

Through the centuries, fishing boats had developed from the small clinker-built open boat with oars; then boats of perhaps 15 to 18 feet in length with oars and sail; half-decked boats up to 25 feet in length; fully decked boats with a fo'c'sle but no bunks or fitments; and then boats of over 30 feet, fitted with bunks and lockers, sometimes carvel-built and with a mainmast and a mizzen. By the 1820s, Scottish fishermen were drift-netting for herring off both the east and west coasts and there were many types of fishing boats in use, mostly two-masted sailing vessels, until the advent of steam. On the east coast, the Fifie with its vertical stem and stern, and the Scaffie with rounded bows and raked stern, were superseded by the Zulu developed by William Campbell of Lossiemouth. The Zulu's raked stem and stern gave it more speed and manoeuvrability while its shorter keel was economical in its use of timber. Loch Fyne skiffs fished with the ring-net in the south-west and the Sgoth (pronounced 'sgaw') was used for line fishing in the Hebrides. Steam drifters made their appearance by the end of the nineteenth century and boats of up to 75 feet in length, with steam capstans to pull in the nets, were soon at work. All the bigger boats were carvel-built. The last sailing drifter, built in Buckie, worked out of Stornoway until 1945.

The technique of trawling began to be practised in Scottish waters by sailing trawlers in the 1890s but it did not come into its own until the introduction of steam. Although the fishermen of the Firth of Forth were the first Scots to use steam drifters, when the steam trawler arrived Aberdeen rapidly became the leading Scottish port for white fish: it had the harbour and market, the rail and road communications to distribute sales and the engineering expertise and yards to maintain the boats. Granton on the Firth of Forth rivalled Aberdeen, while Leith and Dundee had small trawler fleets until after the Second World War. Steam-propelled boats from Aberdeen and elsewhere were also used for great-line fishing. By 1955, the oil diesel engine had virtually replaced steam.

Trawlers with engines did not gain an immediate monopoly of the white fish industry. Fishing for cod with anchored nets, or 'gill' nets, continued all around Scotland, particularly in the spring when shoals of cod approached the shores to spawn. All types of boats, including drifters, were used for this method of cod fishing. Regrettably, however, stocks of cod have been seriously reduced as a result of over-fishing by trawlers of all nations, with disregard for the future of the industry.

In the decades between the two world wars, the herring industry declined severely because of the reduction of the Baltic market. There was a switch to seine-netting because white fish catches were more dependable. Fishermen who had manned the drifters began to seek berths in trawlers. Many emigrated to Australia, Canada and New Zealand, but Scotland's trading link with the Baltic just kept the herring fishing going. There were also outlets for fresh herring through retailers all over the country and a steady demand from the kippering and curing market. From about 1930 onwards, however, the smaller ports stopped curing herring and, apart from a few individual operators, only Fraserburgh, Peterhead and Lerwick now continue the curing trade.

After Greenock became a commercial trading port, most of the herring fishing on the west coast was carried on by east-coast fishermen, but Stornoway had a fleet of drifters until after the Second World War. Then fishermen from the 'long island', from as far south as Castlebay in Barra, and from Skye, became more interested in catching white fish and prawns. At the same time, the men from the Moray Firth and the east coast were becoming skilled in seine-netting for white fish, mainly haddock. It was the Scots who first improved on the Danish method by operating without an anchor, chain and mooring buoy – a system that became known as fly dragging, or Scottish seining, and was particularly suitable for catching cod and haddock. However, Scottish seining, using a converted steam drifter, required a crew of at least seven, whereas a small Danish seine-netter required only four, making their operation much more economical. It was not until another very shrewd and experienced fisherman from

Lossiemouth, John Campbell, designed a motor-seiner in about 1930, that Scottish fishermen began to compete economically, and his design rapidly replaced the old converted steam drifters. Catches with seine-nets were lower than with the trawl but they swept a wider area and could be shot from smaller boats with less powerful engines.

Until the outbreak of war in 1939, employment on a trawler generally offered the best financial security in the fishing industry except, perhaps, to a few who had found a niche market for shellfish and crustaceans. Whereas the crew of a herring drifter obtained their livelihood by means of a share system, which meant no money when the herring were proving elusive, on a trawler all the crew had a regular wage except the skipper and mate, who shouldered the responsibility for taking the boat to the most profitable fishing ground. The better the reputation of the trawler skipper for finding good fishing grounds, the easier it was for him to get together a good crew.

The decline of the herring shoals and the growing and lucrative market for white fish proved an incentive for more of the steam drifters to purchase Danish gear and try seine-netting. It is a difficult technique to master and this, coupled with poor facilities for keeping fish on ice, which was sometimes necessary for up to two weeks, meant that only the most skilful of those who tried seine-netting made a success of it. However, there were plenty of plaice in the Moray Firth and elsewhere in coastal waters. Some of the seine-netters moved out to the Dogger and Fisher banks, landing their catches at east-coast ports from Aberdeen to Grimsby. Often there were severe hold-ups when they tried to land fish at Aberdeen in competition with the trawlers, forcing them to land their fish at Peterhead instead. Consequently, Peterhead has become the port where the biggest tonnage of Scottish white fish is now landed – both from seine-netters and trawlers. By the 1970s, the trawler had virtually superseded the drifter in catching both herring and white fish.

⚓ ⚓ ⚓

The importance of shellfish to the Scottish fishing industry cannot be overlooked. Not only have they provided human sustenance from prehistoric times (in a prehistoric shell midden at Polmonthill, Falkirk, there are estimated to be between six and seven million oyster shells!) but they have comprised a large proportion of the bait used for sea fishing and they are now a lucrative part of the industry.

In the Middle Ages, oyster beds in the Firth of Forth were the subject of disputes between littoral proprietors. Oysters were then considered a food of last resort for the urban poor rather than a delicacy for the gourmet and the beds were virtually destroyed in the nineteenth century by over-fishing. When the potato harvest failed in the 1840s, destitute families resorted to the beach to dig for cockles, collect mussels and whelks, or knock limpets off the rocks. As recently as the 1950s, whelks were collected and sent by train in bags to the London fish market and men stood chest-high in the waters of the estuaries that discharge into the Solway Firth to catch shrimps and small fish in nets on long poles. In earlier centuries, lobsters and crabs were mentioned as common food sources and by the late eighteenth century crustaceans, trapped in baited creels, were being sold to the London market. Lobsters are mostly found in coastal waters at depths between 30 and 200 feet, although the best depth for the creels or pots is at about 70 feet. Lobsters seem to prefer rocky coasts and have become an important source of income to fishermen in the Hebrides, the northern isles and on the west coast.

Towards the end of the nineteenth century, the Fishery Board took responsibility for shellfish, although they represented only 2 or 3 per cent of the industry's total output. By the 1920s, Catterline, Crail, Dunbar, Cove, St Abbs, Burnmouth and Keiss in Caithness were among ports which had achieved substantial landings of lobsters and crabs. On the east coast, edible crabs or partans were sought from April to December, after which fishermen would turn to line fishing for cod, ling and halibut. Transport and preservation were always a problem with shellfish until freezing plant and refrigerated transport became available. There is a seasonal variation in production, mainly due to the hazards of operating small boats in stormy and wintry conditions. Because shellfish are for the most part static, they are particularly vulnerable to over-fishing. Nevertheless, they are an increasingly important sector of the Scottish industry and provide valuable employment. At the start of the twenty-first century, excluding shellfish such as mussels and others which are sold either for bait or human consumption, shrimps and prawns constitute more than half by weight of the shellfish catch, followed by scallops, lobsters and crabs. Prawn fishing has become particularly important to the fishermen of Stornoway, Lossiemouth and the ports of the north-west Highlands, Ayrshire and East Lothian. Dredging for scallops to meet a strong consumer demand started in Orkney and the Clyde in the 1960s and there is now a market for anything edible that can be trawled out of the sea. The days of relying on half a dozen popular species are past.

⚓ ⚓ ⚓

Fish farming offers no real threat to the sea fishing industry, except possibly by the transmission of disease. It is a major employer and contributor to

Scotland's gross national product. In 2003 it supports roughly the same number of jobs as the boats in the sea fishing fleet – between six and seven thousand – and claims to produce some seven million pounds' worth of salmon and shellfish per annum, mainly in sea lochs on the west coast. Though an important industry with a promising future, it will always generate high overheads and concentrate on species of high value. It runs the risk of disease and offers an end product which the consumer will not choose in preference to wild fish unless the price differential is substantial or the species is otherwise unobtainable. The closure of the Sea Fish Authority's research station at Ardtoe in Ardnamurchan, with its facilities for the experimental rearing of the larvae of cod, halibut, haddock and lobsters, will be a lethal blow to the industry if the threat is implemented.

The threats to sea fishing stem from defective conservation, poorly framed legislation, subsidies which give some foreign boats an unfair competitive edge, cheating by the use of nets with too fine a mesh, fishing in prohibited areas or exceeding quotas and selling 'black fish' – the catch that exceeds the quotas.

HARD WORK, HARD TIMES, HARD CHOICES

Throughout the eighteenth century, the herring fisheries were encouraged by bounty schemes but there had been a decline in the Forth herring fisheries due to an unexplained change in herring migrations. At the same time, the profitability of the Clyde fishery was rising, although all fisheries had suffered from the imposition of a salt tax by the London government in 1712. Salt doubled in price and could only be bought in quantity from Customs depots. Nevertheless, towards the middle of the century the herring industry began to thrive. Fishing settlements developed into villages and towns and haphazard groups of houses grew into villages, often built on a grid pattern. On the stretch of north-east coast between the mouth of the Findhorn and the mouth of the South Esk at Montrose, there were over 60 settlements, mostly line fishing for white fish from small boats. On the west coast, cod fishing became popular with bigger boats from burghs such as Greenock, Campbeltown and Stornoway and from relatively distant ports such as Fraserburgh and Anstruther. Boats from Peterhead ventured as far as Iceland.

By the 1790s, Wick was becoming an important centre for the North Sea herring fishery, attracting boats from the Moray Firth and the west coast with their following of shore-workers, including the women gutters and packers. When herring were landed at Whaligoe on the east Caithness coast, which was home port to 21 boats by 1840, it was the women who carried the baskets 360 steps up a cliff. The women of the fishing communities were renowned for their strength. Before the days of thigh-length rubber sea boots and where there was no jetty or quay, they habitually carried their men folk out to the boats on their backs so that the men started a trip with dry feet and clothing. Sometimes they walked many miles carrying creels loaded with fish for sale in the nearest town – and then back with the household necessities bought with the proceeds. It is recorded in the *Old Statistical Account* compiled by Sir John Sinclair in the 1790s that three women each carried 200 lb of herring from Dunbar to Edinburgh – 27 miles – in five hours. That they could do this, wearing the traditional voluminous striped skirt and apron, dark blouse, woollen shawl and white bonnet, is hard to believe. Somebody may have given them a hurl!

Not until the Fishery Board was set up in 1809 to promote the industry were curing, packing and marketing methods regularised. The Board persuaded the government to remove the tax on salt in 1824, immediately benefiting the herring fisheries, which began to leave coastal line fishing behind in terms of profitability. Total production of herring – almost entirely from Scotland – increased from less than 200,000 barrels in 1810 to a peak of more than two million barrels (each 32-gallon barrel containing a maximum of 1,270 fish) by 1910. To ensure quality, the Board instituted rigid inspections: the fish had to be gutted and cured within 24 hours of being landed, barrels then stood unsealed for ten days to 'pine', after which they were topped up and the lids put on.

Expertise in curing had been developing since the eighteenth century in the Clyde and Forth areas, where there had been long-established herring fisheries, but the curers soon realised the potential of Caithness, the east coast and the islands. The number of curing firms multiplied to 300 by 1920. Their contribution to the industry was to guarantee prices to fishermen for the summer season – July to September – and to guarantee quality to the buyer by branding with a crown those barrels of fish that had been properly cured. The business of one curer, James Methuen, who started in Scotland in the mid-eighteenth century, soon spread to cover the whole east coast from the northern isles to East Anglia. Companies drew up simple contracts with the women who performed the highly skilled work of gutting, cleaning, grading and packing.

Until the herring fishing began to flourish, most fishing villages had been relatively isolated and intermarriage was the rule rather than the exception, but there was some movement of families between the islands and between the north and south sides of the Moray Firth and other east-coast ports. Eventually herring fishing for the curing and packing trade led to greater mobility, the women of fishing families following the herring fleet, gutting and packing as the boats moved south through the season. Not only were the women involved in gutting and packing, but when at home they gathered the bait, baited the hooks for line fishing, mended nets and carried all the domestic burdens. A wife was as likely to lose her life in childbirth as was her husband at sea.

Fish were not just the livelihood of the fishing communities; they were the currency. Fresh or preserved fish – dried, smoked, or salted – was the mainstay of their diet and was bartered for oatmeal, potatoes or other produce from the surrounding farms or crofts, occasionally supplemented by a rabbit, hare or game bird. This was the basic diet until well into the twentieth century. When boats started spending more than a day or two away from home, each man would take a small wooden chest with him, packed with oatcakes, home-baking, cheese and – if the family could afford it – hard-boiled eggs or salt beef or herring. In earlier days, there was no means of cooking on board – or even of getting a hot drink. It was not until boats began to reach a length of 28 feet or more that they began to carry small coal or wood stoves. The vacuum or thermos flask, invented by Scottish scientist Sir James Dewar late in the nineteenth century, could not be obtained at a price within the reach of most fishermen until well into the following century. Nowadays – depending on the cook, and weather permitting – fishing vessels maintain high catering standards.

By the nineteenth century, fishermen's clothing had almost become a uniform: a calico shirt and heavy serge trousers over hand-knitted, worsted underwear. Over the shirt a heavy knitted jersey was worn. The style of pattern in which a man's jersey or 'gansey' was knitted usually indicated the area he came from. The women knitted them whenever they could, sometimes while walking with creels on their backs. Footwear consisted of thick worsted socks inside short leather sea boots or clogs. Sealskin outer clothing was later superseded by oilskins. Sailcloth dressed with linseed oil was found to be waterproof until a more flexible combination was developed.

Prior to the nineteenth century, fishing communities would have lived in low, thatched, poorly furnished cottages, devoid of sanitation and surrounded by evidence of baiting, gutting and cleaning fish and gear. The floor would have been earth covered in sand – with a peat fire in the middle, probably with a hole in the roof above to let the smoke out. Fishermen were accustomed to cramped spaces and as their wives almost invariably came from fishing families they were used to the same conditions. The Scottish Fisheries Museum at Anstruther has a realistic furnished re-creation of a fisherman's cottage of the 1800s, with a loft for storing nets and gear and an outside stair to save internal floor space. Such a dwelling would probably have been feued from the local laird, who might have entered into an agreement to provide a new boat every six or seven years, as well as the cottage, in return for a rent paid in cash or kind. Such an agreement often also gave the tenant the right to collect bait on certain areas of the foreshore. In places where fishermen did not have legal title to their houses, they were unable to provide security for loans to replace boats or worn-out equipment.

Inevitably the specialist knowledge passed down from father to son, the skills and way of life of the fishing communities, together with the investment in boats and gear, led to the formation of family businesses and dynasties that survived over several generations. The prevalence of intermarriage with other fishing families, and a certain lack of mobility, resulted in villages consisting of families sharing only half a dozen surnames. Gardenstown in Banffshire was almost confined to Watts, Wests and Wisemans; Auchmithie in Angus to Cargills, Spinks and Swankies. The origins of some of the commonest names in Lossiemouth are unusual: the first Edward came from Wales – crew member of a ship landing merchandise; the Mcleods were Jacobite clansmen who took refuge there after Culloden; the Mitchells – a common enough name in the North East – are descended from a Spaniard called Michelle washed ashore from a shipwreck. However, Stewart is still by far the commonest name in the seatown of Lossiemouth, passed down from a young man who had been press-ganged then put ashore in Spey Bay when the Navy released him. In the eighteenth century, and during the Napoleonic wars, fishing communities were an obvious target for the Royal Navy's press gangs, which operated as far north as Shetland. There they could prey on the passing whalers and merchant ships as well as on the local fishermen – hoping to capture experienced seamen whose skills could easily be adapted to man warships. The whole of Scotland's east coast was highly vulnerable to this unwelcome form of recruitment.

Stewarts in Lossiemouth or Watts in Gardenstown and others with common surnames had to be distinguished from one another by pre-fixing a tee-name, or nickname, often the name of their boat.

One well-known fishing family who have been in the industry for three centuries are the Buchans of Peterhead. The crisis of 2003 faced them with a well-nigh insoluble problem. In 1997, after carefully preparing a business plan based on the known facts, John Buchan placed an order with a boatyard in Troon for a £3.7 million state-of-the-art trawler. He had to borrow heavily to do so but in normal circumstances the loan would be paid off in ten years. A Spaniard or Frenchman in his situation could have got a hefty subsidy towards the cost. The boat, the 130-ft *Atlantic Challenge*, was one of the largest in the North East fishing fleet. Her first season went well but unfortunately 'normal circumstances' are the exception in the fishing industry. In the spring of 2000, there was a fuel crisis. In 2003, the industry faced another crisis. What does the future hold for the Buchans as employers of a crew of nine, faced with the prospect of only being permitted to fish 15 days a month under the terms of the agreement reached by EEC governments in December 2002 and with overheads and loan repayments to be met?

⚓ ⚓ ⚓

The distinctive lifestyle of the fishing communities, challenged by the proximity of danger and constant threat of death, was reflected in a range of superstitions and strong religious beliefs and many skippers refused to put to sea or return to harbour on a Sunday. On strong drink, there was a divide. Some fishermen drank heavily between trips – as did a few at sea – but there was a powerful temperance countermovement based on strict religious principles. Scrupulous fairness was characteristic of fishermen. Skippers went to great lengths to ensure that the proceeds of a catch were fairly divided.

As the practice of fishing further away from the coasts increased, so did the risks, although danger was never absent from any kind of sea fishing. Before recorded history there would have been many losses of single boats and occasionally disasters involving whole communities, but in more modern times they have been frequent. In a storm off St Andrews in November 1765, three boats went down, taking twelve men with them. On Christmas Day 1806 the line fishermen of Stotfield, Lossiemouth – 21 of them – put to sea. After hauling in their lines, they turned for the shore but were overwhelmed by a hurricane from the south-west. Every boat sank and all the men were drowned. The oldest male left in the village was a lad of 12, apart from a few too old and infirm for the fishing. An even greater loss of life was incurred in July 1832, when 18 boats were overwhelmed by a storm off Shetland and 105 men were drowned.

On 18 August 1848 over 800 herring boats put to sea from Wick in the afternoon, shortly after high water. At dusk, when they were ten miles out, they shot their drift-nets. By midnight the weather was deteriorating, with the wind strengthening to gale force from the south-east. Many of the skippers wisely decided to haul in their nets and make for Wick harbour, getting in before high water at 1.30 a.m. By 3 a.m. the wind had increased to a hurricane and driving rain reduced visibility to less than a cable (200 yards). The ebbing tide had left only five feet of water at the harbour entrance and huge waves were battering the stone piers. The boats that attempted to enter were flung against the piers or quays and either smashed or swamped, watched by agonised relatives ashore. Forty-one boats were lost. Some had made for Helmsdale, 30 miles to the south, where 24 boats foundered. At Peterhead, fifty-one boats sank and another eight at Stonehaven. Altogether 124 boats went down and 100 fishermen lost their lives, leaving 47 widows and 161 children.

Five boats sank with the loss of thirty-seven fishermen from St Monance and Cellardyke in 1878, when the East Neuk of Fife was hit by a bad storm. The year 1881 was particularly bad. The Shetland fishing fleet was hit by a July storm when fishing off Gloup at the north end of the island of Yell. In what has come to be known as the Gloup Disaster, ten boats went down and fifty-eight lives were lost. This was followed by perhaps the best known of all fishing community disasters: the Eyemouth disaster, which occurred on 14 October 1881 when a hurricane hit the east coast. The tragedy has been movingly described in Peter Aitchison's *Children of the Sea* and commemorated in a haunting song recorded by Cilla Fisher. The fleet of line-fishing boats had put to sea on a calm, sunny morning, although the barometer was low. About an hour after they had left harbour, the sky turned black and the northerly wind quickly reached gale force. The boats hauled in their lines and ran west for shelter but the suddenness of the gale and driving rain and spray, which reduced visibility to a few yards, overpowered them. The boats had to steer between the Hurcars, a line of rocks outside the harbour entrance, and battle their way through fearsome surf to reach the relative shelter of the harbour. Few of them made it and 189 men from Eyemouth and nearby Burnmouth, Cove and St Abbs were drowned. The Church of Scotland had to take some of the blame because the land on which Eyemouth was built had formerly belonged to the Church and the fishermen had to pay a tithe on all their earnings. They needed to put to sea when others could afford to stay in harbour and the drain on their incomes had postponed improvements to the harbour and construction of protective moles known to be essential.

In a November gale of 1890, boats from half a dozen east-coast ports were lost with all hands and in the winter of 1910 the crew of a large line-fishing sailing boat from Buckpool near Lossiemouth were drowned and the bodies washed ashore in Stotfield Bay. Between 1887 and 1961, a total of 303 Aberdeen steam trawlers were lost. The sea continues to take its toll.

⚓ ⚓ ⚓

In 1784 an Edinburgh bookseller named John Knox, who had written an influential book recommending investment in fishing villages, was sent on an official tour by a parliamentary committee. He produced an enthusiastic report describing the abundance of herring in west-coast sea lochs and presented a plan to the Highland Society. The outcome was an increase in the bounties to encourage herring fisheries and the foundation of what became the British Fisheries Society, which set to work to raise money to establish fisheries based on selected villages. Tobermory and Ullapool were among the first. They also sited warehouses nearby to store salt for curing the catch.

The Fisheries Society also became influential in the modernisation of ports and harbours, employing the renowned Scottish engineers Thomas Telford and John Rennie, contemporaries who occasionally worked in partnership. They made an enormous indirect contribution to the Scottish fishing industry between the end of the eighteenth and the beginning of the nineteenth century. Much of the original money for improvements came from the Forfeited Estates Fund, derived from the rents on estates of the Jacobite chiefs and lairds, forfeited after Culloden, and from the Fisheries Society itself, whose functions were taken over by the Scottish Fisheries Board in the nineteenth century.

Wick was one of the first harbours Telford improved. A large tidal basin, well-protected from the weather, was constructed. The development changed Wick from a poor village into a thriving fishing port that could accommodate up to 1,000 herring boats with a seasonal take that sometimes exceeded 100,000 barrels.

Similar improvements were made at most of the principal fishing stations on the Highland and island coasts, and local proprietors who were willing to construct piers and small harbours were given financial help by the two funding bodies. On the east coast, Banff, Burghead, Cullen, Dingwall, Fortrose, Fraserburgh, Kirkwall, Nairn, Peterhead and Portmahomack were improved. Perhaps Peterhead benefited most of all: the south harbour was deepened, piers and jetties extended, the entrance widened, and a road built on the causeway linking the north and south harbours with a wet dock between them. Work was carried out in Peterhead in stages from 1811 into the 1820s. It received a major setback in October 1819 when a violent storm from the north-east hit the coast, inflicting costly damage on any unfinished coastal works from the Firth of Tay to Wick. Nevertheless, the improvements changed a forbidding and dangerous coast into one which offered a choice of safe havens in most conditions of wind and weather.

Telford's most notable harbour works were also on the east coast, at Aberdeen and Dundee. When he first surveyed Aberdeen, he expressed surprise that anybody should have settled in a place so wild and barren.

The mouth of the Dee was blocked by shoals. In 1759 a quay had been built on the north bank of the river, extending towards the village of Footdee (Fitty), beyond which lay a small fishing harbour. From the quay, cured salmon were exported in quantity. A fort or blockhouse, to prevent the entrance of pirates, had been constructed beyond the harbour. Telford planned to confine the Dee to a deepened channel, clear its entrance, protect it with piers and create a tidal harbour. The tonnage of shipping entering the port increased from 50,000 tons in 1800 to about 300,000 in 1860.

In contrast, Dundee started with the advantage of being situated on a deep tidal estuary. In addition to piers and jetties, floating docks and a graving dock for large vessels were added and eventually in 1826 a large floating dock was constructed to take ships up to 170 feet long with a beam of 40 feet.

⚓ ⚓ ⚓

With an expanding population and improved communications, the early part of the nineteenth century saw a rapidly growing internal market for fresh and cured fish, stimulated for a decade from 1820 by bounties granted by the Fisheries Board, which in turn encouraged the construction of bigger boats requiring crews of seven or eight instead of four or five. From 1868 fishing boats had to be registered with the two letters indicating their port of registration and a number, painted on the bows. The introduction of steam propulsion followed in the last quarter of the century, by which time herring were being caught by Scottish drifters in large numbers off Shetland, Orkney, Lewis, Harris, Barra, Oban, Mallaig, the Isle of Man and Ireland – according to season. They were being salted and cured in the spring in Lerwick, Scrabster, Stromness and Stornoway; in the early summer in the Moray Firth ports and Barra, Oban and Mallaig; then later in the summer on the east coast from the Moray Firth to East Anglia.

When the herring fishing was at its zenith, the women folk – the 'gutting quines' – followed the fishing fleet from port to port, to gut, salt and pack the herring into barrels for export. It was gruelling work, standing at the farlans or gutting benches, and it took a heavy toll on health and beauty. The women worked in teams of three: two gutters to one packer. A skilled gutter, fingers bound in 'clouts' – torn fabric rags – to keep out the salt and protect them from the razor-sharp knife, could gut 60 fish a minute. The packer could separate herring into seven grades and fill three barrels or more in an hour. There was some social life for the younger men and women in the evenings and at weekends but few places where they could consort and little money to be spent on recreation. In the course of a season some women might work in more than a dozen ports, starting in May in the north: Baltasound, Lerwick, Stronsay, Stromness, Wick and Scrabster; then west to Stornoway, Castlebay, Mallaig and Oban, or down the east coast to Fraserburgh, Peterhead, Aberdeen, Eyemouth, Berwick, Shields, Scarborough and Grimsby, finishing in December in Yarmouth and Lowestoft. It was a long, hard and comfortless road. The romance of place names afforded no respite to toiling hands and aching limbs and there was scant opportunity to raise eyes from the bellies of fish to the beauty of a distant landscape or sea horizon. More than 6,000 Scots women travelled this road.

Wick gave work ashore to 11,000 in a season, including, among others, coopers and workers in transport. At Fraserburgh, some 300 fishermen provided work ashore for over 2,000. And then there was a winter season for some in the Forth, the Minches and the Irish Sea.

When steam drifters began to dominate the industry, it did not put an end to line fishing. It was still carried on, often by elderly men in boats of 20 to 40 feet, and sometimes by larger boats in the winter months when the herring fishing was out of season. By the beginning of the First World War, marine diesel engines and small auxiliary petrol engines were becoming available. The line-fishing boats came to rely on engines and in most fishing ports a small part of the community kept up line fishing. It was hardly profitable. During the First World War, some of the herring boats continued to work in the summer, in areas patrolled by HM ships, but most fishermen were absorbed into the Royal Navy or found themselves manning steam drifters taken over by the Admiralty for a variety of duties.

At the outbreak of the First World War, the number of Scottish-registered fishing boats had dropped to 8,534 crewed by 32,676 with 52,448 dependants. Nearly 8 per cent of the boats were wartime casualties and 1,127 fishermen perished. When fishing resumed in 1919, it was profitable for a few years but when the great depression came fishermen suffered along with everybody else. Rampant inflation in Germany crippled the continental market for herring and in 1926 some 60 per cent of the British fishing fleet was laid up for want of coal. Wages slumped and thousands emigrated. One courageous skipper who refused to accept defeat was John Robertson of Campbeltown. In 1921 he ordered two boats from James Miller and Son of St Monance, Fife, based on a Norwegian design and became a pioneer of seine-netting.

When the Herring Industry Board was set up in 1935, the east-coast herring boom, which had lasted for more than a century, was virtually over, although 150 drifters were still using Wick harbour in the summer season.

The number of Scottish fishermen had dropped to 22,175, of whom nearly a quarter were crofter-fishermen. In 1937 there were still more than 19,000 Scottish fishermen in total but they were having a hard time.

Following the Second World War, the industry passed through a relatively prosperous period. As fishing for herring declined in importance, the opposite was true of the white fish industry. For a generation, Scottish trawlermen fished the high seas freely. Their only concern was to catch fish and sell it at a profit. The White Fish Authority came into being, earnings were subsidised and a grant and loan scheme was introduced in 1953 enabling boats to be purchased for a down payment of 15 per cent. Boat sizes continued to increase and after the 1960s steel hulls and diesel engines became the norm for new boats. While the Scottish fleet nearly halved, the total trawler catch only dropped by 10 per cent despite the ban on trawling in inshore waters.

The 1970s saw intensification of the disputes over fishery limits and unilateral extension of territorial waters by Iceland and the Faeroes, which deprived deep-sea trawlers from Scottish ports of some of their traditional fishing grounds and resulted in the so-called 'cod wars' – a serious game played between encroaching trawlers and fishery protection cruisers. The issue was resolved to the detriment of Scottish fishermen when the United Kingdom joined the Common Market in 1972 and so became subject to the Common Fisheries Policy (CFP), which in principle opened all fisheries within 200 miles of the coasts of EEC members to the fishing fleets of all members. As a result, Scottish fisheries were plundered by the fishing fleets of continental European countries. This policy was linked to a system of quotas to each member country for each of the main commercial species of fish – Total Allowable Catches – which were supposed to be historically based on each country's past records of catches of that species. Thus Scotland became the dominant UK partner, with 70 per cent of the catch by weight, but some EEC members inflated their records and, thereby, their quotas. Although the CFP should have stalled the threat of big boats from eastern Europe, the 'klondykers' (factory ships) could still legally wait outside the 12-mile territorial limits, buy fish which might or might not be 'within quota' and transport it, lightly salted, for curing elsewhere, by-passing both the CFP and its ineffectual attempts at conservation.

Klondykers were not the only problem to become evident in the 1970s. To prevent over-fishing, a ban was put on trawling in inshore waters, to be replaced in the 1980s by protected areas, but the unprincipled policy of some governments, offering over-generous subsidies for the building of boats, resulted in substantial over-capacity: too many and too big boats were hunting a declining number of commercial fish. Scottish skippers were not helped by the high wages offered by the oil industry to skilled and unskilled workers, which made the recruiting of deckhands more difficult, or by the hike in the price of oil, nets and other gear in 1973–4. Problems were not eased by drift-netters' claims that ring-netters were damaging the herring fisheries, while delaying tactics by Aberdeen dockers forced white fish boats, in self-defence, to take their catches to Peterhead. Stornoway now has the biggest number of registered fishing vessels but these are mostly smaller boats, less than 12 metres in length. Fraserburgh comes next followed by Shetland, Campbeltown, Orkney, Oban, Ayr and Peterhead, with Fraserburgh, Peterhead, Buckie and Shetland having the largest number of big boats more than 24 metres in length – some over 50 metres. Scotland has between 60 and 80 boats big enough to exploit the continental shelf and beyond.

⚓ ⚓ ⚓

In the first decade of the twenty-first century, the Scottish fishing industry faces a bleak future. Cod stocks have reached the point where scientists recommend that the cod fishing grounds around the British Isles should be closed for up to 12 years to enable them to recover and in practice that means a partial ban on haddock, whiting and prawn because they are a 'by-catch' of trawling for cod. In fact, scientists also fear that haddock stocks are in imminent danger of collapse and that – except for shellfish – stocks of only three of the twenty-one commercial species in Scottish waters remain at a sustainable level. Fishermen claim that stock assessments are unreliable but EEC politicians listen to scientists, not to fishermen, although they also listen to the powerful Spanish and French lobbies, which reputedly did a deal with the Dutch and Irish late in 2002. As a result, niggardly quotas were awarded to the British fishing fleet. The quotas for North Sea cod were slashed by 45 per cent and haddock by 50 per cent. This hit the Scottish industry disproportionately hard, although overall quotas are said to be still 30 per cent above the scientists' recommendations. The upshot is that Scottish trawlers will have to spend half of every month tied up, possibly until 2015. Coming so soon after the £27-million deal in 2001 that resulted in the decommissioning of 20 per cent of the Scottish white fish fleet, this is real hardship, and judging by the ban on fishing the cod banks off Newfoundland, even these drastic actions will not guarantee the recovery of stocks.

In January 2003 the Scottish Executive voted £50 million to pay for decommissioning of a further 15 per cent of capacity and compensation for the periods of compulsory tie-up but whatever the outcome the basic situation remains unaltered: too many European boats hunting too few fish and this situation will be further aggravated when four east European countries with Baltic fishing fleets join the EEC.

Are there any answers to this multi-faceted problem? There may be, but the biggest problem of all will be to get any agreement among members of the EEC and then to police it effectively. First, a policy of 'effort limitation' should be followed: banning certain types of fishing entirely in specified areas where endangered species are known to spawn; second, the mesh size of nets should be compulsorily increased to ensure that young fish escape unharmed to grow and propagate, rather than being thrown back into the sea to die simply because they do not conform to quota specifications; third, industrial trawling for 'reduction' to animal feed should be banned; fourth, there must be intense lobbying in the European parliament and Commission to ban any form of grant which further increases the capacity of the continental European fishing fleet; fifth, quotas must be made the legal property of EEC governments and be returned to them if relinquished, not sold to other fishermen; sixth, fuel for British fishing boats should be tax-free; seventh, the Scottish Executive and British government should offer guaranteed prices for some of the excellent but unfamiliar fish which can be caught in the deep-water fisheries off the west coast of Scotland – black scabbard, blue ling, orange roughy and grenadier – and should subsidise a marketing drive to popularise these fish as they come onto the market; and eighth, the sale of fish *at sea* to klondykers and others should be made illegal, to avoid the regulations on size and species being flouted.

Collapse of the industry would leave thousands faced with unemployment. Five wage-earners ashore would lose their jobs for every fisherman who lost his at sea. The future for those Scots who fish the sea is in peril.

⚓ CHAPTER 15 ⚓

Building Ships, Boats and Lighthouses

Scotland's record in the building of ships and the installations for their servicing and safety is second to none. Examples of dug-out canoes made by hollowing out the trunks of trees from the ancient Caledonian forest have been found preserved in the silt of Scottish lochs such as Loch Doon in Ayrshire and Loch Laggan in Inverness-shire. The coracle, or something similar, came next or simultaneously in areas where trees of sufficient size were not available. They could be made from skins stretched over wickerwork or suitably shaped branches. The salmon coble evolved from this basic design. The advance to a hull of planks fixed to cross-timbers was a natural development. Over the course of 2,000 years, the basic technique has not changed. A modern boat or ship is still made of a skin of wood or steel laid over a framework of timbers or steel ribs or frames, built up from a keel laid down when construction starts. The Norse longship illustrated in the picture section would have been about 80-feet long, with a beam about a fifth of its length and a draught of three or four feet, depending on how heavily she was loaded.

In the fourteenth century or even earlier, slipways or yards for the construction of boats and ships were established at many places on the Scottish coast and in the estuaries of the Clyde, the Forth, the Tay and at Aberdeen. Some constructed famous ships; others survived by building fishing boats and pleasure craft; a few disappeared and left little trace. One of the latter is the slipway where ships were built for James IV in the sixteenth century. Traces of it may still be identified: blackened timbers projecting from the mud at low tide on the shore of the Forth estuary, half a mile north-east of Airth.

Andrew Wood's *Yellow Carvel*, probably built at Largo in Fife, was a fairly typical armed merchantman of the sixteenth century. Her clinker-built timber hull, less than 100-feet long with a cargo capacity of perhaps 100 tons, would have been vulnerable to decay. Hulls were sometimes dressed with pitch towards the end of the seventeenth century but copper sheathing was not introduced until late in the eighteenth century. *Yellow Carvel* would have been steered by a whipstaff projecting through the aftercastle, attached by a ring to the tiller, which in turn controlled the rudder.

In 1819 a shipbuilder in Leith, Thomas Morton, developed a patent slip designed to haul vessels out of the water onto a slipway for repair and maintenance. This often had advantages in time, cost and convenience over using a dry dock. By the end of the nineteenth century, not including small boatyards, there were some 16 shipyards on the river and estuary of the Clyde and a dozen or more on the east coast from the Forth to Inverness. There was a huge influx of people into Glasgow after 1830 from the Highlands and from Ireland, and many of the men became involved in shipbuilding.

Aberdeen has witnessed the rise and demise of five major shipyards. Alexander Hall & Co. was established in 1790 and survived until 1957. The yard developed the raked Aberdeen bow and built many clippers and other sailing vessels before moving into steam: trawlers, coasters, tugs and dredgers. Duthie's operated from 1816 to 1925, building a wide range of ships, from clippers to steam trawlers. William Duthie owned ships as well as building them, and used them to carry emigrants to North America and transport timber and the first guano from South America. He set up the first regular run between London and Australia. The Duthie family were also involved in rope- and sail-making, whaling, fish-processing and in captaining their own ships. They built the first Aberdeen screw trawler *North Star* in 1883, but they had to buy engines and eventually were taken over by Hall Russell. Nichol Reid's yard, which opened in 1817, built nearly 50 ships in 24 years. John Lewis & Sons specialised in cargo and fishing vessels, building their first ship in 1917. Their best-known vessel was *Fairtry*, the first purpose-built factory stern trawler. During the Second World War they built more than 30 minesweepers and patrol vessels, eventually being taken over by the Wood Group, which now services the oil industry. The Walter Hood shipyard built ships from 1839 to 1881, mostly for the Aberdeen White Star Line, among them the famous clipper *Thermopylae*. The yard merged with Alexander Hall & Co. in 1881.

Hall Russell & Co. Ltd was the last Aberdeen shipyard to survive. Founded in 1864, it stopped building ships in 1992. It was a partnership of two of Alexander Hall's sons and a Glasgow engineer, Thomas Russell. They constructed engines and boilers and launched their first iron steamer in 1868. They built fishing vessels, cargo ships and trawlers for the Aberdeen Steam Trawling and Fishing Company. During the First World War they built minesweepers and during the Second, frigates and corvettes, returning to the construction of fishing vessels after the cessation of hostilities. *Star of Scotland*, built by Hall Russell in 1947, was the most up-to-date trawler in the world when launched and in 1971 they built their largest ship, a 10,500-ton cargo vessel for a Dutch owner. In 1974 the yard built its last fishing boat – a seine-netter – then passed through several vicissitudes before attaining its present function, servicing the oil industry and undertaking ship repairs.

Dundee did not stake a claim in the shipbuilding industry until the first half of the nineteenth century, when a few yards began producing wooden sailing ships. As iron hulls and steam took over, three yards became prominent. Alexander Stephen & Sons built ships in the Panmure yard from 1844 for nearly 50 years. They built most of the Dundee whaling fleet, including *Terra Nova*, an innovative stern whaler that operated from 1884 to 1908 and was then used by Captain Scott in 1910 for his expedition to the South Pole. Thereafter they concentrated their business on the Clyde at Linthouse near Govan. Stephen's Linthouse yard became well known for passenger liners and cargo ships, particularly banana boats, while their Caledon yard in Dundee built ships for specialised purposes such as the Tay ferry. The Gourlay Brothers started building screw-propelled iron ships in Dundee in 1854 and soon became the biggest shipbuilding yard in the city. They built ships for the whaling industry and specialised vessels such as *Discovery*, used by Captain Scott in his first Antarctic expedition of 1900–04, now open to the public on the Dundee waterfront.

Shipbuilding was a major industry in Bo'ness in the nineteenth century, producing ships of up to 350 tons for the coastal and Baltic trade. Paisley, despite its distance from the Clyde, was building small ships at about the same time on the River Cart, a Clyde tributary. Paisley developed a relationship with the Canadian market, building specialised vessels such as ferries and lighthouse tenders.

The sailing vessel reached near perfection in the nineteenth century, embodied in the superb clippers built in Scottish yards. Among the most famous were *Aeriel, Taeping, Sir Lancelot, Thermopylae* and *Cutty Sark*, the first three built by Steele of Greenock. The fastest was possibly *Sir Lancelot*. She could make the passage from China, fully loaded with tea, in less than 90 days. She once recorded a day's run of 354 nautical miles – an average speed of nearly 15 knots, about half that of the Clyde-built Cunarder *Queen Mary* when she broke the transatlantic record in 1938. When *Aeriel* won the 'Great Tea Race' race in 1866, the captains of the first three ships – *Aeriel*, *Taeping* and *Serica* – were all Scots skippering Scottish-built clippers. *Aeriel* also held the record for the west–east voyage: from Gravesend to Hong Kong in 83 days, anchor to anchor.

Thermopylae was a composite ship of wooden planking on iron frames, displacing 991 tons, and launched in 1868. Her first record was achieved on her maiden voyage from Gravesend to Melbourne, completed in 60 days – still unbeaten by a sailing ship. Her next was to complete the run from Newcastle, New South Wales, to Shanghai in 28 days – less than three-quarters of the accepted time for the voyage. In her later career, under Canadian ownership, she once kept pace for three days with the Canadian Pacific liner *Empress of India*, which was steaming at an average 16 knots.

Cutty Sark was designed and built in Scott and Linton's yard at Dumbarton and launched on the Clyde on 22 November 1869. Her designer, Hercules Linton, born in Inverbervie, Kincardineshire, was familiar with the hulls of east-coast fishing boats and these influenced his design. The ship's owner – a Scot who had set up business in the Port of London – drove such a hard bargain with the builders that they went broke and the fitting out had to be completed by another Dumbarton firm, William Denny & Brothers. Her owner switched her to the Australian wool trade in 1885 and she made her name on that route, repeatedly making the fastest passage home with the season's new wool clip. She owed her speed in part to superlative ship-handling but no less to her hull shape, which was stronger and could take more sail than any other. The Maritime Trust are to be congratulated on preserving her for posterity, even though she is on display at Greenwich, far from her birthplace.

Alexander Hall & Co. of Aberdeen was the pioneer of the 'Aberdeen bow' – extending a strengthened bow further forward above the waterline, which not only reduced the depth of the hull, thereby saving tax based on hull depth, but increased speed and sea-keeping qualities. A two-masted schooner which they built in 1839, *Scottish Maid*, was said to be one of the first 'true clippers'. She could cover the 440-mile run from Leith to London in 33 hours. She displaced only 142 tons and was 92-feet long compared with *Aeriel*'s 1,059 tons and length of 197 feet. *Sobraon*, launched in Aberdeen in 1866, was the largest composite iron and timber sailing ship ever built. Her teak hull was stressed with iron beams and frames, her lower masts of wrought iron and her topmasts of steel. Her spread of canvas with all sails set was over two acres. She was never used as a tea clipper but sailed with passengers and general cargo to Melbourne, returning with passengers, wool and wheat.

Walter Hood of Aberdeen built the 827-ton wooden clipper *Queen of Nations*, launched in 1861 and highly regarded on the runs to Australia, New Zealand and the Far East. Russell & Co. of Greenock were successful builders of medium clippers of around 1,800 tons, such as *Goldenhorn*, a four-masted barque completed in 1883 as a bulk cargo carrier, which achieved a successful compromise between speed, cargo capacity and economy of operation. She could be handled by a crew of only 26 and was awarded the highest possible rating in Lloyd's Registry (*100A1). By the last quarter of the nineteenth century, steamers were replacing clippers on the route to Australia, the last great sailing ship route.

Scottish yards adapted without great difficulty to the construction of steamships. One of the first designed for a regular commercial run was the paddle steamer *Berenice*, launched on the Clyde in 1836. She was ordered by the East India Company for the Bombay to Suez run, 33 years before the opening of the Suez Canal. She displaced 756 tons and could reach 8 knots, driven by a 220-horsepower engine. Built two years later at Greenock and propelled by wooden side-wheels, *Unicorn* operated on the route between Glasgow and Liverpool until purchased by the British and North American Steamship Company, which became the Cunard Line, pioneering the transatlantic route from Liverpool to Halifax and Boston in 1840. The iron barque *May Queen*, built by Alexander Hall & Co. of Aberdeen and launched in 1869, was driven by a screw-propeller. She was slightly smaller than *Berenice* and was chartered by Shaw, Savill & Co. for the New Zealand run.

⚓ ⚓ ⚓

James Watt, whose name is more or less synonymous with steam, was born in Greenock in 1736. He was the grandson of a teacher of mathematics, surveying and navigation and son of a versatile father who was a merchant and shipowner as well as an instrument-maker and building contractor. His brother John died at sea in 1763 but, fortunately for posterity, James was considered delicate and was not encouraged to go to sea. He studied geometry at Greenock Grammar School and demonstrated manual dexterity making models, which encouraged his father to send him to study instrument-making. In 1757 he settled in Glasgow but was prevented from practising as a mathematical instrument-maker because he had not served a recognised apprenticeship. Luckily his best friend from schooldays, Andrew Anderson, had an elder brother who was Professor of Natural Philosophy at Glasgow University. James was appointed mathematical instrument-maker to the university and was able to mix with eminent scientists. He later utilised the scientific work on heat of Joseph Black (1728–99) in his development of steam power.

One day in 1764 James Watt was asked to repair a model of John Newcome's steam pumping engine, which had never worked properly. Its poor performance stimulated James to investigate the cause of its waste of power. The following year he devised a separate condenser, which transformed the engine's performance, and in 1769 patented the Watt Steam Engine. His crowning achievement was the invention of the governor, which regulated the working speed of the engine under varying conditions of load and made it a feasible means of propulsion for ships. He entered into an agreement with the Carron Iron Works to manufacture the engine at Kinnell near Linlithgow and became their engineering adviser.

Watt was responsible for the fuel-saving furnace. He was also employed on surveys for the Caledonian Canal, the Forth–Clyde Canal and for deepening both rivers for navigation. He was directly involved in improvement of the harbours at Greenock, Port Glasgow and Ayr.

It was William Symington, born in the village of Leadhills in Lanarkshire in 1763, who first married boats with steam. William was the son of the engineering superintendent of the Wanlockhead Mining Company and developed his ideas from a steam engine, manufactured by the James Watt partnership of Boulton and Watt and installed at Wanlockhead. In 1786 the manager of the mines, who had observed young William's potential, sent him to Edinburgh University to study scientific subjects.

In 1787 Symington, having previously constructed a working model of a steam road carriage, patented an improved form of steam engine. Patrick Miller of Dalswinton near Dumfries, who had been experimenting with a scheme to propel vessels with paddle wheels, employed him to design an engine for this purpose. An improved two-cylinder engine was made in Edinburgh and fitted to a 25-foot boat with paddle wheels, which achieved a speed of five knots on the local loch at Dalswinton in 1788. Miller decided to experiment on a larger scale on the Forth–Clyde Canal and, with Symington's engine, achieved a speed of nearly seven knots, but could not get any commercial support for his initiative. However, in 1801 Lord Dundas, governor of the Forth & Clyde Canal Company, decided to employ Symington, who had taken out a second patent for a horizontal engine: basically for a piston-rod guided by rollers in a straight line, linked by a connecting rod to a crank attached directly to the paddle-wheel shaft. This is the system that has been used to turn paddle-wheels ever since.

In March 1802 Symington's patented engine was installed in *Charlotte Dundas*, which was fitted with a single large paddle-wheel aft. In six hours she travelled 19½ miles on the Forth–Clyde Canal, against a strong headwind, towing two barges of 70 tons each. She was the first boat ever fitted with a steam engine for practical use. Unfortunately the Forth & Clyde Canal Company were worried about the effect of the steamboat's wash on the banks of the canal and would not support the project commercially. *Charlotte Dundas* was laid up but the project was taken up by Robert Fulton, an American citizen of Scots descent who had actually been on board the *Charlotte Dundas* as an observer and who further developed the idea in the United States.

Henry Bell was born at Torpichen Mill, Linlithgow, son of the millwright. His mother's family were mechanics and Henry was apprenticed to a firm of engineers. He worked under John Rennie, then with boatbuilders Shaw & Hart in Bo'ness. In 1800 he installed a steam engine in a small boat and applied to the Admiralty for support. The Admiralty, incurably conservative, turned him down. In 1803 when he approached them again, his application had the support of Lord Nelson, but again his ideas were rejected. Bell persisted and in 1812 the world's first commercially operational steamship, *Comet*, came into being. Built by Wood & Co. of Glasgow, she displaced 30 tons and was driven by a three-horsepower steam engine built and installed by Henry Bell. When the wind was favourable, she could hoist a large squaresail, set on the funnel, and was capable of six knots. Advertised by her owner as 'a handsome vessel to ply upon the River Clyde from Glasgow, to sail by the power of air, wind and steam', she plied between Greenock and Glasgow for eight years before running aground on Craignish Point. Henry Bell was also closely involved with the first steam ship to operate on the Thames. *Argyll*, renamed *Thames*, was launched at Port Glasgow in April 1814. She was bought by a London engineer and successfully sailed down the west coast, then along the English Channel to the Thames estuary.

Robert Louis Stevenson, literary genius and creator of *Treasure Island* among other classics, who died on the island of Samoa in 1894, came from an Edinburgh dynasty of engineers and lighthouse builders. He wrote movingly of his father Thomas in *Memories and Portraits* and there are parts of the world where Thomas Stevenson is better known than his famous son. He left a legacy to which countless mariners have owed their lives and their peace of mind.

Robert Stevenson, the founder of the engineering dynasty and grandfather of the author, was born in Glasgow in 1772. He came from a family of farmers, maltsters and West India merchants. He studied engineering at the Andersonian Institute in Glasgow, then at Edinburgh University, before joining the Northern Lighthouse Board. At the age of 19, he supervised the construction of a lighthouse on the island of Little

Cumbrae in the Clyde and became engineer to the Scottish Lighthouse Board soon afterwards, holding the office for half a century. He designed and built 20 lighthouses, brought their innovative lighting systems to perfection, invented intermittent or flashing lights and also designed bridges.

Possibly Robert's most famous lighthouse is the Bell Rock, erected in cooperation with John Rennie on a dangerous submerged reef 11 miles off the coast of Angus. In the infamous storm of 1799, 70 sail were wrecked on the reef, including the 74-gun ship-of-the-line *York*. The lighthouse took five years to complete. It was a pioneering structure 100 feet high, tapering from a diameter of 42 feet at the base to 15 feet at the top. The floors of the six storeys were bonded to the walls, thus tying them to ensure maximum strength. Robert Stevenson even invented a lightship to warn mariners while the lighthouse was under construction.

In 1814 the Lighthouse Board Yacht *Pharos*, with Robert on board, made a tour of inspection, sailing from Leith on 29 July by way of Shetland, Orkney, the Pentland Firth, the outer isles, Skye, Iona, Mull, Northern Ireland and finally reaching Greenock on 8 September. In the course of the voyage, Robert made preliminary surveys of Cape Wrath and Skerryvore, south-west of Tiree, with a view to building lighthouses there in the future. Among the guests on this voyage was Sir Walter Scott, whose copious notes were published in 1838 in John Gibson Lockhart's biography.

Robert Stevenson was also responsible for many valuable inventions and innovations: malleable iron rails for railways, hydrophones and the use of greenheart oak for piers and other structures in the sea to avoid worm damage. He was interested in fisheries, the use of the barometer for weather prediction and the compilation of accurate charts by marine surveying and sounding. He was an originator of the Royal Observatory in Edinburgh.

Robert Stevenson had three sons, who were all engineers involved with the sea: Alan, the eldest, built ten lighthouses including Skerryvore; David, who was a pioneer of marine surveying and hydrometry and an authority on rivers, estuaries, harbours and docks, constructed 28 beacons and 30 lighthouses in places as far apart as Newfoundland, New Zealand, India and Japan; and the youngest son Thomas, father of the writer, was an engineer and meteorologist who made scientific contributions in a number of other fields, including optics and waves. He invented the azimuthal condensing system of lighthouse illumination and, like his father and brothers, was an expert on harbours.

A dozen other notable Scottish inventors and engineers contributed in different ways to progress in shipbuilding and port and lighthouse construction. James Taylor, born at Leadhills in Lanarkshire, adapted the steam engine to drive paddle wheels and cooperated with William Symington in his experimental work at Dalswinton and on the Forth–Clyde Canal.

Thomas Telford, born at Westerkirk in Dumfriesshire in 1757, was the son of a shepherd and apprenticed to a local stonemason at the age of 14. He became a civil engineer and went on to design and build bridges, canals and harbours all over the British Isles and beyond. Among his outstanding achievements are the Caledonian Canal, the Ellesmere Canal, two of the bridges across the Severn, the Menai suspension bridge to Anglesey and the Gotha Canal in Sweden. He built 1,200 bridges throughout Scotland, improved numerous harbours and constructed St Katherine's Dock in the Port of London.

John Rennie, born near Haddington in 1761, started life as a farmer. He worked with the millwright Andrew Meikle, inventor of the threshing machine, and was offered a job by James Watt. He built steam engines, using iron for shafting and framing. He then established his own business in London and expanded the scale of his operations. He constructed four canals – the Kennet and Avon, Rochdale, Lancaster and Shannon – before progressing into dock and harbour construction. He built the East and West India Docks in London and the docks at Chatham, Hull, Ramsgate and Sheerness. He built bridges at Kelso and Musselburgh and in London built Waterloo Bridge – a copy of the Kelso Bridge – London Bridge and Southwark Bridge. With Robert Stevenson he built the Bell Rock lighthouse, 25 miles east of Dundee. He constructed the Plymouth breakwater in deep water, which required three and a half million tons of stone, and worked with Thomas Telford on the fundamental improvement of the most important harbours on the coast of north-east Scotland. For good measure, he also invented the diving bell and steam dredging with chain buckets.

Edinburgh scientist and engineer Thomas Drummond specialised in lights for surveying and lighthouses, while James Jardine, a mathematician and engineer born in Dumfriesshire, recorded tidal observations on the east coast and was responsible for construction of the Grand Union Canal linking London with Nottingham and Birmingham.

Admiral Lord Cochrane, tenth Earl of Dundonald, was a powerful proponent of the steamship, but, like his father before him, he was also an inventor and innovator. Thomas's first invention of importance was to aid the management of convoys in wartime conditions: the mast-head lamp he devised in 1813, in which combustion of oil or some other fuel was enhanced by the admission of a free current of air – a principle subsequently taken for granted which greatly increased the brightness and reliability of lights. At the age of seven he was taken by his father especially to meet James Watt. He had steam on the brain ever afterwards and, despite his outstanding skill in sailing ships, continually pressed the Admiralty to experiment with it. In 1818, when appointed vice-admiral of Chile, he had a steamship named *Rising Star* built at home, with the help of a brother, to his own design. It was the first steamship to cross the Atlantic, although an Atlantic crossing without the aid of sails was not achieved for another 20 years.

Cochrane was also a proponent of the rotary engine. In 1843 he succeeded where James Watt had failed by manufacturing what John Bourne in *A Treatise on the Steam Engine* called 'the most perfect engine of the class which has yet been projected'. He took out patents for various improvements, including one for an improved propeller or screw. Instead of the blades being set at right angles to the propeller-shaft, they were set at an angle of around forty-five degrees. In his submission for the patent, he gave a full scientific and technical explanation as to why this greatly improved performance. The principle has since been accepted worldwide. At the same time, Cochrane took out a patent for another invention, which has since been incorporated in most marine steam engines: the double tier of upright tubes through which water circulates within a flue carrying the hot gases from the furnace.

Cochrane made another lasting contribution to marine engineering with his 'best lines' for hull conformation: to use his own words, 'the uniform delineation of consecutive parabolic curves, forming a series of lines presenting the least resistance in the submerged portion of ships and vessels'. He continued to impress on the Admiralty the need for warships of the least tonnage commensurate with the greatest strength, speed and armament and at last, in the latter part of 1843, the Admiralty consented to build a frigate, *Janus*, based on Cochrane's principles. The work was so poorly executed that he had to take up his appointment as C-in-C North American and West Indies Station before she was completed. However, *Janus* did eventually have some beneficial impact on British warship design. When he became First Lord of the Admiralty in 1847, the Earl of Haddington agreed to install one of Cochrane's rotary engines in the small ship *Firefly*, which proved a success. Thomas Cochrane was responsible for at least eight other inventions, the majority of which he patented.

⚓ ⚓ ⚓

Robert Napier, who has been called 'the father of Clyde shipbuilding', was born in Dumbarton in 1791, to a family of engineers, blacksmiths and millwrights. His mother was Jean Denny from another Dumbarton family who would also become famous shipbuilders. Denny's of Dumbarton were the first to open an experimental model ship tank for commercial use in the 1880s. Robert's brother David used such a tank to develop hull designs with wedge-shaped bows more suitable for steamships than the rounded bows of sailing ships. The company later experimented with hovercraft and helicopters.

Napier gained experience working first with his father and then in Edinburgh, before setting up on his own account in Glasgow where the engineering trades were regulated by the Incorporation of Hammermen. He registered as a member and rose to a senior position in the organisation. He made pipes for Glasgow waterworks and manufactured a 12-horsepower steam engine for a Dundee mill. This was his entry into the field of marine engineering.

In 1823 he won the contract to construct the engine for the steamer *Leven* being built by James Lang of Dumbarton. This engine, built at Camlachie Foundry, which Napier had rented from his cousin David, outlived *Leven*, was transferred to *Queen of Beauty* and survives on a permanent site in Denny. He also built the engines for the Glasgow to Belfast steamer *Eclipse* and most of the engines for the Glasgow Steam Packet Company's Glasgow to Liverpool ships. In 1827, when the Northern Yacht Club held their annual August regatta in the Clyde, they offered a cup for a steamboat race. The two winning vessels were both powered by Napier engines. He established the Vulcan Foundry in Glasgow and trained several men who subsequently became prominent in shipbuilding on the Clyde, notably both James and George Thomson, who formed the company J. & G. Thomson on Clydebank, later taken over by the legendary John Brown & Co., which survived into the twenty-first century. In 1834 he built the engines for the Dundee to London steam packets.

In 1836 Napier leased his cousin's Lancefield Works and expanded into more powerful engines for ocean-going vessels. In 1836 he built the 220-horsepower engine for *Berenice*, one of two new paddle steamers for the East India Company. English engineers were critical of the company for giving the contract to a 'provincial' builder, but when *Berenice* beat her Thames-built sister ship by 18 days on their maiden voyages to India, criticism was silenced and he was given an order for a 280-horsepower engine for their next ship, *Zenobia*. This contract was followed in 1839 by an order for engines for *British Queen*, designed for the transatlantic run from Liverpool to New York.

A Canadian businessman, Samuel Cunard, planned a transatlantic liner service underpinned by the valuable government contract to carry the mails. London and Liverpool interests tried to warn him off the Clyde shipbuilding industry but Robert Napier was able to produce satisfactory specifications for the 800-ton 300-horsepower ships Cunard wanted. Napier then persuaded the Canadian to go for something bigger. A contract was eventually signed for the first of four 1,150-ton 420-horsepower ships, all to be built on the Clyde: *Britannia*, *Acadia*, *Caledonia* and *Columbia*. *Caledonia* was built at Charles Wood's yard in Dumbarton. Cunard had some difficulty in raising the capital for these bigger vessels but Napier's excellent reputation persuaded Glasgow investors to support the venture and Napier himself made an investment. The startling increase in size between *Britannia*, built by Napier in 1840, and the massive *Queen Mary*, built for Cunard in John Brown's yard on Clydebank nearly a century later, can be seen in the illustration in the picture section. Robert Napier's wooden steamers were so successful that nine more, successively larger and more powerful, were built for Cunard over the following decade.

In 1838 Napier got his first Admiralty contract for engines for two paddle sloops, *Stromboli* and *Vesuvius*. The perennially conservative Admiralty was reluctant to employ shipbuilders outwith the areas familiar to them: London and the Royal Dockyards at Portsmouth, Devonport and Sheerness. Although the Napier-built engines were completely successful, the Admiralty reverted to their traditional builders until a parliamentary question asking for details of costs, repairs and time out of commission proved that Napier's engines were both cheaper and more reliable than the English-built versions. Thereafter Napier became a regular contractor to the Admiralty.

Until 1841 Napier only built engines and contracted out the hulls to shipbuilders such as John Wood at Port Glasgow but the demand for iron hulls was growing fast and he decided to meet it. A wooden hull had to be as heavy as the weight of the cargo carried in order to be strong enough, whereas an iron hull could carry a cargo twice its own weight. Robert took his brother as a partner, then bought Lancefield and land at Govan where he established a yard to build iron ships. He also brought in his cousin William Denny and in cooperation with his other brother, David, built the 680-ton *Vanguard* for the Glasgow–Dublin run. This was followed by the first iron steamers for the Royal Navy: the gunboats *Jackal*, *Lizard* and *Bloodhound*. In 1849 they built *Leviathan*, the world's first train ferry, which plied across the Forth from Granton to Burntisland. In 1850 they began building iron-hulled ships for P&O; then in 1854 the world's largest ship to date – the 3,300-ton *Persia* for Cunard and in 1860 the ironclad warship *Black Prince*.

Before Robert Napier's retirement at the end of the decade, more than

300 ships had been built, either for the government or for great shipping companies. Warships were built for the French, Turks, Danes and Dutch. Patents were taken out for armoured decks and turrets. He found time to train engineer officers for the Royal Navy and to build a valuable art collection. When he died, an obituary in the *Glasgow Herald* described him as 'a noble workman with a soul above money and meanness in all its forms'. At his funeral in Dumbarton, 1,400 of his workmen accompanied the coffin for the last mile of its journey.

Robert Napier's brother David, who was just a year older, was a distinguished shipbuilder and marine engineer in his own right. He was the first to introduce British coasting steamers and steam packets for mail delivery. He started the first steamer service between Glasgow, Greenock and Liverpool and built the steamer *Talbot*, fitted with two 30-horsepower engines, to run between Holyhead and Dublin. In 1826 he built the 200-horsepower engine for the largest steamship yet designed, *United Kingdom*. Constructed by Steele of Greenock, she was 160-feet long with a beam of 26½ feet. David Napier also invented the steeple engine, which occupied much less space than the side lever engine, and he was the first to apply the surface condenser to marine engines.

As a result of the Napiers' initiative, shipbuilding on the Clyde gained worldwide recognition and renown. In addition to those at Clydebank, Dumbarton and Greenock, yards came into being at Fairfield, Govan, Partick and Port Glasgow. Lower down the Firth, there were yards at Ardrossan, Troon and Fairlie which became famous for yachtbuilding. On the east coast, Aberdeen, Bo'ness, Dundee, Grangemouth, Inverness, Kirkcaldy, Leith and Peterhead all developed important yards and there were many lesser boatyards up and down both coasts. The emphasis changed from wood and composite hulls to iron and steel. Among the pioneers of iron ships was the firm of William Laird, Birkenhead, founded by a Scots family. John Laird, born in Greenock in 1805, built the first iron vessel ever seen in American waters and also built iron steamers for the Nile and Euphrates.

John Scott Russell, born in Glasgow in 1808, studied engineering at Glasgow, Edinburgh and St Andrews. He carried out research into the nature of waves in order to improve hull shapes. He became manager of Caird & Co., shipbuilders in Greenock, and put his research into practice in the construction of four ships for the West India Royal Mail Company. He moved to London and was responsible for building *Great Eastern*, designed by Brunel and launched in the Thames in 1858. Her huge propeller was cast in the Lancefield forge on Clydeside. This vessel was intended for the eastern trade, to ascertain the correlation between size and economy, but was used instead for cable-laying across the Atlantic in 1865 and 1866, from Bombay to Aden in 1870 and to Newfoundland in 1870. Russell also built the first sea-going armoured frigate HMS *Warrior* at Blackwall. He was a founder and president of the Institute of Naval Architects.

⚓ ⚓ ⚓

The Scottish shipbuilding industry continued to expand with the development of boilers of increased efficiency, the steam-turbine, the triple expansion engine and the transition from hulls of wood and iron to steel. The steamer *Aberdeen*, launched in 1881, was the first to be fitted with the new triple expansion engine.

In 1883 the coaster *Daphne*, when launched at Linthouse, rolled over and sank with the loss of 124 workmen's lives. This led to a commission of inquiry and, indirectly, to the founding of a Chair of Naval Architecture at Glasgow University by Mrs Isabella Elder, widow of ship designer John Elder.

The liner *King Edward*, launched at Dumbarton in 1901, was the world's first steam turbine-powered passenger ship. Also in 1901, six months before Marconi made the first transatlantic wireless transmission from Cornwall to Newfoundland, the Clyde-built Cunarder *Lucania* was undergoing trials of wireless telegraphy at sea.

In 1903, faced with massive expansion of the German navy, the Admiralty took the decision to construct a naval base at Rosyth. Merchant fleets grew bigger and naval rearmament in the years before the First World War brought more work, particularly to the Clyde. William Denny & Co. worked on a number of designs for helicopters between 1905 and 1910. By 1912 they had found an engine with a sufficient power-to-weight ratio to get the craft off the ground, but not for long. Their experiments were overtaken by the First World War, when the need to build warships became paramount.

In 1913 Clyde shipbuilders used one and a half million tons of steel and between 1908 and 1914 a quarter of all ships for the Royal Navy were built on the Clyde. The quays of the Broomielaw had been built by a tax on every pint of beer sold in the city of Glasgow. Some 6,000 dockers were employed in the shipyards; as many as 2,500 workers would be employed on building a single medium-sized ship, with a management staff – ranging from foremen to managing director – of nearly one-tenth of the total workforce.

The Cunard liner *Lusitania*, sister ship of the *Mauretania*, was launched at John Brown's yard on Clydebank in 1907 and equipped with steam turbines. In October *Lusitania* took the 'blue riband of the Atlantic' from Germany, crossing in 4 days, 19 hours, 52 minutes, cutting nearly 12 hours off the German record. Sadly she was destined to be sunk by a German U-boat on 8 May 1915, with the loss of 1,200 lives – most of them civilian passengers, including 120 Americans. This atrocity was a major influence on the United States' decision to declare war on Germany. Millions of tons of shipping were sunk during the war, leading to a vast rebuilding programme in the years 1919 to 1923, when Scottish shipbuilding accounted for 60 per cent of UK output of all types of ship.

⚓ ⚓ ⚓

Although the first liner to have oil-fired electric turbine engines, *Viceroy of India*, was launched for P&O from the Clyde yard of Alexander Stephen & Sons in 1929, the post-war recession of the 1920s and early 1930s hit hard at Scotland's shipyards. The Clyde, which was geared to building big ships, suffered most. As industrial production fell, not just in shipbuilding, unemployment in the area rose inexorably from 2 per cent to 18 per cent, never falling below 10 per cent for 20 years. Orders for ships and heavy engineering equipment – even without allowing for any profit margin – became scarce. One in three shipyard workers were out of work. Three out of five were unemployed for at least part of this period of intense depression. One-third of a million – 6 per cent of Scotland's population – were forced to emigrate; 12,000 per month in 1923.

The poverty of those who remained bred the politics of extremity. For a time parliament ran scared, fearing the repercussions of the revolution that had fractured Russia. Only the common sense and compassion of men like James Maxton, described by Winston Churchill as 'the greatest parliamentarian of his day', kept revolt within the boundaries of parliamentary democracy. Maxton, a teacher who had been an anti-war campaigner, imprisoned as a conscientious objector, lost his teaching post and in 1917 went to work in a shipyard at Polmadie as a plater's mate. The yard was constructing barges for neutral countries. He went on to be a general labourer and shipping clerk before taking an organisational post in the Independent Labour Party and eventually becoming its leader in parliament.

The keel of the great Cunarder *Queen Mary* was laid down at John Brown's yard in December 1930. Known as contract no. 534, she became a symbol of the fortunes of Clyde shipbuilding. Economics forced the owners to stop work on her a year later and for two years her rusting hull loomed over the yard and nearby streets. National unemployment rose from one to two million between 1929 and 1931. By 1932 it was approaching three million. Clyde shipbuilding, which had still launched a million tons a year in the 1920s, launched only 133,000 tons in 1933. At last, in April 1934, the impasse was broken: government loans, combined with an agreement to merge Cunard with the competing White Star Line, enabled work to start again. Then the keel of the *Queen Elizabeth* was laid down. The two *Queens* eventually completed their maiden voyages in 1936 and 1940 respectively.

To attribute the recovery of Scottish shipbuilding to Adolf Hitler would be a ludicrous and distorted allocation of credit, but it is one paradox of human activity that war, or the threat of it, benefits at least a few of those on the periphery.

⚓ ⚓ ⚓

The brothers James and George Thomson had a marine engineering business in Glasgow before opening a shipyard and launching the paddle steamer *Jackal* in 1852. They specialised in building passenger ships of high quality and moved to a 'green field' site at Clydebank in 1872. By 1899 Thomson Brothers had become the Clydebank Shipbuilding and Engineering Company. They were then taken over by Sheffield steel-maker John Brown. Among the famous ships built in this Clydebank yard, in addition to the three *Queens*, were *Lusitania*, HMS *Hood* and HMS *Vanguard*. The 44,500-ton battleship HMS *Vanguard*, in which the author served as senior sub-lieutenant in 1947, was launched in 1944 and completed just too late to join the British Pacific Fleet before the Japanese surrender in August 1945. In 1947 she took King George VI and Queen Elizabeth, accompanied by their daughters the princesses Elizabeth and Margaret, on a cruise to South Africa. Not long afterwards she was put into reserve, then broken up for scrap. She needed a complement of over 2,000 men and was too expensive to be kept operational in peacetime.

Queen Elizabeth II, launched in 1967, was the last major contract to be completed in John Brown's yard before it was absorbed by Upper Clyde Shipbuilders. This firm sadly went into liquidation in 1971, with the loss of 4,000 jobs. The yard is now destined to become another of those sites for housing and offices. It is to be hoped that employment will be found for those who live in the houses and that they will not be haunted by the tramp of feet of thousands of shipyard workers or of the sound of hammering and riveting; or be overshadowed by the ghosts of great ships.

Some yards attempted alternatives to traditional shipbuilding. William Denny's Dumbarton shipyard was among the leaders in experimenting with hovercraft. Their first craft, *Denny Enterprise*, was acquired in the early

1960s by the Norwest Hovercraft Company to operate a high-speed service from the Isle of Man to Morecambe Bay in Lancashire. It was not a true hovercraft, being an air-cushioned vessel that was not amphibious. A sister craft was used to operate an experimental service on the River Thames in 1963 before being sent to the Bahamas and then to Florida. It was a noisy craft, spray obscured the view from the windows and Denny's could not claim it was a commercial success.

Because wages and the cost of materials are relatively high in Scottish yards, foreign competition, particularly from the Far East, has rendered many of them uncompetitive. Boatbuilding in Scotland may yet thrive but the future of shipbuilding rests with three yards on the Clyde and one on the Forth: Govan, Scotstoun, the yard at Port Glasgow that specialises in ferries and vessels related to the oil industry, and the former Royal Naval Dockyard at Rosyth. There are other yards around the coast with the capacity and skills to construct oil rigs and platforms. Dry docks at Greenock and elsewhere are capable of undertaking ship repairs or modifications, but shipbuilding will largely depend on government contracts.

BAE Systems, who operate the Govan and Scotstoun yards, already have six Type 45 destroyers under construction at Scotstoun, with six more in the pipeline. Their plan to construct two huge aircraft carriers was endorsed by the Ministry of Defence in January 2003. Winning this contract against fierce competition from other British and French yards gave an enormous boost to Scottish shipbuilding and particularly to the Clyde, but other British yards, those with specialist skills, and manufacturers of numerous products from electronics to textiles, will also benefit.

The contract awarded to BAE is worth ten billion pounds, the sum of three billion pounds in construction costs and seven billion pounds for maintenance and upgrading spread over the 30-year predicted lifetime of the two carriers. They will be three times as big as the three they will replace and much more sophisticated. About 950-feet long, each vessel will displace about 60,000 tons. This makes an interesting comparison with the last great liner built at Clydebank by John Brown & Co. and launched in September 1967 – *Queen Elizabeth II*. She is 963-feet long, displaces 70,327 tons and cost £29 million. Inflation since 1967 and the difference in category invalidate any comparison of costs. Work on the carriers is due to start in 2004 and they should be in service by 2015, manned by crews of about 1,600 and carrying up to 50 jump-jet aircraft.

Although BAE Systems are the prime contractors, the work of construction will be shared between four yards and numerous subcontractors. The Govan yard, which employs 500, will carry out most of the steel work, while Scotstoun, with 1,500 workers, will take responsibility for design and sub-assembly. The massive components will be put together by Babcock at Rosyth, who employ a workforce of 2,300. Two English yards – Swan Hunter on Tyneside and Vosper Thornycroft at Portsmouth – will do some of the sub-contracting. The massive project will ensure continued employment for 10,000 and create another 2,000 jobs.

The future construction of warships – destroyers, landing craft and fleet auxiliaries – is a field where the main competition will come from Europe. The Clyde's reputation for quality and traditional engineering skills should win a fair share of the available contracts, provided essential modern skills in electronics and computer-aided design are readily accessible.

Just as aircraft have revolutionised naval warfare, so they have revolutionised the carriage of passengers and freight. It is cheaper and faster for passengers and freight with a high value-to-weight ratio to be transported by air; but ships have a future in transporting bulk cargoes where speed is not the major consideration, and in carrying passengers on short hauls and for pleasure, when comfort and having room to stretch the legs are more important than speed. However, in the building of merchant ships and liners, Scottish yards are faced with competition, not only from modern yards in America and Europe but from government-subsidised yards in Asian countries which employ highly disciplined workers at relatively low wages.

⚓ CHAPTER 16 ⚓

Merchant Shipping, Maritime Trade and Oil

The history of Scotland's merchant navy started when the first vessel, propelled by oars and assisted by a sail, set forth to barter smoked or salted fish, wool or hides, for something more exotic. In AD 80, when Calgacus the swordsman stood against the Roman General Agricola on Benachie, Caledonia was trading with Cornwall for tin, with Gaul for fruit and wine, with Spain for iron and oil. A Gaelic-speaking Celt is reputed to have sailed to Greenland with the Vikings in AD 1000 and set foot in the New World. Four hundred years later the Earl of Orkney, Henry Sinclair, sailed to Greenland to trade manufactured goods for whale oil, by which time there was already a Scottish fishery off Iceland. By 1600 a Dundee merchant was trading with Newfoundland and 20 years later Scots migrated to that island. The following year and again in 1623 Scottish expeditions to establish trading posts in Nova Scotia were unsuccessful but by the 1630s Scots were trading with the American colonies – Dutch, English and French.

There is no obvious reason why merchant shipping should not continue to transport bulk or containerised cargoes for as long as the human species exists. Both Grangemouth and Greenock are eminently suitable for this traffic. Air transport is faster but unlikely to become cheaper; intercontinental pipelines or tunnels are possible but enormously costly to construct and maintain. So-called globalisation will inevitably lead to the ownership of legitimate merchant shipping being concentrated in the hands of a few huge international companies but, although the tonnage of merchant shipping owned by Scottish-registered companies greatly decreased in the twentieth century, Glasgow is still an important centre of ship management, arranging cargoes and itineraries for the owners. Denholm Ship Management, for example, with tramp ships and ore carriers of their own, manage a large tonnage of shipping of different nationalities and are among the world leaders. Scotland's major ports are headquarters to numerous shipping agents, brokers and chandlers.

England's Navigation Acts, dating from 1381, ruled that exports from and imports into English ports could only be carried in English ships. There was, therefore, little maritime trade between Scotland and England until after the Union of 1707. Although isolated ships from Scotland traded in the Baltic and across the North Sea, there was no regular maritime trade to and from Scottish ports until the middle of the thirteenth century. Restrictions imposed by the Hanseatic League, which exercised a shipping monopoly over much of the Baltic and Scandinavia, forced Scotland into a close relationship with France and Flanders. From the French viewpoint this was largely an expedient relationship, as Scotland represented an ally at England's back.

A nation could adopt one of two opposing principles in its attitude to maritime trade: mercantilism or free trade. In this context, mercantilism meant controlling trade by legislation, by the imposition of import and export duties or taxes and by blockades when considered necessary. Free trade ideally meant the exchange of commodities at their real value and the processing of raw materials in the country of origin. The former, which benefited colonial powers, was usually adopted by England; the latter, of necessity, by Scotland – until the Union.

Scottish enterprise was not entirely stifled, however. When an English expedition of three ships set out in 1553 to explore a possible route to the Far East along the north coast of Asia, they were scattered by a storm; two ships were lost but the third, putting in to Vardo in the extreme north of Norway, 150 miles beyond the North Cape, found a Scottish trading post.

By the 1680s Port Glasgow had been built and seven ships a year were plying the Atlantic from the Clyde and more from Leith and Aberdeen. The first cargo of tobacco from New England reached the Clyde in 1640. The tobacco trade was to bring unprecedented wealth to the City of Glasgow. The financial benefits concealed its insidious damage to health and the nefarious links between a minority of the tobacco merchants and the slave trade, despite the concept of slavery being widely abhorred in Scotland.

Between the middle of the eighteenth century and the outbreak of the American War of Independence, the tobacco trade between Great Britain and Chesapeake Bay in New England was at its most prosperous. It increased sixfold in value between 1741 and 1771 and the Scottish share of the trade, mainly through Glasgow, rose over the same period from 10 per cent to 52 per cent. Much of this was re-exported to France, leaving very substantial profits in the hands of Glasgow's elite tobacco lords, such as John Glassford, and merchants who owned shares in ships.

The exclusive ownership of ships by families became more common in the following century. In the two decades before 1771 the value of Scottish imports increased two and a half times and exports three and a half times. Tobacco comprised 85 per cent of the former and 52 per cent of the latter, but there were simultaneous increases in trade with Russia, mostly dependent on the import of flax for the thriving Scottish linen trade, for which home production of flax was insufficient. Sailings to Russia increased from 12 ships in 1730 to 120 in 1770.

During the eighteenth century the merchant navy expanded and its activities and structure were increasingly controlled by legislation. Following the Act of Union, merchant vessels were ordered to fly a distinctive flag – a red ensign, with the Union Flag replacing the St Andrew's or St George's cross in the upper canton next to the mast. Marine insurance became customary in 1720, when a London corporation was granted a charter to undertake marine risks and in 1760 Lloyd's Register of Shipping developed from 'Lloyds List', which had started as a publication of shipping news in 1734. Whereas some 3,281 vessels totalling 260,000 tons were registered at British ports at the beginning of the eighteenth century, by the outbreak of the French revolution in 1789 the number of ships had increased by nearly fivefold and the tonnage by nearly sixfold. By 1815 British-registered tonnage was about two and a half million. In the following century and a half this tonnage would increase eightfold. Due to the complexity of partnership agreements and the tendency of shipping lines to open up offices in the south as they expanded, it is impossible to identify what proportion of this tonnage was Scottish. However, Scottish shipping companies and merchant houses proliferated in the nineteenth century. For example, there were fourteen Scots merchant houses involved in trading from Calcutta, as compared to ten English. Trade with the Far East, and particularly with China, encouraged the design of the fast clipper ships built in Scottish yards. Tea had to be fresh or its value plummeted.

Until 1814 the London-based East India Company retained its monopoly of all trade east of the Cape of Good Hope. In that year, under pressure from rival interests, its charter was not renewed. It was the start of the era of the fast clipper, which lasted until Indian tea began to dominate the market, shipped by steamer through the Suez Canal which opened in 1869. Most clippers then moved to the Australian run. Wool did not deteriorate as quickly as tea but the new wool clip had to reach the London market ahead of its rivals in order to get the best price.

The traffic in opium from India to China, which had been a profitable sideline for the East India Company and its employees, was now pursued by the captains of small, fast, locally built clippers, many of them ex-employees of the Company. The sale of opium had long been an important source of revenue to India, and China was the principal consumer, while there was a valuable and growing market for tea in the British Isles. Two Scots, William Jardine and James Matheson, were quick to spot the gap in the market. The opium trade was unprincipled but not yet illegal and the demand in China was vast.

William Jardine had been born near Lochmaben in Dumfriesshire in 1784. He studied medicine in Edinburgh, qualified when very young and joined the East India Company as a ship's surgeon at the age of 18. The ships' officers were permitted to trade privately. William did so well that he set up on his own account in 1817. He met James Matheson in Canton, a trader 12 years his junior who was originally from Sutherland. The two of them established the famous company of Jardine Matheson & Co. in 1832. Two years later the partners sent home the first shipments of Chinese tea not consigned by the declining East India Company. Jardine Matheson & Co. invested in land in Hong Kong, expanded into mainland China and became the first foreign trading house in Japan. The first clipper had been launched in Aberdeen in 1839. The Glen Line bought out Jardine Matheson's ships 72 years later to form the Glen-Shire Line, which was eventually bought by the Blue Funnel Line of Liverpool.

John Laird and his brother MacGregor were Clydesiders, both born in Greenock, but the family moved to Liverpool, where their father founded the shipbuilding firm of William Laird, Birkenhead. They became pioneers of iron shipbuilding. They built *John Randolph* for Savannah in the United States – the first iron vessel ever seen in America – and also built steamers for the Euphrates and the Nile.

MacGregor Laird, born in 1808 and educated in Edinburgh, was partly motivated by a hatred of slavery, which had been largely responsible for Liverpool's prosperity. He was convinced that if the River Niger in west Africa could be opened up, legitimate trade would overtake the slave trade. In 1832 the Laird brothers sent the *Alburkah*, which they had designed, to the Niger – the first iron ship to make an ocean voyage. MacGregor himself traced the course of the Niger and of the Indus in Kashmir, before becoming involved in promoting the North American Steam Navigation Company, established to run steamers between the British Isles and New York.

In 1853 MacGregor Laird won the contract for operating monthly mail boats to west Africa, against competition from powerful Liverpool traders. He won because he put the emphasis on providing a service for small traders, both British and African. He also won a subsidy to explore the Niger to see how far upriver a ship could be piloted. He himself took the ship through the delta and up the river. By his skill and forethought, and the use of quinine, he achieved another first: his exploration into the African interior was achieved without the loss of a single life. It was his fellow-Scot Mungo Park who had famously explored the source of the Niger in 1806. With government support, MacGregor sent another expedition up the Niger in 1854, led by yet another Scottish explorer, William Baikie.

⚓ ⚓ ⚓

The Reciprocity of Duties Bill, enacted in 1823, superseded the Navigation Acts and encouraged free trade, ushering in the era of the great shipping lines. Among the first in the field were Pollok, Gilmour & Co. of Glasgow. Originally a grocery business, they started importing timber from Canada, then constructing their own ships in Nova Scotia. By 1824, with a fleet of 78 ships, they were probably the biggest shipowners in the world.

By the middle of the century, trade with China and Japan was opening up and the clipper really came into its own. The first 'tea race' from China to Britain was held soon after Shanghai was opened to trade in 1843. The fastest clippers were built in Scotland and owned by individual merchant shipowners before the famous shipping lines were established. The first true clipper, built in Aberdeen in 1839 for Alexander Nicol and George Munro, with the famous raked 'Aberdeen bow', was *Scottish Maid*. She was small – 142 tons, 92-feet long – and designed for the Leith to London run. *Queen of Nations* was built in Aberdeen in 1861 for the Aberdeen White Star Line. *Aeriel*, which won the 'Great Tea Race' in 1866, had been built in Greenock the previous year for Shaw, Lowther, Maxton & Co. *Sobraon* was built in Aberdeen for the same company in 1866 and later bought by Devitt & Moore, who ran ships to South Australia. *James Nicol Fleming* was built in Glasgow in 1869 for Patrick Henderson's Glasgow-based Albion Shipping Company. *May Queen*, an iron barque, was built in Aberdeen in the same year for Shirris Leslie & Co. of Aberdeen but was chartered to Shaw Savill & Co. for the New Zealand run. The famous *Cutty Sark* was built in Dumbarton in 1870 for Jock Willis, a Scottish shipowner based in the Port of London. At 212 feet, she was more than twice as long as was *Scottish Maid* and six or seven times her tonnage.

The Aberdeen Line, founded by George Thomson in 1825, was one of the earliest shipping lines. It operated a passenger service to Canada and traded in general cargo to the St Lawrence, returning with timber. By 1837 the Aberdeen Line had a dozen ships and had extended trading to South America and the Pacific. Early in the twentieth century it was taken over and managed jointly by the White Star Line, the Albion Line and Shaw Savill. The Albion Line, which pioneered the service to New Zealand, was founded in 1856 by Patrick Henderson, an insurance broker from Pittenweem in Fife, and survived into the 1930s. The line gave such good service to the French government during the Crimean War that it was given permission to use the French tricolour – with a small Union Jack in the centre – as its house flag. The Albion Line was the first to import refrigerated mutton from New Zealand in 1882, the year it amalgamated with Shaw Savill. The combined company also included John Leslie & Partners. It was recognised as the main trade link with New Zealand and was permitted to use the New Zealand ensign as its house flag. In 1875 the White Star Line began a service in the Pacific, between San Francisco, Japan and China, and in 1883 the combined company began to replace sailing ships with steamers. The Loch Line of Glasgow began running ships to Australia and New Zealand in 1867, initially chartering ships belonging to other companies before having iron-hulled clippers built to its own specifications in Clyde yards.

The Lyle Shipping Company was originally a partnership between a cooperage making barrels for sugar and molasses and the shipping required to bring the raw materials back from the West Indies, Mauritius and India, set up by Abram Lyle of Greenock in 1827. On the outward voyage the cargoes were coal, iron and railway sleepers. Competition from European sugar beet forced Lyle to seek economies which led to amalgamation with Tate's of Liverpool and the establishment of Tate & Lyle's sugar refining factory in Greenock.

Abram Lyle, however, loved sailing ships and wanted to stay in Scotland. His shipping company developed into a fleet of tramp steamers based in Glasgow. The tramping trade was free of cartels and not bound by an advertised schedule. Some small tramp steamers, typified by the *Vital Spark*, described immortally in Neil Munro's *Para Handy* series, plied the Scottish and neighbouring coasts in a leisurely fashion with very mixed cargoes. Inheritors of this tradition are the landing craft, operated commercially in competition with MacBrayne's, capable of landing cargoes varying from gas cylinders to sheep on beaches anywhere in the Western Isles.

The Anchor Line, established in 1838 for Baltic commerce, expanded into the Atlantic trade in 1852 when Thomas Henderson of Glasgow entered the partnership. From 1865, its ships linked Glasgow and New York with fortnightly sailings and then expanded into the Mediterranean and established a passenger service to Bombay and Karachi. They were the first to send a merchant ship through the Suez Canal after it opened.

The Ben Line, founded in 1839 by Alexander and William Thomson of Leith, started with a run to Leghorn in Italy but soon expanded into Atlantic traffic. They operated sailing ships until the 1890s. After the opening of the Suez Canal in 1869, their cargoes were mostly grain and sugar because there were no facilities for taking sailing ships through the canal. They were said to have a contract to carry sherry casks full of new whisky to the Far East and back because the warmth and movement of the ship greatly improved the whisky. A century later the company was absorbed by a big container group.

The Glen Line sprang from the Glasgow shipbroking business of James McGregor and Leonard Gow, although their ships were registered in London. They specialised in the import of China tea using fast clippers.

For the first third of the nineteenth century, mails from Britain to the Mediterranean were carried in government ships but in 1837 a mail contract was concluded with the Peninsular Steam Navigation Company, which had been operating between London, Portugal and Spain for three years. This company was founded by Arthur Anderson, who hailed from Shetland. Born in 1795, he joined the Royal Navy as a boy then worked as a shipbroker in London. He established the company in 1837 and won a contract to carry the mails to Gibraltar, stopping en route at Spanish and Portuguese ports. In 1840 the company won a further contract to carry the mails to India by way of Alexandria and the Red Sea. Operations were extended to the Far East and the company's name was changed to Peninsular & Orient. When the Navigation Acts were repealed and the Suez Canal opened, many of the company's ships became obsolete. Thomas Sutherland from Aberdeen, who had been head of their operations in Hong Kong and had made the route to that destination profitable by trading in opium, extended their operational area to include Australasia. Scottish ownership was diluted but half their fleet was still registered in Greenock. Arthur Anderson had been MP for Orkney and Shetland, and Thomas Sutherland represented Greenock in parliament from 1884 to 1900. P&O eventually amalgamated with the British India Steam Navigation Company under James Mackay.

The British India Steam Navigation Company, which was established in 1862, had grown out of the Calcutta and Burmah Steam Navigation Company, set up in Calcutta in the 1840s by three Scots – Robert Mackenzie, William Mackinnon and James Hall. James Mackay worked for William Mackinnon in Calcutta, where he was a strong supporter of Indian interests. The company dealt in textiles between Scotland and India and in general goods with Australia. It was mainly a shipping business – a carrier subsidised by the mail contract to Calcutta and Burma. Mackinnon was the driving force. He joined the board of the City of Glasgow Bank, invested boldly and expanded the company after the completion of the Suez Canal. With associated companies, they came to own 180 ships and ruled a huge commercial empire. Mackinnon cultivated Clyde shipbuilders and was particularly supportive of William Denny & Brothers of Dumbarton. Originally from Kintyre, Mackinnon would only allow Campbeltown malt whisky to be served on his ships, though this rule must have been difficult to police.

Since the introduction of cotton in the 1790s, the manufacture of cloth had become vital to the Scottish economy and it was exported world wide. Unfortunately the City of Glasgow Bank failed, the manufacture of textiles in Scotland declined and with the opening of the Suez Canal William Mackinnon moved the offices of the company to London. It was he who negotiated the amalgamation with Thomas Sutherland of P&O, but it was Sutherland who chose James Mackay, later Lord Inchcape, to succeed him as boss of the combined company. It is interesting to note that several Glasgow shipping lines other than the Calcutta and Burmah Steam Navigation Company did business with Burma. The Glasgow-operated Irawaddy Flotilla grew into the Burmah Oil Company, the parent of British Petroleum.

Imports of palm oil to Glasgow prompted the formation of the British and African Steam Navigation Company in 1861, which merged into Elder, Dempster & Co. in 1868. The company eventually became the leader in the West Indian fruit trade in addition to its African trade. Christian Salvesen of Leith diversified from whaling into tankers and refrigerated transport when whaling ceased to be viable in the 1950s.

Cunard has probably had a greater influence on Clyde shipbuilding and consequently on employment and the Scottish economy than any other shipping line. Samuel Cunard was a shipowner from Nova Scotia with the vision to see the possibilities of a fast and comfortable transatlantic passenger service, so long as it was subsidised by a government contract to carry the mails. He founded the British and North American Royal Mail Steam Packet Company and, risking his own personal fortune, convinced other investors to subscribe sufficient capital to build the company's first ships. Clyde engineer and shipbuilder Robert Napier won the contract against tough opposition from shipyards south of the Border. He persuaded Cunard to build bigger ships than he had originally intended and personally invested substantially in the project. The government duly awarded the mail contract to Samuel Cunard, reassuringly underpinning the whole venture. His managing partners were George and James Burns and David and Charles MacIver of Glasgow, whose own ships had recently entered the Mediterranean trade after competing with each other on the Glasgow to Liverpool run until 1853, when they amalgamated. The Cunard, Burns and MacIver families were to control the company for the next 40 years.

Britannia was the very first Cunarder. She was launched on the Clyde on 7 February 1840 by Miss Isabella Napier, sister of Robert, and was just 200 feet in length with a beam of 32 feet and a draught of just over 21 feet. On her maiden voyage, with Samuel Cunard on board, she reached Halifax in 12 days and 15 hours. So successful was the venture that within eleven years nine new wooden-hulled steamers had been added to the fleet, making possible a service of weekly sailings on a route encompassing Boston and Halifax as well as New York. Their operations were later extended to the West Indies and into the Mediterranean. Cunard acquired their first iron ships in 1853. Screw propulsion soon followed and by 1867 their steam-powered, iron-hulled, screw-propelled ships were crossing the Atlantic in eight days. But Cunard did not have it all their own way. The White Star Line inaugurated a service from Liverpool to New York in 1869. The tragic loss of their flagship *Titanic* on 15 April 1912 did not improve the company's reputation, however. Among the many lost were the engineering staff, including seven Scots, who had gallantly remained at their posts to keep the pumps, lighting and wireless operating.

For three decades the competition between the Cunard and White Star companies was intense until Cunard came out on top after a reorganisation in 1889 that involved moving their base to Liverpool because it was nearer to London – a fatal attraction to successful Scottish-based businesses. After weathering the depression with the aid of government grants, the building programme culminated in the launch of *Queen Elizabeth II* from John Brown's yard at Clydebank in 1967. During the two world wars, Cunarders moved many thousands of American and Canadian troops across the Atlantic and others were converted to serve as armed merchant cruisers. One such was *Ascania*, captained by the author's father in 1942–3. Ships of the P&O, Union Castle, Pacific Steam Navigation Company, Royal Mail and Canadian Pacific Lines were all heavily involved in transport of troops to and from different war theatres. Winston Churchill suggested that the participation of *Queen Mary* and *Queen Elizabeth* as fast troopships shortened the Second World War by a year.

The Union Castle Line was formed from the amalgamation of the Union Steamship Company with the Castle Mail Packets Company in 1900, under the management of Donald Currie, who came from Greenock. He had started as an employee of Cunard but set up his own shipping line from Leith to Hamburg. When he won the mail contract to South Africa, he extended his services and transferred most of his business to London.

The Clan Line bucked the trend by moving its offices north from Liverpool to Glasgow. It was founded in Liverpool in 1877 by Charles W. Cayzer, a Londoner, trading with India. When Captain William Irvine joined the company, his name was incorporated. There were substantial investments in the firm by John Muir of James Finlay & Co. and Alexander Stephen of Govan Shipbuilders, whereupon the offices were moved to Glasgow under the management of Cayzer Irvine. In 1890 the company adopted the name The Clan Line of Steamers Limited, then bought the ships belonging to the Persian Gulf Steam Ship Company and successively took over the Scottish Shire Line, the Houston Line and the British and South American Steam Navigation Company. In 1956 they merged with the Union Castle groups to form British & Commonwealth Shipping Limited. After a further series of amalgamations and mergers the Clan Line ceased trading, although Cayzer Irvine stayed in ship management until 1988. In the course of its varied history, the company had managed ships on routes between the UK and Africa, the Persian Gulf, India, Pakistan, Australia and North America.

In the past century Glasgow shipping companies have serviced every continent except Antarctica: P. Henderson and Company to Alexandria, Bombay, Rangoon and Sydney; the Donaldson Line to Quebec, Buenos Aires, Montevideo and San Francisco; the City Line to Tripoli, Istanbul, Port Said and Calcutta; and the Clyde Shipping Company to destinations closer to home – Southampton, Cork and Limerick.

The unarmed *Athenia*, a 13,500-ton passenger liner of the Anchor Donaldson Line, was the very first ship to be sunk in the Second World War – within 12 hours of the declaration of war, at dusk on 3 September 1939. Most of her passengers had time to take to the lifeboats before she sank, but 112 lives were lost. The ship was torpedoed off the Rockall Banks within hours of leaving the Clyde bound for the St Lawrence. Her loss made a particularly heavy and sombre impact in Scotland because many of the passengers were women and children of Scottish families with relatives in Canada and the USA. The crew of *U-30*, which fired the torpedo, claimed afterwards that they thought they were attacking a troopship or cruiser.

⚓ ⚓ ⚓

There can be few Scots who are not familiar with the name MacBrayne. It is synonymous with communication in the Western Isles, the islands' lifeline and the main factor in enabling some islands to remain inhabited. If ever MacBrayne's ferries are compelled to compete commercially with other operators under a private enterprise system, the less economic routes would simply disappear and the smaller and more remote islands would either become uninhabited, or playgrounds for those wealthy enough to afford motor cruisers or aircraft.

Caledonian MacBrayne was founded in 1851 as David Hutcheson & Co. The three partners were David and Alexander Hutcheson and David MacBrayne. Their fleet consisted of eight paddle steamers and two boats confined to the Crinan Canal between Ardrishaig and Loch Crinan. In 1855 a year-round service to Tobermory, Portree and Stornoway was inaugurated. Thereafter routes were extended, one by one, to encompass virtually every inhabited island off the west coast, delivering mail, passengers and commodities. Unfortunately the exigencies of the First World War obliged the company to curtail services to such an extent that it could no longer tender for the Royal Mail contract. In effect, this meant the withdrawal of a substantial subsidy. However, the London Midland and Scottish Railway came to the rescue in 1928, a new partnership was formed and four new ships were ordered. MacBrayne was able to secure the Royal Mail contract again. One of the new vessels was Britain's first diesel, electrically propelled ship, *Lochfyne*.

The Second World War also hit MacBrayne's hard but the government and armed forces had to rely on the company for communication with the strategically important islands. Nationalisation of the railways in 1948 underpinned the company's operations. Their resources were combined with those of McCallum, Orme & Co., formerly MacBrayne's opposite number in the commercial cargo field. This resulted in improved shore and terminus facilities and the provision of car ferries to Mull, Skye and the Outer Isles. Over the next 45 years, MacBrayne's underwent a variety of traumatic changes at administrative and managerial level, emerging in 1990 as Caledonian MacBrayne, a company wholly owned by the government – now by the Scottish Executive: probably the best outcome, so long as its owners fully meet their obligations to the inhabitants of Scotland's remote and beautiful islands, which are among the last outposts of natural living in Europe's increasingly polluted urban environment.

⚓ ⚓ ⚓

From the beginning of the twentieth century, foreign competition in the shipping business became intense. British shipping lines only just managed to keep ahead on routes serving the Commonwealth and where they were not subjected to unfair competition by ships operating under flags of convenience with skeleton, underpaid crews and uncertificated officers. 'Shipping Conferences', another term for cartels, provided a partial solution to this problem and many reputable companies joined them. With profits allocated by agreement, shipping lines could only expand by planned programmes of building and development, sometimes aided by government subsidy. Some shipbuilding companies were linked with shipping lines. Denny's of Dumbarton, for example, had agreements with 19 shipping lines. In the three decades preceding the First World War, Denny's sold 770 ships to these lines but, one by one, shipbuilders have succumbed to foreign competition which utilises low-cost labour and government subsidies.

British shipping and fishing companies were not helped by the loss of some 44,500 skilled officers and seamen, and some 15 million tons of shipping in the course of two world wars. No seaman would wish to belittle the courage and self-sacrifice shown by the fighter pilots of the RAF in the Battle of Britain, but without the sailors of the navies, which kept open the lifelines to the British Isles, defeat would have been a certainty. In his autobiography, *A Sailor's Odyssey*, Admiral of the Fleet Viscount Cunningham of Hyndhope, who more than any other single man was responsible for victory at sea in the Second World War, refers frequently to the vital role performed by the Merchant Navy and to the 'fine sea discipline and fighting qualities shown by their personnel'.

⚓ ⚓ ⚓

A new element in Scotland's relationship with the sea came with the discovery of oil off the Scottish coast. While shipbuilding and fishing both declined after the Second World War, there was a hiatus before the oil industry became the dominant industry of the Scottish coastline. Following the discovery of gas in the Netherlands, geologists located gas in the North Sea in 1965. The rock formations convinced them that oil would be found near the Scottish coast. In 1969 drills first struck oil in Amoco's field off Arbroath, but another six years passed before the first North Sea oil came ashore at Cruden Bay, north of Aberdeen. By the early 1990s, a hundred oilfields were in production in UK waters and Aberdeen had become the oil capital of the North Sea. Oil terminals were soon developed at Sullom Voe in Shetland, at Flotta in Orkney and at Nigg in Easter Ross, with operational yards at Nigg, Ardersier on the Moray Firth, Methil on the Firth of Forth, Kishorn on the west coast and

Hunterston on the Clyde. Pipelines can be fabricated in more than one of these yards.

By the end of the twentieth century, oil and gas were providing more than 100,000 jobs in Scotland, employing 6 per cent of the work force, three-quarters of them in the North East: not only men and women on the oil rigs but workers in more than 2,000 small innovative companies which service the industry and derive a significant part of their income from international activities. At the rate of production of oil and gas achieved at the end of the twentieth century, reserves in the North Sea could last beyond 2015 – but not much longer. Oil will then have to come from the deep waters of the Atlantic or further afield and hopefully much of our power and heat will be derived from renewable sources: wind, waves, tides and hydro-electricity. The government aims to obtain 10 per cent from renewable sources by 2010 but ideally the graph should be much steeper. It is questionable how much longer the supply of oil and gas off our shores will continue to exceed demand, leaving a surplus for export.

Employment in the oil industry increased the population of the North East by 15 per cent over the 30 years following the first strike in 1969. North Sea oil has generated enormous wealth for the multinational companies – something now approaching ten billion pounds per annum from the combined international sales of services and primary products. A small part of that wealth has filtered into east-coast towns and villages and further inland, but many Scots consider that the oil and gas off Scotland's coasts are a Scottish resource and that government revenue accruing from it should be invested in Scotland.

It is commonplace to meet families living 30 or 40 miles from the coast who have husbands, sons and brothers working in the oil industry – either on the rigs or in one of the servicing and supply companies. This emphasises the feeling that Scotland is a land surrounded and dominated by the sea – some would say threatened. Many families have harrowing memories of 6 July 1988, when the Piper Alpha oil platform caught fire and blew up. Nearly three-quarters of the 228 on board lost their lives. It was a tragically expensive way to learn the need for meticulous control of working practices in a dangerously volatile environment.

Life on the oil rigs is well paid but risky. The conditions on some rigs are Spartan, with poor domestic facilities, unappetising food and little in the way of recreation. Without good pay and alternate fortnights ashore, few would be willing to do the dangerous work. The suspicion persists that health and safety considerations may be subordinated to company profit: out of sight, out of mind. It has been suggested that foreign workers, who do not require work permits if employed outwith UK territorial waters, are being exploited and are depriving home-based workers of employment. There is a long haul ahead before all the big oil companies accept full accountability for the health, safety and welfare of their oil rig workers. Comparisons with Norway do not reflect favourably on the Scottish situation, either in terms of the proportion of oil wealth reinvested in Scotland, or in terms of pay, welfare and job security.

Measures to limit oil spillage are strictly enforced but, as demonstrated by the sinking of the stricken tanker *Prestige* off the north-west coast of Spain in November 2002, the lesson that oil tankers must be double-hulled and compartmented has not been completely implemented in the first decade of the twenty-first century. The threat remains. It is more than a decade since the oil tanker *Braer* ran aground off Sumburgh Head in Shetland, carrying some 130,000 tons of oil. Fortunately the stormy weather, which hampered the well-organised clean-up by Shetland Islands Council, helped to disperse 70 per cent of what was a light crude oil by natural means, but the evidence is still there. The spilt oil had serious effects on primary industries and wildlife, but it could have been a great deal worse. This must not be allowed to happen again.

⚓ ⚓ ⚓

The twenty-first century holds countless uncertainties for Scottish shipping, shipbuilding and the men and women who are employed in these industries. The future is overshadowed by the question marks which loom over oil production and the extent to which it will be replaced by alternative fuels and the harnessing of energy from sustainable sources. Ships propelled by a combination of wind, wave and solar power are not beyond the bounds of human ingenuity. The future of ships and shipping must be sustainable.

⚓ CHAPTER 17 ⚓

World Power to World War

In the century between the outbreak of the Boer War in 1899 and the restitution of a Scottish parliament in 1999, Scotland underwent a fundamental transformation in status. From being a minority shareholder in the biggest empire the world had ever seen, covering one-fifth of the globe, she became a nation with powers limited by membership – direct or in partnership – of several layers of organisation, from the United Kingdom to the United Nations. By the dawn of the new millennium, a global economy was progressively transferring real power from national governments to international conglomerates, but in the twentieth century maritime trade and sea power were still of prime importance, although increasingly under the wings of air commerce and air power.

Two realities had to be accepted before the end of that century: that commodities and people could be moved more quickly by air than by sea and that in wartime sea power without adequate air cover could not be sustained, except perhaps when exercised from beneath the sea. The submarine almost defeated the United Kingdom in two world wars. Had Germany not surrendered in 1945, it is possible that a new generation of submarines, capable of long endurance, high speeds and of launching rockets while submerged, would have severed our lifeline across the Atlantic and made invasion of mainland Europe impossible.

One man who lived through most of that century and provides a strong link between the epoch of the British Empire and the age of the United Nations was Andrew Browne Cunningham, Admiral of the Fleet Lord Cunningham of Hyndhope. Nobody in that century carried a greater burden of sustained personal risk and heavy responsibility – or made fewer mistakes.

So far as is known, Andrew B. Cunningham (known universally as ABC) had no naval forebears. His mother was the eldest daughter of Andrew Browne, parish minister of Beith in Ayrshire. His father Daniel was the son of John Cunningham, who had been parish minister of Crieff in Perthshire and Moderator of the General Assembly of the Church of Scotland in 1886. Daniel Cunningham went to Edinburgh University to study medicine. He became Professor of Anatomy at Trinity College in Dublin, where Andrew, the third of their five children, was born on 7 January 1883. 'Though born in Ireland I am a Scot,' Cunningham states unequivocally on the first page of his autobiography.

ABC went to school in Edinburgh before joining HMS *Britannia* as a naval cadet in 1897. At the start of the Boer War, he was serving as a midshipman on the South African station and for six months was ashore with the Naval Brigade, gaining useful experience of military campaigning. His first taste of 'small ship' life came as sub-lieutenant in the destroyer HMS *Locust*. Its appeal was such that destroyers dominated his early career. He never specialised but remained what the Navy called a 'salt horse' all his life.

In the years between 1906 and the outbreak of the Great War in 1914, ABC accumulated vast experience of small ship handling and tactics. He was captain of three destroyers successively before his appointment to the destroyer HMS *Scorpion*. He was to command this ship until January 1918, while he rose in rank from lieutenant to commander, won a DSO with two bars and became the doyen of destroyer captains.

Early in the First World War, the 3rd Destroyer Flotilla, of which *Scorpion* was part, became involved in the ill-conceived plan to land troops on Gallipoli and force the Dardanelles. The dual objective was to open a route through the Black Sea to Russia and to knock Turkey out of the war. Neither was achieved. For two years *Scorpion* was deployed escorting battleships, which were either bombarding well-manned Turkish forts or trying unsuccessfully to blast their way through the straits; minesweeping; or covering troop landings. The military planning was disastrous and the Navy suffered heavy losses but fire support from the destroyers was highly effective. When Churchill and the generals finally admitted failure, it was the Navy's task to evacuate the battered remnants of the Army – a task they successfully achieved over two nights in December 1915. Commander Cunningham was awarded the DSO for his services in the Dardanelles.

Meanwhile the unrestricted German U-boat campaign in the Atlantic was posing an increasing threat. On 7 May 1915, *U-20*, cruising off southern Ireland, fired a single torpedo at the Clyde-built Cunarder, *Lusitania*. She sank within 18 minutes, taking nearly 1,200 men, women and children with her, amongst them 128 Americans. American public opinion now swung dramatically in favour of the French and British cause.

In May 1916 Grand Admiral Scheer, C-in-C of the German High Seas Fleet, decided to break the British blockade of German ports and emerged hoping to destroy some part of the British Home Fleet. The German force, comprising 22 battleships and 70 or more cruisers and destroyers, proceeded north-west from Heligoland. The Royal Navy, warned that the German fleet had put to sea, steamed east from their Scottish anchorages in Scapa Flow, the Cromarty Firth and the Firth of Forth. The combined squadrons and flotillas of the Royal Navy outnumbered the German High Seas Fleet by approximately 3 to 2 but their command was divided and communications were unreliable. The opposing fleets met some 100 miles west of Jutland, off the coast of Denmark. Visibility was poor, signalling difficult and orders confused. The author's father, Alastair Davidson, then a junior lieutenant in HMS *Martial* of the 11th Destroyer Flotilla, described the battle as 'total chaos'. Some destroyers fired their torpedoes, while others did not because they were unsure whether the grey shapes looming ahead through the mist and smoke were friend or foe.

Although the British ships secured a greater number of hits, it seems that German guns and shells were more effective because the Royal Navy's losses were greater than those of the enemy. The British losses of fourteen ships included three battlecruisers, as against German losses of eleven ships, which included a battleship and one battlecruiser. In personnel, the difference in casualties was greater. Many Scots were among the 6,007 British killed and 510 wounded – more than double the German casualties. However, the German High Seas Fleet retreated and never put to sea again until their surrender in 1918, when they sailed to Scapa Flow, where some 70 ships were ignominiously scuttled.

After the evacuation of troops from the Dardanelles, Cunningham was sent to establish a base on the Greek island of Leros, with the object of harassing the supply lines between the Turkish-held islands. He continued these operations until January 1917. Thereafter *Scorpion* was employed mainly on convoy duties across the Mediterranean. Cunningham did not lose a single ship from convoys he escorted in the Mediterranean in 1917 but in the Atlantic the situation was desperate. In May more than 100 merchant ships, many of them American, were sunk. The introduction of Q-ships by Captain Gordon Campbell RN, who won the Victoria Cross for his exploits and subsequently reached flag rank, helped to reduce the losses. Q-ships were merchantmen, their crews appropriately dressed, with hidden guns. When it appeared advantageous, German submarines would surface and attack with gunfire instead of with torpedoes. A Q-ship would then raise its gun-ports and open fire, often before the submarine had time to man its own gun.

In the final months of the war, Cunningham commanded the destroyer *Termagent* in the famous Dover Patrol. Between more arduous duties, *Termagent* was chosen to take a succession of VIPs to France: the future King George VI, Admiral Beatty, the First Sea Lord – Admiral of the Fleet Lord Wemyss, another Scot who was on his way to represent the Royal Navy at the signing of the Armistice – and lastly Prime Minister Lloyd George.

The armistice had a sting in its tail for many families in the Isle of Lewis. The steam yacht HMS *Amalthea*, attached to the naval base in Stornoway, was entering harbour with sailors returning home from war service when she struck the reef known as the Beasts of Holm outside the harbour entrance. Two hundred and eighteen lives were lost.

After service in the Baltic, on the North American and West Indies Station, then as captain of the battleship HMS *Rodney*, ABC was appointed Commodore of RN Barracks, Chatham, in 1931. He became aware of the growing gap between lower deck and wardroom, which was potentially disastrous. Severe government economies, which had pruned officer numbers, were reflected in pay cuts on the lower deck, damaging both discipline and recruiting. On 15 September 1931 there was a mutiny in ships of the Royal Navy at Invergordon. When they heard about impending pay cuts, ships' companies held mass meetings and refused to take the fleet to sea. At Chatham Barracks Commodore Cunningham, sensitive to the difficulties faced by sailors' families, offered to see personally any man with a complaint. He interviewed more than 500 men face to face to explain the dire economic situation the country was in. At the same time, he put pressure on the Admiralty to mitigate the pay cuts. Discipline was restored in the fleet when the Admiralty reduced the pay cut from 25 per cent to 10 per cent.

In January 1934, ABC was appointed Rear-Admiral (Destroyers) Mediterranean, flying his flag in the cruiser *Coventry* and commanding four flotillas of nine destroyers each. Lord Mountbatten, then captain of the destroyer *Daring*, watched the Admiral manoeuvre the 36 ships virtually single-handed: 'No move escaped his eagle eye. It was the greatest one-man performance I have seen on the bridge of a ship. I never forgot it.'

By July 1936, Cunningham had been promoted to vice-admiral, flying his flag in the ill-fated battlecruiser *Hood* – a deceptively beautiful but fatally flawed ship. As a child on the beach at Nairn in the summer of 1938, the author recalls watching with fascination as HMS *Hood*, in company with the Navy's two other battlecruisers, *Repulse* and *Renown*, steamed out of the Cromarty Firth between the red Sutars, turned east and eventually disappeared over the horizon.

By 1937 it had become obvious to realists that a major war was becoming inevitable. British fleets met in Gibraltar for day and night exercises involving surface, air and submarine forces. At this point the Navy still did not fully appreciate the vulnerability of ships to air attack when air cover was inadequate; this knowledge would come through painful experience. Fortunately, however, radar had just been invented. Without it, Great Britain would have been defeated.

Scottish scientist and inventor, Robert Watson-Watt, while superintendent of the National Physical Laboratory from 1932 to 1936, had established the science of radar – radio detection and ranging. When first secretly fitted in HMS *Rodney* in 1938, it was called RDF or Radio Direction Finding. Watson-Watt, knighted in 1942, was director of communications development at the Air Ministry from 1938 to 1940 and later their scientific adviser on telecommunications. Without his brilliant contribution, the Battle of Britain, the Battle of the Atlantic and many other Second World War battles could not have been won, but it would be several years before radar could be fitted to all ships and aircraft.

When war was declared against Nazi Germany on 3 September 1939, Vice-Admiral Sir Andrew B. Cunningham had been C-in-C Mediterranean for three months. He flew his flag in HMS *Warspite*, one of the old battleships that had been present at the Battle of Jutland. In June 1940 he had some sixty ships under his command, including four battleships, nine cruisers and the aircraft carrier *Eagle*. From 11 June, Britain was also at war with Italy, whose fleet greatly outnumbered the Royal Navy in the Mediterranean. Malta was the Mediterranean HQ, although it was well within the range of Italian airfields and was continually bombed. ABC preferred to operate from Alexandria, whence he could protect shipping using the Suez Canal.

When the French capitulated on 14 June 1940, it became vital to prevent the French ships from falling into enemy hands. The flag officers in command were given the choice of joining the Royal Navy, scuttling their ships, or handing them over while the crews were repatriated to France. By skilful negotiation, and ignoring ill-considered signals from the Admiralty, which he suspected had emanated from Churchill, ABC was able to neutralise the French ships in Alexandria harbour. Oran was a different story and a tragic one. There ABC's subordinate, Rear-Admiral Somerville, followed Admiralty orders. His ships opened fire, blowing up the French battleship *Bretagne*. Over 1,000 French sailors died and French goodwill died with them.

There was some talk at the Admiralty of abandoning the eastern Mediterranean to concentrate on safeguarding Gibraltar and the Atlantic sea routes, but Cunningham, aware that the route round the Cape to India, Australia, New Zealand and the Far East exceeded the voyage through the Suez Canal by something like 6,000 miles and six weeks, fiercely opposed this suggestion and was able to win Churchill's support. All but vitally essential personnel and stores were evacuated to Alexandria from Malta, which became an isolated fortress.

ABC's primary strategic objectives were firstly to keep the Mediterranean open for the convoys that supplied both Malta and the Eighth Army in North Africa – initially through Alexandria – and secondly to disrupt the supply lines between Italy and the enemy forces in Libya. On 9 July 1940 his ships were in action off Calabria. An Italian fleet of three battleships, and some seventeen cruisers and twenty-seven destroyers, had been covering an important convoy to Benghazi. ABC's ships were south of Crete, steaming north-west and under attack from Italian shore-based aircraft. The British cruisers came under heavy fire but when *Warspite* came within a range of 13 miles she secured a hit with her 15-inch guns on the battleship *Giulio Cesare*. During this action, two British convoys sailing from Malta for Alexandria were attacked by Italian aircraft which dropped more than 100 bombs without scoring a hit. *Warspite* and her escorting destroyers suffered twenty air attacks in ten hours. There were seventeen attacks on the cruisers and three on *Eagle*, but the only hit was one on *Gloucester* and three enemy aircraft were shot down. The two convoys got through safely to Alexandria. When his ships carried out a bombardment of Bardia in August, Gladiator fighter aircraft from *Eagle* and RAF Blenheims shot down 12 enemy aircraft.

Operation HATS, an important convoy bringing reinforcements and supplies, left the UK in August. It also carried 50 desperately needed tanks for the Army in North Africa. ABC left Alexandria on 30 August to meet the convoy west of Crete. Aircraft from HMS *Illustrious*, assisted by the anti-aircraft cruisers, shot down five enemy bombers. ABC was constantly prodded from London to be more aggressive and to take the initiative – an irritation to a naturally aggressive attacking admiral. He explained that the prerequisites to successful operations were complete air reconnaissance and an adequate number of destroyers, neither of which he had.

Three Italian destroyers from a flotilla which attacked a Malta convoy in October were sunk. ABC, always humane, signalled their position to the Italian admiralty so that the survivors could be picked up. Meanwhile Italian anti-submarine forces were having unwelcome success against ABC's very limited submarine fleet. By the end of October, seven of the twenty-one available to him had been lost.

In November 1940 ships of ABC's fleet carried out diversionary airstrikes on the Italian battle fleet in Taranto harbour. This time the RAF provided good photographic reconnaissance. The whole of the Italian battle fleet was there, including six battleships. The British force comprised *Illustrious*, with her own aircraft, and some of *Eagle*'s Swordfish torpedo bombers, four cruisers and four destroyers. Two waves of thirteen and nine aircraft delivered the attack on Taranto harbour, meeting intense anti-aircraft fire. The first wave got two torpedo hits on battleships for the loss of one aircraft. The second wave scored three more hits for the loss of one more aircraft. While Swordfish were attacking the capital ships in Taranto harbour, the cruisers and destroyers sank four merchant ships, convoyed by a destroyer and a torpedo boat, in the Straits of Otranto.

ABC and the Army and RAF Chiefs of Staff then resisted a verbal campaign by Churchill to mount an operation to capture the tiny island of Pantelleria between Sicily and Tunisia. They realised that, if successful, it would simply stretch their resources and increase their obligations to keep another vulnerable island provisioned and protected.

In January 1941 German Stuka divebombers were seen for the first time in the Mediterranean. Operating from airfields in Sicily, 150 of them, accompanied by 120 long-range bombers and 40 fighters, attacked *Illustrious* and the capital ships escorting a convoy to Malta. The carrier suffered six direct hits and heavy casualties but managed to get to Malta. The cruisers *Gloucester* and *Southampton* were also hit by bombs on 11 January and *Southampton* had to be abandoned, but the convoys did get through. While undergoing repairs in Malta dockyard, *Illustrious* was bombed again. She managed to get to sea on 23 January but she was too severely damaged to be operational and was obliged to go to America for long-term repairs. This left ABC desperately short of air cover. When he was awarded the KCB in February, he commented that he would far sooner have had three squadrons of RAF Hurricanes for Malta.

Next the Germans attacked Greece and on 22 February 1941 the Chiefs of Staff in London decided to send troops to help the Greeks. To ABC, whose resources were already overstretched, fell the task of landing 68,000 men with their mechanised transport, weapons and equipment.

On the morning of 27 March an Italian fleet was reported to be 60 miles south of Crete, steering south-east, its strength roughly equivalent to that available to ABC. Ahead of ABC's force, which was steering north-west towards the Italians, was his cruiser squadron. It came under fire from the leading Italian battleship – the first shots in the battle off Cape Matapan. As a result of three attacks by carrier aircraft and accurate gunfire by ABC's flagship *Warspite*, the Italians lost three cruisers and two destroyers and had a battleship severely damaged – all for the loss of one aircraft – but the rest of the Italian fleet escaped to their home ports. The Royal Navy's ships were just not fast enough to catch them. Hundreds of Italian sailors were rescued and taken prisoner.

After Matapan, the Italian navy stopped interfering with British convoys but air attacks continued ceaselessly. ABC was becoming increasingly irritated by Churchill's interference in strategic matters, which were strictly the responsibility of the C-in-C on the spot, who was in possession of the facts. He felt that he should either be given maximum intelligence and material support and left to get on with it – or should be replaced.

It was becoming apparent to the Chiefs of Staff and even to Churchill that another Dunkirk was looming in Greece and that the Army would have to be evacuated. Piraeus, the port of Athens, was under heavy German air attack. The Clan Line freighter *Clan Fraser*, loaded with ammunition, was hit and blew up, sinking 11 other ships and virtually destroying the port. ABC was faced with the prospect of evacuating the Army from the beaches with very limited air cover and at night because of overwhelming German air superiority. Despite these odds, more than 50,000 troops were taken off the beaches and lived to fight again, but there were 12,000 casualties, 7,000 were taken prisoner and a massive quantity of equipment was lost. ABC reported on the 'courage, skill and determination of the officers and men of the merchant ships' involved who 'behaved magnificently' and took their ships into 'difficult anchorages with no navigational marks and often without adequate charts'.

Crete had now become strategically important to both sides. Some 50,000 Greek, British and Commonwealth troops, including 5,300 Royal Marines, were garrisoning the island, which had only two small ports (Suda Bay and Heraklion) and three landing strips – all on the north coast. The Germans mounted a massive attack on the island with over 1,000 aircraft of all types as against 29 British aircraft, half of which were obsolete. ABC's task was to prevent any German landings by sea but he could do little to prevent the enemy from landing troops by parachute or transport planes.

While the German assault on Crete was being launched on 20 May, the world's newest battleship, *Bismarck* – the most heavily armoured ship afloat – was on the point of breaking out into the Atlantic, accompanied by the cruiser *Prinz Eugen*. After sinking HMS *Hood*, she was sunk by ships of the Royal Navy on the morning of 27 May, but overwhelming German air superiority was winning the battle for Crete. They flew in thousands of troops but the Royal Navy, despite losing the cruisers *Gloucester* and *Fiji*, three destroyers and five motor torpedo boats, prevented any landings from the sea. The Germans machine-gunned men in the water but hundreds of survivors were picked up by the other destroyers.

In Cairo the joint planning staffs of the Royal Navy, Army and RAF prepared a paper assessing the situation as hopeless and recommended to the Joint Chiefs of Staff – Cunningham, Wavell and Tedder – that the Army in Crete should be ordered to surrender. When they met, two important representatives of the Commonwealth were present: the Prime Minister of New Zealand, Peter Fraser, and the C-in-C of the Australian forces in the Middle East, General Sir Thomas Blamey – both extremely concerned about the fate of their soldiers, who comprised a substantial proportion of the Army in Crete. Fraser, Blamey, Wavell and Tedder all agreed to accept the unanimous recommendation of their staffs, but Cunningham did not. He argued that it had always been the duty of the Navy to land the Army where required and to re-embark it when necessary. He did not underestimate the enormity of the task, but refused to accept that it could not be done. By sheer personality he overcame the arguments of the other four and a decision was taken to organise the evacuation. It was a decision of tremendous moral courage that would never have been taken without ABC's determined stand. Even his own personal staff expressed doubts about the feasibility of the operation.

There were some 24,000 troops to be evacuated, all on the north side of the island. The airfield and harbour of Heraklion were still held by 4,000 soldiers of the 14th Infantry Brigade and the 1st Battalion of the Argyll & Sutherland Highlanders but the majority of the troops were in the region of Suda Bay. They could not be evacuated because the Germans held both the port and airstrip. The soldiers would have to cross the mountains to beaches on the south side of the island.

The evacuation began on the night of 28 and 29 May. Air attacks were incessant. The ships arrived off Heraklion at 11.30 p.m. By 3.20 a.m. the whole garrison had been embarked, although, as a result of air attacks en route to Alexandria, one-fifth of the 4,000 were lost at sea. Over the following three nights, everything possible was done to evacuate the remaining troops from the beaches on the south side of the island. Some soldiers never found their way there but in the final count some 16,500 British and Commonwealth troops were successfully brought off. The Navy lost 1,828 men and hundreds were wounded. Three cruisers and six destroyers had been sunk and a carrier, two battleships, two cruisers and two destroyers seriously damaged. Nine other ships had been less seriously damaged and nine of the flotilla of little ships servicing Suda Bay were lost. The Germans did not get off lightly. More than 5,000 soldiers and airmen, many of them from the elite airborne divisions, were killed or wounded; 220 of their aircraft were shot down and 148 damaged.

Malta's situation was now becoming desperate. A convoy had to be forced through at all costs. While ABC carried out diversionary operations in the eastern Mediterranean, a vital convoy escorted by Somerville's Force H, based in Gibraltar, got through to Malta from the west with the loss of one destroyer and two ships damaged. In a second convoy, all but one out of nine merchant ships got through. When Somerville was knighted for the second time, ABC sent him a signal: 'Fancy – twice a night at your age. Congratulations.'

In August 1941, the Australian government, short of soldiers at home and understandably nervous of the Japanese threat to the Australian mainland, demanded the withdrawal of their troops from the garrison in Tobruk, still under siege by the Germans. ABC organised a dangerous operation spread over successive moonless nights. Fast minelayers and destroyers took in 6,000 Polish troops with thousands of tons of stores and brought out 5,000 Australians. In September the operation was repeated. The ships took in 2,100 tons of stores and 6,300 troops brought over from Syria and evacuated 6,000 more Australians. In October, despite the heavy naval losses involved, General Blamey insisted that his remaining men be brought out. Over a period of two weeks, more than 7,000 troops and 1,400 tons of stores were taken in and nearly 8,000 more Australian troops were brought out. The Navy's losses directly attributable to the Tobruk operations were 539 killed and 241 wounded, of whom 70 and 55 respectively were Merchant Navy. Thirty-four ships were sunk – 7 of them merchant ships – and 33 damaged, 6 of them merchant ships.

The eventual relief of Tobruk by the Eighth Army was good news, as was the implementation of ABC's proposal for an RAF Coastal Command for the Mediterranean, and the arrival of reinforcements: two cruisers and two destroyers. Renewed efforts to disrupt enemy convoys to North Africa were made: the first one to be attacked was virtually annihilated. The next enemy convoy turned back after two of its escorting cruisers were torpedoed. The percentage of enemy convoys failing to reach North Africa increased from 16 to 62. However, some 20 German U-boats had got into the Mediterranean. Force H's carrier *Ark Royal* was torpedoed and sunk. Then on 25 October the battleship *Barham* was hit by three torpedoes and blew up. ABC, with his flag in HMS *Queen Elizabeth*, was steaming just ahead of her when she sank with the loss of 861 lives – two-thirds of her company.

During ABC's remaining five months as C-in-C Mediterranean, from December 1941 until April 1942, two brilliant actions – known as the First and Second Battles of Sirte – were conducted by ABC's subordinate, Rear-Admiral Philip Vian, protecting vital convoys by holding off superior Italian naval forces while under incessant air attack. Barely sufficient supplies won through to enable Malta to survive.

In December three two-man submersible 'chariots' were launched from an Italian submarine outside Alexandria harbour. They penetrated the harbour defences and managed to lay explosive charges under the hulls of the battleships *Valiant* and *Queen Elizabeth*. Two of the 'charioteers' were captured before the charges went off and gave some warning, but both ships were crippled. ABC was on board *Queen Elizabeth* at the time. The third pair of 'charioteers' fixed a charge to a tanker. From the Italian viewpoint, it had been a brilliantly successful operation.

April 1942 was not a good time for a trusted C-in-C to be leaving the Mediterranean but the Americans were by now in the war and ABC was chosen to head an Admiralty delegation to Washington to discuss future combined strategy. Before he left, he paid a heartfelt tribute to the Merchant Navy's unobtrusive courage and tenacity, as well as sending a farewell message to his 'magnificent' but hard-pressed fleet.

⚓ CHAPTER 18 ⚓

Into Europe

Filmgoers have become accustomed to Hollywood productions that imply that the USA won both world wars virtually single-handed, sometimes attributing acts by their allies to US servicemen. A particularly galling example of this genre was the film *U-571*, which purported to show how Germany's secret Enigma codes were retrieved from a U-boat by American sailors. The retrieval of these codes was an intelligence coup with massive significance for the outcome of the anti-U-boat campaign in both the Atlantic and the Mediterranean. The Americans had nothing to do with either the capture of the machine and codes, or with the deciphering of them, although they benefited greatly from them. In May 1941 – before the USA entered the war – the British had captured a U-boat in the Atlantic complete with her Enigma coding machine, books, tables and settings, which, after brilliant work by the boffins of Bletchley Park, enabled signals to the U-boat packs to be decoded, convoys to be re-routed and losses reduced by some 30 per cent. However, there were still pieces missing from the jigsaw puzzle.

Shortly after ABC left to head the Admiralty delegation to Washington, the destroyer HMS *Petard* attacked a U-boat, *U-559*, in the Mediterranean and forced her to the surface, where she surrendered. After the crew abandoned her, she began to sink. Lieutenant Anthony Fasson, from Lanton near Jedburgh, knew that *U-559* would contain the vital decoding equipment with the new inserts and codebooks. There was no time to lower a boat. Calling for volunteers to come with him, he twice swam to the sinking submarine, a hundred yards there and back. With two volunteers, he entered the conning tower, removed as much relevant material as they could carry and swam back to *Petard* with code books, a machine and inserts. However, Fasson knew there were more vital codes to be salvaged. Disregarding his captain's order, he and one of the others, Colin Grazier, swam back a third time and went below in the sinking submarine to save the rest of the invaluable material. The U-boat went down before they could get out.

There has rarely been a greater act of selfless bravery. Both men won posthumous decorations, which should have been VCs. The name of Lieutenant Francis A.B. Fasson GC RN is recorded on the War Memorial in Jedburgh and in Edinburgh Castle. He had already been mentioned in dispatches for bravery in rescuing two Maltese stewards from a ship which had struck a mine. The Hollywood film *U-571* was an insult to three very brave men.

⚓ ⚓ ⚓

In Washington ABC found the Americans congenial and cooperative, with the notable exception of Admiral Ernest J. King, the Chief of Operations and C-in-C US Fleet. Smarting from Pearl Harbor and innately anti-British, King, when asked by ABC for the loan of four or five submarines for work on the European side of the Atlantic, was 'abominably rude' and overbearing. ABC, who considered that the US Navy's contribution to the Battle of the Atlantic was wholly inadequate, told King what he thought of his method of advancing Allied unity and amity. He noticed that there was bitter rivalry between the US Army and Navy – unlike the excellent relationship between the British Army and Royal Navy.

The Americans argued for a cross-channel invasion of the European continent in 1942. The British Chiefs of Staff considered this would be premature and proposed a landing in North Africa in 1942 – subsequently named Operation Torch by Churchill – to be followed by a landing in southern Europe after a firm platform had been established with air superiority and airfields along the whole North African coast. ABC was a powerful proponent of the Mediterranean strategy and of a patient approach to the concept of a cross-channel invasion.

Operation Torch was finally agreed upon. ABC was invited – with the authority of President Roosevelt and of General Eisenhower, who was to be supreme commander of the operation – to be the naval commander. Admiral Ernie King accepted Cunningham's appointment, provided no US ships were under his direct command. Vice-Admiral Kent Hewitt USN, who was given command of US ships, subordinate to ABC, said, 'It would be a privilege to serve under Admiral Cunningham.' ABC also forged an exceptionally good and lasting relationship with Eisenhower, who said of him years later, 'I considered him one of the finest individuals that I ever met . . . I had the utmost respect for his military judgement as well as for his great human qualities.' Even Admiral King said later, '. . . they got a man. A fighter. He would fight like hell . . . '

Operation Torch was planned for 8 November 1942. Troops direct from the United States would land near Casablanca in French Morocco and a combined force of British and Americans would sail from the Clyde and land close to Oran and Algiers. ABC's command embraced an area of the Atlantic and Mediterranean that included the approaches and landing areas of both forces.

The naval side of the operation was planned with emphasis on economy and meticulous attention to detail. There were to be two advance convoys of 45 ships, followed by the main convoys of more than 200 ships with 100 escorts, carrying 38,500 American and British troops. ABC's orders covered all Allied naval and merchant ships at Gibraltar and in the Mediterranean. Cooperation between the British and American staffs, based in Gibraltar, was excellent. Morale was boosted by General Montgomery's victory at El Alamein in the Libyan desert, two weeks before the landings were to take place, but a huge question mark hung over the French in North Africa. Nobody could predict their attitude.

In the event, the landings went well. At Casablanca, the Americans were unopposed. At Algiers and Oran, there was French resistance and dissension between the various French factions. Eventually Vichy Admiral Darlan offered to negotiate and an agreement was reached whereby the French admiral repudiated the Vichy government of Marshal Pétain and was made governor-general of French North Africa, while General Giraud was to command the French army there.

ABC had wanted Operation Torch to include a landing further east of Bizerta but that was one argument he did not win. Consequently the enemy had weatherproof airfields, which the Allies did not, and the Germans retained a measure of air superiority over Tunisia. They continued to fly troops into Tunis and the Allies lost the race for that important city and port. As the Allies advanced east, ABC took responsibility for supplying the armies by sea, under constant air attack, because the roads were so poor. The Axis armies were now fighting on two fronts.

In January 1943, Churchill, President Roosevelt and the Combined Chiefs of Staff met in Casablanca to decide the next move. They agreed on Operation Husky, the invasion of Sicily. Promoted to admiral of the fleet, ABC was appointed naval C-in-C for the operation and was reappointed as C-in-C Mediterranean. The Germans and Italians were bottled up in the

Cape Bon peninsula, across the straits from Sicily, and ABC's ships were there to prevent a 'Dunkirk'. On 13 May the enemy forces in North Africa admitted defeat. A quarter of a million men surrendered with all their equipment.

In the Atlantic, too, things were looking up. Not only were the signals to the U-boat packs being decoded but anti-submarine tactics had also been developed to a fine art. By May 1943 German U-boat losses became unsustainable. So far, they had lost 650 U-boats and 30,000 trained officers and crew. Grand Admiral Karl Donitz ordered his boats to withdraw from the North Atlantic while he reconsidered his strategy.

ABC's task was now to clear the Mediterranean for through passage to Alexandria and Port Said and thence by the Suez Canal to the Far East, thereby saving shipping, time and fuel. The route was literally a minefield, but by 15 May a passage had been cleared. The first unopposed convoy reached Malta on 24 May. Pantelleria was taken on 11 June. In July planning for Operation Husky started in earnest. ABC moved his headquarters to Malta, but there was a personality clash between him and Montgomery. He found Montgomery's theatricality and arrogance repugnant. ABC and the Air Commander, Air Marshal Tedder, saw the capture of the Sicilian airfields as the first priority after securing more than one bridgehead, whereas Montgomery wished to concentrate effort on the south-east beaches. The whole plan had to be recast by Eisenhower to keep Montgomery happy, at the cost of overruling his own staff, ABC and Tedder.

In the course of the massive build-up for Operation Husky, only four ships were lost by U-boat attack. It was to be the greatest amphibious operation ever undertaken to date. Some 160,000 troops, 14,000 vehicles, 600 tanks and 1,800 guns were to be landed on a heavily defended island. ABC had the ultimate responsibility for landing them. The operation could not be kept secret. The RAF and USAAF heavily bombed all airfields within range of Sicily's beaches for days in advance.

Ship movements had already begun when a gale blew up from the north-west on 9 July, making the sea almost too rough for landing craft. To postpone the operation could have caused fatal confusion. Eisenhower, on ABC's advice, decided to go ahead. It was a bold decision but the right one. The weather had lulled Sicily's defences into a false sense of security. The landings were successful, although only 12 out of 137 gliders carrying paratroopers reached their correct dropping zones and a quarter of the men were drowned.

After the landings, the Navy's task was to take in supplies and reinforcements, carry out anti-submarine and aircraft patrols and provide fire support when requested by the Army. Initially, naval losses were relatively light: 16 ships, the largest a destroyer, and a hospital ship that was attacked despite being brilliantly lit for identification. Subsequently the aircraft carrier *Indomitable* was damaged by a torpedo, as were two cruisers. Four merchantmen and two LSTs (Landing Ship, Tanks) were sunk by submarines, but ten enemy submarines were sunk before the end of July.

By the second week in August, the Germans realised that Sicily was lost and they began to pull out. The three-mile-wide Straits of Messina were covered by enemy-held batteries of heavy artillery on both sides. The Germans managed to evacuate most of their troops to the Italian mainland successfully. Montgomery claimed that the Navy delayed the crossing by the Eighth Army by three or four days. In fact, he had not even conferred with the Senior Naval Officer tactically responsible – Rear-Admiral Roderick McGrigor – and went over Cunningham's head direct to Eisenhower. In the event, the crossing was carried out with complete success. Heavy naval bombardments of the defences on the mainland side of the straits were carried out on 31 August and 2 September. The next day a British and a Canadian Division of the Eighth Army were ferried across in 22 LSTs and 270 landing craft under cover of a continuous bombardment. Five thousand three hundred vehicles were ferried across the straits in three days.

ABC was already involved in naval planning for Operation Avalanche – the landing proposed by Eisenhower at Salerno, 200 miles up the coast, south of Naples, but just within extreme range of Allied land-based air cover. On 8 September, Italy surrendered. It was arranged that the Italian fleet should rendezvous with the Royal Navy some 20 miles off the coast of Tunisia, west of Bizerta. The main body of Italian ships, including three battleships, six cruisers and eight destroyers, were attacked en route by German bombers with radio-controlled bombs. The battleship *Roma* was sunk but the remainder duly reached the rendezvous. ABC had embarked with General Eisenhower in the destroyer HMS *Hambledon* to witness the event. He was deeply moved to see his former flagship HMS *Warspite* leading his erstwhile opponents into captivity. The rest of the Italian fleet was directed to Malta, from where, on 11 September, ABC made a memorable signal to the Admiralty: ' . . . the Italian Battle Fleet now lies at anchor under the guns of the fortress of Malta'.

The landings at Salerno before dawn on 9 September met with tough resistance. The Germans counter-attacked but a combined air and sea bombardment from ships and carriers under ABC's command eventually turned the tide. *Warspite* was hit by a radio-controlled bomb and had to be towed back to Malta. The carriers' Seafires maintained patrols over the beaches until the bridgehead was considered secure by the middle of the month, when patrols were taken over by the USAAF and RAF. The Seafires had flown nearly 1,000 sorties. Only two were shot down, but due to the frailty of their construction and the short decks and slow speed of the utility escort carriers, more than 40 were lost or damaged beyond repair.

The Salerno landings, followed by the signing of the Italian surrender on board HMS *Nelson* in Grand Harbour, Malta, on 29 September 1943, were the final chapters in ABC's Mediterranean saga. The First Sea Lord, his old friend Admiral of the Fleet Sir Dudley Pound, died in harness, after years of stress and overwork, on Trafalgar Day, 21 October 1943. Churchill's first choice to replace him was Admiral Sir Bruce Fraser, C-in-C Home Fleet. He was taken aback when Fraser refused and told Churchill that he thought Cunningham was the right man for the job. 'I have the confidence of my fleet but Cunningham has the confidence of the whole navy . . . ' The post was offered to Cunningham.

ABC heard from Churchill on 28 September and asked the opinion of Eisenhower as to whether or not he should accept. Eisenhower was in no doubt and told him it was his duty to do so. Cunningham's departure from the Mediterranean, from the fleet which he loved, from his colleagues, staff and friends, was a tremendous wrench but duty always came first. His recommendation of Admiral Sir John Cunningham – no relation – as his replacement was accepted. He was given an emotional farewell by all who had worked with him, although some may have felt that life would become a little bit easier. After seeing the prime minister, ABC went to the Admiralty on 16 October to take up his duties.

ABC and his fellow members of the Chiefs of Staff Committee – General Sir Alan Brooke and Air Chief Marshal Sir Charles Portal – the ultimate armed services body responsible to the prime minister – settled down as a balanced, determined and cohesive unit comprising immense experience, sound judgement and intellectual capacity. They argued between themselves, reached decisions, then stuck to them – sometimes in opposition to the prime minister.

Preparations for the cross-Channel invasion of Europe, codenamed 'Overlord', provisionally planned for May 1944, were already in their early stages. In November 1943 Churchill held a meeting with the British and American Chiefs of Staff in Cairo. The Americans, Admiral Ernest King and General 'vinegar Joe' Stilwell in particular, both anti-British, gave Pacific and Far Eastern operations priority. The British insisted that operations against Nazi Germany must come first. It was eventually agreed, after a further meeting in Tehran, that the campaign in Italy should continue until Rome had been captured and the Pisa–Rimini line reached, in order to prevent German troops being transferred to the Russian front. The date of Overlord was postponed until the end of May 1944. A decision on Anvil, the proposed landing in the south of France, was postponed until sufficient shipping for an assault should become available.

On Boxing Day 1943, the German battleship *Scharnhorst* was sunk off the North Cape of Norway by HMS *Duke of York*, wearing the flag of Admiral Sir Bruce Fraser, accompanied by the cruiser *Jamaica* and four destroyers. Only 36 of her crew of more than 2,000 could be rescued from the icy Arctic waters.

Meanwhile ABC, as First Sea Lord, was preoccupied with planning for Overlord. The portable Mulberry harbours, parts of which had been designed and built on Clydeside, were being tested in Scottish waters off the Wigtown coast between Garlieston and Isle of Whithorn. Admiral Sir Bertram Ramsay was appointed Allied Naval Commander Expeditionary Force (ANCXF). While the Germans were aware that a major operation was afoot, they did not know where the main attacks would come. They concentrated their operational U-boats on the European coast. ABC responded by ensuring that 20 hunter-killer anti-submarine groups, supported by the whole of RAF Coastal Command, were also available between the English south coast and the invasion beaches. Describing Winston Churchill at a lunch on the eve of D-Day, ABC said he was 'in an almost hysterical state. He really is an incorrigible optimist . . . ' It is fortunate, it must be said, that the prime minister was just that through the darkest days of the war.

In the event, the D-Day landings in Normandy on 6 June caught the German High Command, including Donitz, by surprise. There were 12 U-boats at sea but none near the invasion beaches, although 35 had sailed by midnight. In the whole of the period June to August, U-boats sank 18 ships but they lost at least 35 of their own number. Attempts by German E-boats and destroyers to interfere were thwarted.

Towards the end of June, a meeting of Allied Chiefs of Staff took place in London to discuss future strategy both in Europe and east of Suez. The Americans insisted on a landing in southern France to assist Overlord and wanted the British effort in the Far East to be aimed at Borneo and the Malay Peninsula. ABC felt strongly that the Royal Navy should be involved in the Pacific. Admiral Sir Bruce Fraser had to be allowed to depart to take up his post as C-in-C British Pacific Fleet before a broad strategy had been agreed. Churchill was India-orientated and obsessed with what ABC called 'this island idiocy': a desire to capture some island and then use it as an airfield for bombing Singapore and other Japanese-held bases. ABC considered that striking at the heart of Japan should be the priority. He eventually converted Churchill to his strategy: to deploy a British Pacific Fleet around the nucleus of all available fleet aircraft carriers.

At the Quebec conference in September 1944, President Roosevelt – tired and ill – Churchill and all the Allied Chiefs of Staff were present. It went well until the subject of a British presence in the Pacific was raised. Ernie King flew into a temper and had to be brought to order by his American colleagues, who finally overruled him. Admiral King only gave way on condition that the British provided their own bases, support structure and logistics, and a 'fleet train' in the forward area to provision and fuel their task forces. Fortunately for all concerned, Fraser got on well with US Admiral Chester Nimitz, under whose immediate command he operated.

With ultimate victory in sight, 1944 ended with a final upsurge in U-boat activity in the Atlantic but it was soon contained. By the end of March 1945, the Allies had crossed the Rhine. On 30 April, Adolf Hitler committed suicide and a week later the Germans surrendered but Allied naval air attacks continued on Japan. On 26 July, Clement Attlee succeeded Sir Winston Churchill as prime minister. In Churchill's resignation Honours List Admiral of the Fleet Sir Andrew B. Cunningham GCB OM, DSO** was created Viscount Cunningham of Hyndhope in the parish of Kirkhope in the County of Selkirk. He accepted the honour with reluctance as a tribute to the Royal Navy. On 5 August, when the first atomic bomb was dropped on Hiroshima, ABC was fishing in Scotland and caught 15 sea trout. When the second fell on Nagasaki, he contemplated retiring as First Sea Lord. In the event, he stayed on for a further year and was created a Knight of the Thistle by George VI – the ultimate distinction available to anybody of Scottish ancestry. No admiral in British history had carried such responsibility for so long, nor achieved such success with limited, often inferior, resources, frequently in the face of poor decisions by those in power.

Scots played a creditable part at every level in winning the war at sea, but without the individual contributions of Robert Watson-Watt, Anthony Fasson and Andrew B. Cunningham, it is more than possible that Britain and her allies would not have prevailed.

⚓ CHAPTER 19 ⚓

Courage at Sea

The history of Scots and the sea is punctuated by many examples of courage, physical and moral, some of which have been touched upon in preceding chapters. The non-stop circumnavigation of the world by Sir Chay Blyth from Hawick – the first under sail westabout against the prevailing winds and currents – set a standard of sustained courage which will rarely be equalled. Emma Richards from Helensburgh showed outstanding courage of the enduring kind when she set sail from New York in September 2002, single-handed, in a 60-foot monohull yacht, on a 29,000-mile voyage round the world in the Around Alone race. The race result is not important but her courage in setting out was. The same can be said of Ellen MacArthur, great-granddaughter of a Skye crofter, and her epic circumnavigation of the world in 2001, alone in *Kingfisher*. Joe Watt, skipper of the armed drifter *Govanlea* of Inverallochy near Fraserburgh, fought off three enemy cruisers in 1917. He won the Victoria Cross and his mate, Fred Lamb, was awarded the DSM. Two midget submarine captains of Scots ancestry won the Victoria Cross in the Second World War: Lieutenant Donald Cameron for penetrating a Norwegian fjord and placing explosive charges under the German battleship *Tirpitz* and Lieutenant Ian Fraser for a similar feat, damaging the Japanese heavy cruiser *Takao* anchored off Singapore.

⚓ ⚓ ⚓

Not surprisingly, the coast of Scotland is littered with wrecks of ships of all ages, from every seafaring country. Many are anonymous and forgotten except where they are marked on charts as hazards to navigation, but most, if not all, are hidden memorials to unrecorded acts of courage by crews or individuals. A few have histories which have become legends; for example the *San Juan de Sicilia*, a galleon of the Spanish Armada lying in Tobermory harbour. Another Spanish galleon lies on the bottom with other ships off the dangerous Farland Head on the Ayrshire coast south-east of Little Cumbrae Island.

Perhaps the most famous wreck is the elusive *Blessing of Burntisland*, the ferry which was carrying the baggage of King Charles I when it sank in a squall in the Firth of Forth on 10 July 1633 while the unpopular Charles was returning from his belated coronation tour of Scotland. It is supposed to contain the royal banqueting service commissioned by Henry VIII, Charles's personal possessions and all the paraphernalia associated with a lavish royal progression. The probable site off Burntisland has been located at a depth of 15 fathoms. The Burntisland Heritage Trust was formed in 1999 and archaeologists and other experts started a methodical search and recovery operation.

The wartime wreck of the cargo ship *Politician* lies off the island of Eriskay, between South Uist and Barra in the Outer Hebrides. She was the origin of Compton Mackenzie's novel *Whisky Galore*. The ship left Liverpool on 3 February 1941 with a strangely mixed cargo, including 28,000 cases of finest malt whisky, bathroom fittings, furnishings, motorcar parts and £145,000 in ten-shilling notes. She was bound for New Orleans and for Jamaica, where British currency was then used.

The North Atlantic was teeming with German U-boats, so the ship headed north to join a convoy before starting the transatlantic part of her voyage. She ran aground in a westerly gale and broke in two on the rocks off the islet of Calvay. The crew all got ashore and were looked after for a few days by the hospitable Gaelic-speaking locals, who, when they learned of her cargo, decided to save some of it before the customs and excise officials arrived. As much whisky as could be unloaded by hand was removed and well hidden. A few years later, ten-shilling notes of the relevant serial numbers began turning up in banks as far apart as Ireland, America, Switzerland and Malta. The author's uncle, a former Cameron Highlander and wounded veteran of the First World War, was a senior Home Guard officer who was regularly offered a dram of 'politeecian' when on visits of inspection to the Outer Isles.

⚓ ⚓ ⚓

The courage of the volunteer lifeboat crews, who are continually on stand-by to go out in the vilest weather, not for glory or for any reward other than the satisfaction of saving lives, may be the ultimate illustration of selfless courage at sea. Just a few examples from Scottish waters are recounted here.

There are over 40 lifeboat stations on the coasts of Scotland and the islands. In one typical year recently, the Royal National Lifeboat Institution's lifeboats from stations all around the British coasts were launched 6,800 times and assisted 5,300 people. Of these, 1,430 owed their lives to the dedication of lifeboat crews, sometimes assisted by the Coastguard and RAF helicopters.

The harbour of Eyemouth on the Berwickshire coast faces north, flanked by rocky points. Its name will always be associated with the tragedy of 14 October 1881, when the village was struck by a terrible gale which sank half its fishing fleet – 24 boats – with the loss of 189 lives. For two centuries, Eyemouth had been notorious for smuggling but its maritime traditions go back to before the sixteenth century, when James VI made the town a free burgh of barony with free port status. On 6 October 1990 another hurricane was blowing, driving 20-foot waves into the harbour entrance. A report was received at the RNLI station that four divers were in difficulty off St Abb's Head, three miles to the north-west. The lifeboat was launched and Acting Coxswain James Dougal skilfully negotiated the narrow exit and set course into a sea with waves more than 35-feet high. Off the rocky point the lifeboat crew of seven, secured by lifelines, with the boat rolling gunwales under, half-blinded by rain and spray, began their search for the divers. Two were sighted on rocks, appearing and disappearing under enormous seas. The boat approached and at the third attempt a line was thrown to them. Hampered by diving gear, they were eventually pulled on board, suffering from shock, hypothermia and seasickness. After landing the divers in St Abbs harbour, James Dougal and his crew continued a fruitless search for the other two, assisted by the Dunbar lifeboat and a helicopter. Eventually the search had to be abandoned. It was discovered later that the missing divers had been washed ashore and were safe. James Dougal received an award for the bravest act of lifesaving in 1990.

St Abbs shares Eyemouth's fishing and smuggling traditions. There are smugglers' caves in the headland on which the lighthouse stands. Fast Castle, on a cliff four miles to the north-west, was Sir Walter Scott's inspiration for Wolf's Crag in *The Bride of Lammermoor*. On 9 September 1976 a storm out of the north with Force 10 winds and furious seas was endangering a yacht moored in the outer harbour. With three people on board, it was half-swamped and about to part its cable. Great skill was required to launch the inshore lifeboat from the slipway into the wind. Although the surface was awash with nets and lobster creels, swept off the pier, which threatened to foul the lifeboat's propellers, the two-man crew managed to get the craft alongside the yacht. The three occupants were taken off and safely landed in the inner harbour.

Dunbar has been renowned in Scottish history for at least eight centuries and became a royal burgh in 1369. The square tower of its prominent parish church is a landmark for fishermen and navigators. On 13 October 1905 a Welsh-registered steamer was reported in difficulty off Barns Ness some five miles to the south-east. The weather was fast deteriorating. The lifeboat *Coxswain Walter Fairburn* was launched into a strong wind and swell. On reaching the vessel, they found that her machinery had broken down. In heavy seas the lifeboat stood by for four hours while the engines were repaired, then returned to Dunbar. But the steamer's engines broke down again and she had to anchor. In an increasing northerly gale, the anchor began to drag and the lifeboat was called out a second time. The helpless vessel was now seven miles from Dunbar, in danger of drifting onto the rocks. The lifeboat was taking heavy seas on her port quarter and the crew were constantly drenched. On reaching the vessel, lifelines were fired over her and the six crew members were brought off, one by one. It took three hours, heading into heavy seas, for the lifeboat to get back to Dunbar. The steamer later ran aground and was wrecked near Thorntonloch.

Broughty Ferry has a reputation for wealth from the jute trade and has had a lifeboat station since 1859. On 5 December 1939 an Aberdeen trawler ran aground in the dark on the Bell Rock, 19 miles to the east of the station. Being wartime, the lighthouse was not operating and the navigation lights in the Tay estuary were doused. It was a dark, bitterly cold night, with squalls of sleet borne on a strong northeasterly wind. There was a heavy swell across the sand bars. The Arbroath lifeboat had also been called out but the Broughty Ferry lifeboat *Mona*, Coxswain James Coull, was first on the scene. The trawler was stuck fast by the bow, with her stern under water, so it was impossible for the lifeboats to go alongside her. The Arbroath boat played her searchlight on the trawler while *Mona* anchored to windward and allowed herself to drift downwind towards the stricken vessel. Heavy seas swept across the lifeboat and one member of the crew was nearly lost. However, the manoeuvre was successful and, one at a time, the trawlermen, half-frozen, were able to jump across. It took more than half an hour for all nine of them to leap to safety.

Just two months later, an unarmed vessel on passage from Aberdeen to Methil was attacked by a German aircraft and immobilised. By the time the Arbroath lifeboat arrived on the scene, two of the crew had been killed and the aircraft was continuing to strafe the vessel. The lifeboat went alongside, under fire, and took off seven survivors while a second German aircraft joined the attack. Shortly afterwards an RAF fighter appeared and drove off the German attackers. The survivors were landed at Arbroath and the damaged vessel was taken in tow. The lifeboat Coxswain, William Swankie, was awarded the BEM. Sadly, thirteen years later another Arbroath lifeboat engaged on a rescue mission capsized in atrocious conditions with the loss of six lives, including two members of the Swankie family.

In the last ten days of January 1937, Aberdeen suffered the worst gales for a century. One harbour breakwater was washed away. The motor lifeboat *Emma Constance* was called out three times and the second lifeboat, propelled by oars, called out once. On 26 January the coastal steamer *Fairey* found herself drifting out of control towards heavy surf whipped up by the on-shore gale, six miles north of the city. *Emma Constance* was launched into a black night of intense cold and driving snow. A trawler had tried but failed to take *Fairey* in tow. As the steamer neared the line of surf, the crew asked to be taken off. *Emma Constance*, repeatedly swept by heavy, icy waves, put herself alongside *Fairey* and some of her crew jumped into the lifeboat. She had to sheer off and make a second attempt. This time the rest of the crew jumped desperately, but one man fell between the steamer and the lifeboat. John Masson of the lifeboat crew risked his own life to grab the man and haul him out of the water. Moments later *Fairey* drifted into the surf, where none of her crew could have survived. It was too dangerous for Coxswain Thomas Sinclair to take the lifeboat back across the bar into Aberdeen harbour. Short of fuel, they made it to Macduff – the only safe harbour within range. *Emma Constance* arrived at 4.30 a.m., having been at sea in appalling conditions for 12 hours.

Peterhead could claim 'the most' in several contexts: the most easterly point on the Scottish mainland (Shetland is further east); the most whales landed at a Scottish port in one year (103 in 1820); the most popular Scottish harbour for the landing of white fish; and the most medals awarded to a Scottish lifeboat station by the RNLI – closely followed by Lerwick and Fraserburgh – an indication of their exposed situations and proximity to North Sea shipping routes. Of the many rescues from Peterhead, those carried out in January 1942 are perhaps the most notable. The week of 23 to 26 January was one of gales, with gusts of over 100 mph, driving snow and spindrift from the crests of huge waves. On 23 January, Coxswain John Buchan McLean took the lifeboat out to three steamers damaged in a collision and escorted all three into Peterhead Bay, where they anchored. On 24 January, one of them dragged her anchor and was driven onto the rocks. McLean's boat rescued the whole crew of 44 in appalling weather conditions. The following day the other two ships were driven ashore. The lifeboat stood by while coastguards attempted unsuccessfully to rescue the crews; then it was the turn of the lifeboat. One ship was on the rocks, almost submerged. McLean's crew got a line aboard and despite an enormous swell the lifeboat stayed alongside for 50 minutes while the crew of the doomed vessel jumped, in twos and threes, each time the decks of the two vessels were level. All the 26 crew were rescued. The third ship was on the beach with waves breaking over her. The lifeboat struck a rock on the way in and a heavy sea nearly washed several members of the crew overboard, but they got alongside and managed to rescue all 36 of the ship's crew. On the way out, the lifeboat struck rocks again but contrived to return to harbour, the crew having shown superb seamanship, courage and endurance. In three days and three hours the lifeboat crew had less than twelve hours' rest and had saved 106 lives.

Fraserburgh harbour, which dates from the first half of the sixteenth century, has had a lifeboat since 1806. In Scotland only Montrose (1800), Aberdeen (1802) and Arbroath (1803) have had one for longer. The station has suffered some misfortunes and several crew members have been drowned while on rescue missions.

Buckie, 35 miles to the west, has the busiest harbour on the Moray Firth and has had a lifeboat since 1860. On 21 February 1968, a fishing boat ran aground at the mouth of the River Spey. She was being battered by a heavy swell, less than a quarter of a mile from the beach, with waves breaking across her. Rescue from ashore was not feasible. The lifeboat was launched and Coxswain George Jappy succeeded in bringing her alongside the fishing boat and manoeuvring so that the crew of six could jump to safety.

Aith station was only established in 1933 to make a lifeboat available on the west coast of Shetland. This was as well for the trawler *Juniper* from Aberdeen, which went aground in a Force 8 gale at the bottom of 200-foot cliffs in Lyra Sound on 19 February 1967. None of *Juniper*'s accompanying trawlers was able to help because of the heavy seas. The lifeboat was launched and Coxswain John Nicolson piloted her through uncharted rocks towards the grounded trawler. He got close enough for a line to be thrown across and one by one the trawler's crew were helped into the lifeboat. Just as the last of them got clear, the trawler rolled over and smashed into the lifeboat, damaging it but not fatally. Coxswain Nicolson manoeuvred his boat away from the rocks, out of the dangerous Sound and succeeded in landing all the trawler crewmen safely.

Lerwick, on Shetland's east coast, has an almost unparalleled record for rescues at sea. On 19 November 1997 the weather was atrocious, with Force 11 winds and 50-foot waves. The station was informed that the cargo ship *Green Lily* was out of control, drifting towards the rocky shore of Bressay, just east of Lerwick, and that the tugs trying to take her in tow had been unsuccessful. A coastguard helicopter, attempting to hover above the stricken vessel's heaving deck, had been unable to winch off any of the crew. Lerwick's new lifeboat, *Michael and Jane Vernon*, was the last hope. Coxswain Hewitt Clark, attempting to get alongside the ship, repeatedly had to sheer off to avoid fatal damage but he managed to get five of the fifteen crew into the lifeboat. By this time, *Green Lily* was within 200 yards of the shore. With great skill, one of the tugs contrived to grapple the ship's anchor cable and pull her bows round, head to sea, so that her deck became stable enough to allow the helicopter to winch off the remaining ten crew members. While helping them, the gallant helicopter winchman, Bill Deacon, was washed over the side and could not be found in semi-darkness, huge seas and thrashing debris. Hewitt Clark was awarded a gold medal. The courage of the crews of the lifeboat and helicopter received formal recognition, including a special posthumous award to Bill Deacon.

In Kirkhope Cemetery on the Orkney island of Hoy there is a memorial to the eight members of the lifeboat crew who lost their lives on 17 March 1969, when their boat capsized in mountainous seas on a rescue mission to a ship in peril. Six of those lost had been involved in a gallant rescue just a year previously. In gale-force winds and sleet a Grimsby trawler was shipwrecked on shoals 50 yards off the island of Hoy on 1 April 1968. The lifeboat manoeuvred within 20 yards of her but could not get a line across and was nearly carried onto the rocks by tidal eddies. At the second attempt, a rocket line was fired from the lifeboat across the trawler and attached to one of her life-rafts. One by one the trawler's crew were hauled across the heaving gap onto the life-raft. An exceptionally heavy sea swamped both lifeboat and life-raft, nearly washing the raft away, but the rescue continued until all the fishermen had been transferred to the lifeboat. The operation took 40 minutes. Coxswain Kirkpatrick received an award for the bravest life-saving act of 1968.

Stromness, facing Hoy Sound on the west side of Orkney's Mainland, is built in the Norse style like Kirkwall and Lerwick. Its seafaring traditions go back to the Vikings. The town has been engaged in the Baltic trade since the seventeenth century but it did not have a lifeboat until 1867. On 14 February 1929 the Grimsby trawler *Carmania II* was wrecked on the rocks at the entrance to Hoy Sound. The lifeboat was launched into very heavy seas with blinding snow driven by a southwesterly gale. On reaching the wrecked trawler, the lifeboat had to wait for over two hours, until the tide turned, before she could get close enough to fire lines across. She anchored and dropped stern-first towards the wreck. Five men were hauled aboard the lifeboat before a huge wave parted the anchor cable and drove her towards the shore. Coxswain William Johnston brought his boat under control and steered her through heavy breakers, right up to the stricken trawler. Five more men were rescued from one of the trawler's boats, which had been washed overboard, and eventually the remaining members of the trawler's crew were pulled on board the lifeboat. They were all landed safely in Stromness.

The former Viking settlements of Wick and Thurso in Caithness have both had lifeboat stations for well over a century and have each built up a fine record of rescues from the notorious Pentland Firth and stormy North Atlantic coast. Late on the evening of 18 March 1931, the schooner *Pet* of Chester ran aground on Brims Ness, five miles west of Thurso Bay. She was in danger of breaking up. The Thurso lifeboat was launched in total darkness. A heavy swell was running. A flare guided the boat to the stranded schooner but submerged rocks prevented Coxswain Angus McPhail from taking her alongside. A line was fired across the schooner and one man was brought off to the lifeboat by breeches buoy. The remaining three members of the schooner's crew were elderly and Angus McPhail decided not to risk dragging them through the water in the breeches buoy but to go in among the rocks and take them off. With outstanding seamanship and at great risk, the lifeboat went alongside the stranded schooner, took the three men off, returned to deeper water without touching the rocks and landed the schooner's crew in Wick because of heavy swell in Thurso Bay. Soon afterwards, the schooner broke up.

The lifeboats at Stornoway and Barra, 80 miles apart, are the only ones in the Outer Hebrides. On 20 January 1962 a fishing boat broke down in a gale and ran aground on the rocks off Battery Point in Stornoway Bay. The lifeboat was launched for the second time that day. The crew had already been out for eight hours, standing by a Swedish coaster which had gone aground off Skye but been refloated. Coxswain Malcolm MacDonald steered the lifeboat inside the rocks in a heavy swell to get close enough to fire a lifeline across the fishing vessel. It took several attempts before this was successfully achieved. Then the fishermen were told by loudhailer to climb over the rocks, one by one, with the lifeline attached. One man made the attempt without the lifeline and was washed away and drowned. The other two remained, clinging to the mast of their boat. The fishery protection vessel HMS *Malcolm*, which was standing by, provided a rubber raft that was floated down to the fishing boat on a line. While the lifeboat mechanic took over, Coxswain MacDonald and another member of the crew used the rubber raft to get on board the stranded fishing boat. They managed to drag the two survivors into the lifeboat and eventually landed them safely in the small hours of 31 January. The whole rescue operation had been carried out by the light of flares and searchlights from HMS *Malcolm*.

On 5 September 1943 the Barra lifeboat carried out an outstanding rescue operation in gale-force winds and heavy seas. The steamer *Urlana* had run aground under the cliffs on Idrigill Point west of Uig on the Isle of Skye. It took five hours for the lifeboat to reach the point from Barra. They found *Thurland Castle*, from the same wartime convoy, standing by. Huge waves were sweeping over *Urlana* but she had managed to get away a boat with all her survivors on board. This boat, steering for *Thurland Castle*, nearly collided with the lifeboat, as Coxswain Murdo Sinclair steered her under the grounded vessel's stern. Then the engine of the ship's boat broke down. The lifeboat tried to take her in tow but the towrope parted. At the second attempt, the lifeboat succeeded in getting a line across and towed the ship's boat to *Thurland Castle*; then she stood by until all the crew of *Urlana* were safely on board *Thurland Castle*. After further problems, the lifeboat eventually got back to Barra late in the afternoon of 7 September.

The harbour of Campbeltown, at the head of the loch on the east coast of the Kintyre peninsula, is deceptively sheltered. Beinn Ghuilean and the island of Davaar shelter it from south-west to south-east, the peninsula and the Isle of Arran from the north, but the full force of the Atlantic is just around the other side of the Mull. On 2 October 1981 the Campbeltown lifeboat station was informed that a Spanish trawler with its main engine out of action and damaged steering gear was aground on the west side of the Mull. The lifeboat was launched and emerged from Campbeltown Loch into a Force 6 wind from the north-east. By the time the lifeboat reached the trawler, the wind had become a Force 9 gale, whipping the sea into short, steep, breaking waves. The trawler had drifted across the North Channel between Kintyre and County Antrim to within two miles of the Irish coast. The Scottish coaster *Ceol Mor* was standing by providing assistance but left the scene when the lifeboat arrived. The Spanish crew refused to be taken off so the lifeboat got a towline to the trawler to prevent her from running aground again. Soon afterwards, the towline had to be let go because it was threatening to capsize the lifeboat in 15-foot beam seas. *Ceol Mor* was signalled to return and came back but attempts by the lifeboat to secure a towline between the coaster and the helpless trawler failed because the line repeatedly parted. Then *Ceol Mor* had to leave because she was low on fuel. At last the Spanish trawler skipper agreed to abandon ship. Coxswain Alexander Gilchrist took the lifeboat alongside through waves 30-feet high, breaking over both lifeboat and trawler. Five times Gilchrist had to approach the trawler to take off the Spanish crew of fourteen in twos and threes before the abandoned trawler ran aground. The lifeboat slowly returned to Campbeltown in heavy, breaking, beam seas, which constantly threatened to capsize her. When they reached harbour, they had been out in dangerous conditions for more than 12 hours.

The holiday resort and yachting centre of Largs on the Ayrshire coast of the Firth of Clyde, scene of the defeat of Norse invaders in 1263, has had an inshore lifeboat station since 1864. On 24 July 1983, the boat was launched to assist a motor cruiser capsized a mile out in the Firth. The lifeboat crew found that two men had already been picked up but a young girl was still trapped in the cabin, surviving in a small air pocket. Crew member Arthur Hill removed his life jacket and dived three feet down to get under the top of the cruiser's cabin. He found the desperate girl, tried to reassure her and attempted to push her beneath the water, out of the cabin door and under the cruiser's gunwale. His first attempt failed. The second time he succeeded and the girl was pulled on board the lifeboat and quickly taken ashore.

Troon, with its famous golf course, five miles north of Ayr, has had a lifeboat since 1871. On 12 September 1980, a Dutch dredger, which had been working off Irvine harbour, was in danger of breaking her moorings in a Force 10 westerly gale with 20-foot waves surging across her deck. The lifeboat was launched and headed for three miles into huge seas that broke over her and, more than once, laid her on her beam-ends so that the starboard side of her wheelhouse was nearly under water. Coxswain Ian Johnson and his crew found the dredger nearly aground in thundering surf, held by a single mooring. The crew of five could only leap into the lifeboat one by one from her lee side. Five separate approaches had to be made. Had the dredger's last mooring parted, the lifeboat would have been trapped between her and the surf. On the return passage, full power was needed to make way through the heavy, confused seas off the harbour entrance before the rescued Dutchmen could be landed.

Portpatrick on the west coast of the Rhins of Galloway was at one time the Scottish terminus of the sea link with Northern Ireland, but that is now the role of the better-sheltered Stranraer. However, Portpatrick still has the lifeboat station, which has been there since 1877. On 31 January 1953, there was a hurricane-force gale accompanied by snow squalls. The ferry *Princess Victoria*, on passage from Stranraer to Larne, radioed for assistance before she foundered in mountainous seas. On board were 125 passengers and 49 crew. The Portpatrick lifeboat *Jeanie Spiers* had been given the wrong position of the stricken ferry, but she battled her way through colossal waves, found the wreckage and searched for survivors. She found just two on a life-raft. The Donaghadee lifeboat from County Down had saved 33 and 8 others had made it to land in one of the ferry's boats, but 133 were drowned.

Such are the risks in the seas around us. But for the courage of the volunteer crews of the lifeboats stationed on our coasts, the casualty list would be far longer.

⚓ CHAPTER 20 ⚓

Power from the Sea

Unlike a marriage, which will end inevitably in death or divorce; or an affair, which may be terminated by either partner, Scotland's relationship with the sea is as permanent as Earth's with the sun. Longships and galleys will never again sail or row the Minches — except, perhaps for some film producer; privateers will not lurk off St Abb's Head to intercept merchantmen from the Baltic or the Low Countries — although a nuclear submarine may do so; fleets of herring boats will not congregate in the harbours of Wick and Peterhead — though trawlers may still land their catches or yachts seek shelter there; great liners and battleships will not be launched on the Clyde — but aircraft carriers, destroyers or marine platforms to extract power from the molten core of the earth, from the tides, currents or winds may yet be built on the banks of that great river. Whatever transpires, the relationship between Scots and the sea will endure until some cataclysmic collision destroys the planet we live on.

Scottish yards may yet build bulk freighters, tankers and container ships — but they will tend to specialise in vessels and rigs to service the oil industry or provide communications between harbours and islands. A Scottish-based company, British Underwater Engineering, already has a sizeable share of the international marine services market. Scottish yards will continue to construct ships for the Royal Navy, appropriate to the needs of a nation without pretensions to world power or a far-flung empire, a nation which has accepted the role of partner in an Atlantic defence organisation: anti-submarine and anti-aircraft frigates or hunter-killer submarines to safeguard our maritime lifelines; fast patrol boats to deter drug-smuggling or illegal immigration; and fast carriers for vertical take-off aircraft. Without control of the air, sea power is history.

International regulations must be framed to conserve stocks of fish and the regulations must be policed internationally to prevent cheating. Fair allocation of fishing rights must restrict the size of fishing fleets and the methods they employ to a capacity sufficient for their domestic needs and not allow them to scour the seabed and decimate the spawning areas for short-term profit. Prevention and control of disease in the fish farms established in sea lochs and tidal inlets is a priority.

Communications to the islands off Scotland's northern and western coasts will have to be improved so that the populations can take maximum advantage of a healthy but challenging living environment. There is no reason why worldwide business cannot be conducted electronically from the islands, using the sustainable power of sun, wind and water. People can thrive there and raise families in clean air and inspirational scenery. It has already been demonstrated that landing craft carrying cargoes of less than 50 tons can cut the cost of transport to and from the islands by embarking or delivering commercial goods wherever there is a beach with a hazard-free approach. There are huge advantages in living on the outer fringe of Europe, facing the New World across an ocean of limitless natural power.

The Scottish parliament has set a target for 40 per cent of all electricity to come from non-polluting sources by 2020. The target should be set higher. Scotland has about 23 per cent of the total European wind energy resource both on- and off-shore. We are a windy country! The ports group, Clydeport, which is responsible for a huge Glasgow harbour redevelopment programme, is set to construct a substantial wind farm at Hunterston. Comparing wind power with other sustainable sources, a Scottish Minister announced in 2002 that 'the prospects for wave and tidal power are equally exciting while there are now a number of solar power experiments in hand, most notably to power the new Gaelic college on Islay'. To dam some of our west-coast sea lochs and generate hydro-electric power from the tides is one possibility for the future. A well-designed and well-placed dam need not diminish scenic beauty. Gates could enable boats to enter and leave at high tide.

The study commissioned by the Scottish Executive and published in December 2001 quantified Scotland's enormous potential wealth in untapped sources of renewable energy – mostly from wind, waves and tides. Peak demand for electricity in Scotland in 2002 was about six gigawatts. The untapped resources could meet ten times this demand – an estimated 58.9 gigawatts to be precise. To put this in context, the installed electricity generating capacity in the UK, including Scotland, was 80 gigawatts in 2001. In the simplest terms, this means that if the untapped sources were fully developed, Scotland would have a surplus of 53 gigawatts for sale – more outwith times of peak demand – and could become one of the wealthiest countries in Europe, without causing pollution or exploiting the natural resources of poorer countries. The prospect is almost too good to be true!

No estimates have been published of the total cost of the developments essential to exploit these enormous resources, but the cost of nuclear power has been shown to be double that of on-shore wind power. With electricity at its current price, environmental pollution a worldwide problem of horrendous proportions and the safe disposal of nuclear waste an impossibility, the requisite investment *has* to be worthwhile. What is needed? Hundreds of underwater turbines to utilise the enormous power of the tides, sited in the Pentland Firth and elsewhere where there are strong tidal currents; thousands of devices such as those which have been developed on Islay, carefully sited around the coast to tap the power of the waves; 8,000 or more wind turbines on platforms out at sea, well clear of shipping lanes and conservation areas; 4,000 or more wind turbines sited on land, clear of conservation or inhabited areas, to catch the on-shore winds; new hydro-electric schemes where feasible on lochs and rivers, supplemented by 'heat and power' stations to compost and burn industrial, agricultural and forestry waste.

Man has been on this planet for a minute fraction of the millennia since its surface cooled after breaking away from the sun. In those terms, Scotland's relationship with the sea, which embraces nearly 99 per cent of our perimeter, has only just begun.

Ports, Harbours, Ferry Terminals and Shipyards

Aberdeen	Major port; shipyard; maritime museum
Airth (Stirling)	Former burgh and port
Alloa (Clackmannan)	Small port on the Forth
Anstruther (Fife)	Fishing harbour; Scottish Fisheries Museum
Arbroath (Angus)	Fishing and boatbuilding port
Ardersier (Inverness)	Moray Firth fishing village and construction yard
Ardrishaig (Argyll)	Fishing village
Ardrossan (Ayr)	Long-established port, part of Clydeport
Auchmithie (Angus)	Ancient fishing village with smuggling traditions
Ayr	Ancient port
Balmeanach Ferry (Skye)	Ferry terminus for Raasay
Baltasound (Shetland)	Fishing village
Banff	Belonged to the Northern Hansa – a league of trading towns – before 1124; fishing harbour
Berwick-on-Tweed	Fishing harbour and ancient port
Blackness (West Lothian)	Former seaport
Bo'ness (West Lothian)	Important port which has declined; museum
Brodick (Arran)	Has a pier for steamers
Buckhaven (Fife)	Has a small harbour and fisheries museum
Buckie (Banff)	The busiest harbour on the Moray Firth; formerly a centre of the herring industry; maritime museum
Buckpool	*See* Lossiemouth
Bunessan (Mull)	Harbour used by fishing boats and yachts
Burghead (Moray)	Fishing harbour
Burntisland (Fife)	Former coaling port which has declined with mining industry
Burnmouth (Berwick)	Small fishing village
Cairnbulg (Aberdeen)	Cairnbulg, Inverallochy and St Combs are three fishing villages, satellites of Fraserburgh
Cairnryan (Wigtown)	Small port built during Second World War
Campbeltown (Argyll)	Fishing port and harbour
Cardross (Dunbarton)	Closely associated with Robert the Bruce
Carradale (Kintyre)	Fishing and yachting harbour

Carsethorn (Kirkcudbright)	Fishing village formerly involved in the coastal schooner trade and emigrant trade
Castlebay (Barra)	Ferry terminus
Castletown (Caithness)	Small harbour built for the trans-shipment of paving stones from the local quarry
Catterline (Kincardine)	Fishing harbour
Clydebank (Dunbarton)	Shipyard constructed in 1871; museums
Clydeport	Group of Clyde ports from Ardrossan to Glasgow
Cockenzie (East Lothian)	Has a small boatbuilding yard and fishing fleet
Colintraive (Argyll)	Car ferry point to Isle of Bute
Collieston (Aberdeen)	Has a pier and small harbour
Connel Ferry (Argyll)	On the south side of the former ferry crossing, where Loch Etive enters the Firth of Lorn
Corran (Inverness)	The ferry here crosses Loch Linnhe between Ardgour and the road linking Fort William and Glencoe
Corrie (Arran)	Tiny harbour on the north-west coast
Craighouse (Jura)	Has a pier used by the ferry and a good anchorage
Craignure (Mull)	Has a pier used by the vehicle ferry from Oban
Crail (Fife)	Fishing and trading port
Cramond	*See* Queensferry
Creetown (Kirkcudbright)	Former seaport used for exporting granite
Cromarty (Ross)	Formerly a royal burgh, it has a small harbour; *see also* Invergordon
Cruden Bay (Aberdeen)	Sandy bay and resort, formerly a fishing village; oil pipeline
Cullen (Banff)	Ancient royal burgh and fishing village
Culross (Fife)	Royal burgh formerly trading with Scandinavia, Germany and Holland
Dalmuir (Dunbarton)	Shipbuilding town on the Clyde
Dumbarton	Ancient shipbuilding centre and port with museum
Dunbar (East Lothian)	Royal burgh and fishing port and harbour
Dundee	Major port with museum
Dunoon (Argyll)	Ferry terminal and yachting centre on the Clyde
Dunstaffnage (Argyll)	Naval repair base during the Second World War
Dunure (Ayr)	Fishing village with a good harbour
Dysart (Fife)	Formerly an important port trading with Holland
Earlsferry and Elie (Fife)	Natural harbour with quays; a base for inshore fishing and formerly for North Sea trade
East Wemyss (Fife)	Small coal port
Eyemouth (Berwick)	Famous fishing harbour; museum
Fair Isle (Shetland)	Midway between Shetland and Orkney, it has a pier for the mail-boat and lobster fishing
Fairlie (Ayr)	Former fishing village; yacht-building and naval depot
Faslane (Dunbarton)	Submarine base
Finnart (Dunbarton)	Oil terminal in Loch Long, part of Clydeport
Findhorn (Moray)	Former fishing village popular with yachtsmen

Findochty (Banff)	Fishing harbour
Findon (Kincardine)	Fishing harbour
Fionnphort (Mull)	Terminus of the ferry to Iona
Fort William (Inverness)	Terminus for ferries from Oban and the southern end of the Caledonian Canal
Fraserburgh (Aberdeen)	Major fishing port
Gairloch (Ross)	Has a small harbour used by fishing boats
Gardenstown (Banff)	Fishing village closely linked with neighbouring Crovie
Garelochhead (Dunbarton)	Naval base
Garlieston (Wigtown)	Small port in Wigtown Bay
Garmouth (Moray)	Formerly a port at the mouth of the Spey, now a mile from the sea; was involved in the export of timber
Gatehouse of Fleet	Aspired to become a commercial port – now largely disused
Gigha (Argyll)	Island served by ferry from West Loch Tarbert
Girvan	Fishing centre and commercial port
Glasgow & the Clyde	Major port and shipbuilding centre; part of Clydeport; museums
Glencaple (Dumfries)	Formerly a busy port now used mainly by yachts and pleasure craft; was much used by emigrants
Glenelg (Inverness)	Ferry crosses to Skye
Golspie (Sutherland)	East-coast fishing village
Gourdon (Kincardine)	Fishing village; *see also* Inverbervie
Gourock (Renfrew)	Terminus for ferries to Bute; famous for the curing of herring; popular with yachtsmen
Grangemouth (Stirling)	Important modern container ship port
Granton (on Forth)	Fishing and yachting harbour
Greenock (Renfrew)	Historic fishing harbour, shipbuilding centre and container port; part of Clydeport
Helensburgh (Dunbarton)	Centre for yachting and short cruises; Henry Bell, designer of the steamboat *Comet*, did his experimental work here
Helmsdale (Sutherland)	Natural harbour and fishing village linked with Portgower two miles to the south
Hillswick (Shetland)	Small seaport on the Shetland Mainland
Holy Loch (Argyll)	Protected anchorage used for servicing nuclear submarines
Hopeman (Moray)	Fishing harbour
Hunter's Quay (Argyll)	HQ of the Clyde Yacht Club at the south end of Holy Loch
Hunterston (Ayr)	Container port developed by Clydeport
Hynish (Tiree)	Fishing village; museum
Innellan (Argyll)	Coastal village near Dunoon with a pier
Inverary (Argyll)	Royal burgh and former fishing village on Loch Fyne
Inverbervie (Kincardine)	Closely associated with the fishing village of Gourdon
Invergordon (Ross)	Former naval base
Inverkeithing (Fife)	A royal burgh and former seaport which now has a major shipbreaking yard

Inverkip (Renfrew)	Village on the Clyde once noted for smuggling
Inverness	Small commercial port; northern terminus of Caledonian Canal
Iona (Argyll)	Linked by ferry both to the Isle of Mull and Oban
Irvine (Ayr)	Small port with shipbuilding facilities; Scottish Maritime Museum
Keillmore (Argyll)	Ferry from Keillmore used to cross to Jura
Keiss (Caithness)	Fishing harbour; shellfish
Kennacraig (Argyll)	Ferry terminus on the Mull of Kintyre linking it with Islay and Jura
Kessock (Ross)	Former terminus of a ferry from Inverness, replaced by a bridge
Kilchattan (Bute)	Formerly a fishing village and ferry terminus
Kilchoan (Argyll)	Ferries from Tobermory run to Kilchoan, Ardnamurchan
Kilcreggan (Dunbarton)	Ferry terminus on the Roseneath peninsula opposite Gourock
Kilmun (Argyll)	Village on Holy Loch with a good anchorage
Kincardine-on-Forth (Fife)	Small port now bypassed by road and rail
Kinghorn (Fife)	Royal burgh formerly the northern terminus of a ferry across Firth of Forth; fishing and boatbuilding
Kingston (Moray)	Former shipbuilding harbour at the mouth of the Spey, now landlocked
Kinlochbervie (Sutherland)	Fishing harbour
Kippford (Kirkcudbright)	Fishing and smuggling were the main activities, now yachting is predominant
Kirkcaldy (Fife)	Has a harbour serving the industries of the town
Kirkcudbright	Royal burgh with a harbour on the Solway Firth
Kirkwall (Orkney)	Adjoins the natural harbour of Scapa Flow; ferry terminus
Kirn (Argyll)	Linked to Dunoon; popular with yachtsmen; has a pier
Kyleakin (Inverness)	Was the Skye end of the ferry from Kyle of Lochalsh
Kyle of Lochalsh (Inverness)	Formerly the mainland terminus for the Skye ferry before completion of the road bridge
Kyle Rhea (Inverness)	Small ferry terminus on Skye, linking island with Glenelg
Lamlash (Arran)	The bay is an anchorage sheltered by Holy Island
Largo (Fife)	Former fishing village and birthplace of two well-known sailors, Sir Andrew Wood and Alexander Selkirk
Largs (Ayr)	Yachting centre with a safe anchorage and ferry services to the Clyde
Latheron (Caithness)	Sheltered natural harbour
Leith (Midlothian)	Major port and fishing centre
Lendalfoot (Ayr)	Used by inshore fishermen and formerly by smugglers
Lerwick (Shetland)	Commercial and fishing port
Leven (Fife)	Small coal port on Largo Bay
Leverburgh (Harris)	Small fishing port
Lochaline (Argyll)	Mainland terminus of the ferry from north-east Mull
Lochcarron (Ross)	Fishing village

Loch Ewe (Ross)	Natural anchorage with the small naval depot of Aultbea on the east shore
Lochgilphead (Argyll)	Village at the south-east end of the Crinan Canal
Lochinver (Sutherland)	Fishing port
Lochmaddy (North Uist)	The port and chief village of North Uist with a coastguard station
Lochranza (Arran)	Its pier serves ferries from the mainland
Loch Ryan (Wigtown)	Its sheltered bay was once a Roman naval base; once famous for oysters
Lossiemouth (Moray)	Historic fishing harbour; fisheries museum; linked with Stotfield
Lybster (Caithness)	Fishing harbour on the east coast of Caithness
Macduff (Banff)	Fishing harbour
Maidens (Ayr)	Fishing village with a pier and breakwater
Mallaig (Inverness)	Fishing harbour
Meikle Ferry (Ross)	Former ferry across the Dornoch Firth between Tain and Dornoch
Methil (Fife)	Has had a harbour since 1665; a coal port
Millport (Great Cumbrae)	The capital and port of the island; ferry terminus from Largs
Montrose (Angus)	A royal burgh with an excellent harbour and a history dating from the fourteenth century and trading links with the European continent
Muchalls (Kincardine)	A smugglers' tunnel linked the castle with a cove on the coast; nearby is the former fishing village of Stranathrow
Musselburgh (Midlothian)	Royal burgh and a port since Roman times; the fishing industry gave rise to the manufacture of fish-nets and twine
Nairn	Fishing harbour was designed by Telford and built in 1820; museum
Newburgh (Aberdeen)	The small harbour is mainly used to export grain
Newhaven (East Lothian)	*See* Port Seton
Newport-on-Tay (Fife)	Formerly the Fife terminus of the ferry from Dundee, now at the south end of the road bridge
Nigg (Ross)	Base for construction and repair of oil rigs
North Berwick (East Lothian)	The harbour accommodates fishing boats and yachts and is the pilot station for ships entering the Forth
Oban (Argyll)	A historic harbour and ferry terminus; fishing port
Onich (Inverness)	At the entrance to Loch Leven; has a pier for ferries
Otter Ferry (Argyll)	Terminus of a ferry that formerly crossed Loch Fyne to Port Ann on the road to Lochgilphead
Palnackie (Kirkcudbright)	The harbour on the Urr estuary, busy in the eighteenth century, is now used occasionally by pleasure craft
Pennan (Aberdeen)	Fishing harbour
Perth	Although inland on the Tay, it has been an important port since medieval times and still actively imports and exports

Peterhead (Aberdeen)	Major fishing port, particularly for white fish
Pitreavie (Fife)	HQ for the RAF's northern Air Sea Rescue operations
Pittenweem (Fife)	Ancient harbour and royal burgh with strong fishing and smuggling traditions
Plockton (Ross)	Fishing village on Loch Carron, a sea loch
Port Askaig (Islay)	Terminus for the ferry to west Loch Tarbert, Port Ellen and the Isle of Jura
Port Bannatyne (Bute)	An anchorage and slipway popular with yachtsmen
Port Edgar (West Lothian)	Former ferry terminus and small ship naval base; now a yacht marina
Port Ellen (Islay)	The principal village and port on Islay and ferry terminus from the mainland
Port Glasgow (Renfrew)	Port and shipbuilding centre
Portgower (Sutherland)	*See* Helmsdale
Portknockie (Banff)	Fishing harbour
Port Logan (Wigtown)	Small fishing village with a tidal fish pond on the opposite side of the bay
Portmahomack (Ross)	Fishing village on the Dornoch Firth
Port of Ness (Lewis)	Fishing village near Butt of Lewis
Portpatrick (Wigtown)	Fishing harbour
Portree (Skye)	Island capital, harbour, used as a base for control of the Hebrides by James V
Port Seton (East Lothian)	Harbour built in 1880 but fishing largely transferred to Newhaven
Portsoy (Banff)	Fishing harbour
Port William (Wigtown)	Small port on the east side of Luce Bay, with a good harbour constructed in 1770
Queensferry	Former ferry crossing the Forth; fishing harbour at Granton
Renfrew	Ancient port
Rhu (Dunbarton)	Yachting centre on the Gare Loch once noted for whisky smuggling
Rodel (Harris)	Village with a pier
Rosehearty (Aberdeen)	An obsolescent harbour, virtually replaced by Fraserburgh
Roseneath (Dunbarton)	Yachting centre on the Gare Loch
Rosyth (Fife)	Naval base, ship repairs and construction
Rothesay (Bute)	A port since the twelfth century, it is now a ferry terminus and yachting centre
St Abbs (Berwick)	Fishing village formerly used by smugglers
St Cyrus (Kincardine)	Village whose fishing industry was destroyed by a tidal wave during an easterly gale in 1795
St Monance (Fife)	Fishing village for seven centuries; it has two harbours
Salen (Mull)	Ferry terminus on Mull looking east to Morven
Saltcoats (Ayr)	A small coastal town with a harbour
Sandbank (Argyll)	Village on the south side of Holy Loch famous for boat building

Scalloway (Shetland)	Terminus for ferry to Foula
Scapa Flow	Naval and oil industry base and anchorage
Scrabster (Caithness)	Harbour for Thurso and fishing port
Shieldaig (Ross)	A small fishing and crofting village
Soay (Inverness)	The island has a natural harbour popular with yachtsmen, formerly a base for fishing for basking sharks
Stonehaven (Kincardine)	Ancient port and fishing harbour
Stornoway (Lewis)	An important harbour and ferry terminus
Stotfield	*See* Lossiemouth
Strachur (Argyll)	Village on the Cowal peninsula, with a pier used by yachtsmen
Stranraer (Wigtown)	Port at the head of Loch Ryan; terminus for ferries to Larne in Northern Ireland
Stromeferry (Ross)	The southern terminus of the former ferry across Loch Carron
Stromness (Orkney)	Fishing port and ferry terminal
Tail of the Bank (Clyde)	An important anchorage, part of Clydeport
Tarbert (Argyll)	Fishing and boat building harbour, Kintyre
Tarbert (Harris)	Main township on Harris and terminus of the Skye ferry
Tayport (Fife)	Formerly the ferry port and harbour for the crossing to Dundee
Tighnabruaich (Argyll)	On the narrowest part of the Kyles of Bute, it is a yachting centre and terminus for cruises down the Clyde
Tobermory (Mull)	The main port on Mull; island capital
Tolsta (Lewis)	Fishing community
Troon (Ayr)	A good harbour with shipbuilding and breaking yards
Turnberry (Ayr)	Robert the Bruce's landing place when returning from Arran on his campaign for Scottish independence
Uig (Skye)	Port for ferries to the Outer Hebrides
Ullapool (Ross)	Fishing port on Loch Broom since the sixteenth century
Ulva (Mull)	A small island off Mull; a centre of the kelp industry in the nineteenth century; birthplace of David Livingstone's father and of Lachlan Macquarie, the 'father of Australia'
Unst (Shetland)	Northernmost of the Shetland Isles; fishing and crofting
Wemyss Bay (Renfrew)	Has a pier for ships cruising on the Clyde; formerly the ferry terminus from Arran
Whitehills (Banff)	Fishing harbour
Whithorn (Wigtown)	Has a small harbour and coastguard station
Whiting Bay (Arran)	Has a pier for ferries from the mainland
Wick (Caithness)	Fishing port; a centre of the herring fishing industry

A Chronological Framework

1292	*John Balliol* becomes king with English support
1296	Second interregnum (to 1306)
1297	William Wallace victorious at Stirling Bridge
1306	*Robert I* (Robert the Bruce)
1314	Battle of Bannockburn re-establishes Scottish independence
1320	Declaration of Arbroath
1329	*David II*
1371	*Robert II*
1390	*Robert III*
1406	*James I*
1437	*James II*
1460	Treaty of Ardtornish between the Lord of the Isles and English king
1460	*James III*
1468–9	Orkney and Shetland Isles acquired by Scotland
1476	Lord of the Isles submits to James III
1488	James III killed at Sauchieburn
1488	*James IV*
1493	Lordship of the Isles assumed by James IV
1511	*The Great Michael* launched by James IV
1513	Battle of Flodden – James IV dies
1513	*James V*
1542	*Mary Queen of Scots*
1559	John Knox returns from exile
1561	Mary Queen of Scots returns from France
1567	*James VI*
1587	Mary executed on the orders of Elizabeth I of England
1588	Spanish Armada
1603	*James VI of Scotland and I of England* – union of the crowns
1625	*Charles I*
1633	Charles I visits Scotland – *Blessing of Burntisland* sinks
1638	National Covenant
1643	Solemn League and Covenant
1649	*Charles II*
1651	Commonwealth and Protectorate
1660	*Charles II* restored
1685	*James VII and II*
1689	*William II (III of England)* and *Mary II* joint sovereigns Battle of Killiecrankie
1692	Massacre of Glencoe
1695	Bank of Scotland established
1698	First Darien expedition
1701	Captain Kidd executed for piracy and murder
1702	*Anne*
1707	Act of Union between Scotland and England
1708	France attempts invasion of Scotland
1714	*George I*
1715	Jacobite rising. Battle of Sheriffmuir

1727	*George II*
	Royal Bank of Scotland established
1745	Second Jacobite rising
1746	Battle of Culloden
1760	*George III*
	Carron Iron Works founded
1768	Captain James Cook embarks on first voyage of exploration
1769	James Watt patents his steam engine
1776	American Declaration of Independence
1783	United Kingdom recognises United States of America
1790	Opening of Forth–Clyde Canal
1797	Battle of Camperdown
1805	Battle of Trafalgar
1809	Action in Aix Roads
1811	Bell Rock lighthouse completed
1812	The first commercial steamboat, Bell's *Comet*, launched
1815	Battle of Waterloo
1820	*George IV*
1824	Royal National Lifeboat Institution founded
1830	*William IV*
1837	*Victoria*
1853–6	Crimean War
1861–5	American Civil War
1866	World's fastest clipper *Sir Lancelot* launched
1901	*Edward VII*
1910	*George V*
1914	First World War
1918	Armistice
1936	*Edward VIII /George VI*
	Cunarder *Queen Mary* enters transatlantic service
1939	Second World War
1941	June – Germany invades the USSR; December – Japan attacks Pearl Harbor
1945	Germany (May) and Japan (September) surrender
1952	*Elizabeth I of Scotland and II of England*
1999	Scottish parliament re-established

Glossary

Nautical terms have only been used where there is no simple alternative. The following explanations may be helpful to those unfamiliar with them.

Athwartships	Across the vessel, at right angles to the fore and aft line
Barque	Ship with three or more masts, with the foremast square-rigged and the other masts rigged fore and aft
Beam	The width of a ship; on the beam (port or starboard) – bearing at right angles to a ship's fore and aft line
Bear, bearing	Compass direction of an object
Bear up	To bring a ship's bow closer to the wind
Beat, beating	Making ground to windward by sailing close-hauled *q.v.*
Boom	A spar along the bottom edge of a sail, or a floating obstruction to prevent vessels from entering a harbour or anchorage
Bowsprit	A spar projecting from the bows of a sailing vessel
Brig	A two-masted, square-rigged ship
Brigantine	A two-masted ship with the foremast square-rigged and the mainmast rigged fore and aft
Bring to	To take the way off a ship; stop by turning into the wind
Captain	Naval rank between commander and commodore, but captain is also simply the person in command of a vessel
Carvel-built	With the planks flush, not overlapping
Clinker-built	With each plank overlapping the plank below
Close-hauled	Sailing as close as possible into the wind without losing way or getting 'in irons' *q.v.*
Commander	A naval rank of nineteenth-century origin between lieutenant-commander and captain; previously the captain of 'sixth-rate' *q.v.* or lesser ship was ranked master *q.v.* and commander
Commodore	An intermediate naval rank between captain and rear-admiral which is often bypassed by direct promotion to rear-admiral
Con	To manoeuvre or direct the steering of a ship
Draught	Depth between a vessel's waterline and the bottom of her keel
E-boat	A German motor torpedo boat (MTB)
Field-piece	A piece of field artillery capable of being moved on wheels
Flag rank	Admiral's rank; flies a flag denoting rank – from rear-admiral through vice-admiral and admiral to admiral of the fleet

Fleet train	A term dating from the Second World War describing the convoy of tankers, store and repair ships maintained in a war zone to supply a fleet, task force or task group of warships
Fore and aft	The straight line from bows to stern
Frigate	Fast warship, fifth-rate or smaller (*see below*), intended for escort duties, reconnaissance or (before radio telegraphy) communication
Furl	To roll or tie up, but hammocks are lashed
Gaff	A spar with its end attached to a mast, suspending a fore-and-aft sail
Gig	A ship's boat or tender propelled by oars or engine; sometimes a kind of fishing line with unbarbed hooks
Go about	To change from one tack to the other by steering the ship's bows through the wind – the opposite to wearing or gybing *q.v.*
Gunwale	The top edge of a vessel's hull; 'gunwales under' means heeled over so that the gunwale on one side is under water, e.g. the leeward gunwale when a sailing boat is heeling over in a strong wind
Gybe (gibe or jibe)	To change from one tack to the other by allowing the stern to pass through the wind (*see* Wear *below*)
Heave to	To stop (e.g. by turning into the wind, furling sails or putting engines astern)
In irons	Unable to get away on either tack, having lost way
Jury-mast	A makeshift mast to replace a damaged one
Kedge	To haul a vessel along, usually by hawser or cable attached to an anchor (*see* Warp *below*)
Keel	The main structural member running fore and aft along the bottom of a vessel
Lee, leeward	The opposite to windward (up wind), i.e. downwind
Line-of-battle ship	Origin of 'battleship'; the same as ship-of-the-line – a ship intended to form in a line of battle opposite an enemy. In the nineteenth century they were rated according to size and armament from first- to sixth-rate. The following is a very rough comparison:

	Crew	Guns	Tonnage	Length
First-rate	900	100+	2,500	180ft
Second-rate	750	90+	2,000	170ft
Third-rate	600	64+	1,700	160ft
Fourth-rate	350	50	1,100	150ft
Fifth-rate	250	32+	800	130ft
Sixth-rate	160+	20+	600	120ft

Lugger	A vessel with a four-sided sail hoisted on a yard *q.v.*
Masts	Most modern ships have a foremast and a mainmast. A yacht or small sailing boat has a mainmast and possibly a mizzen mast astern. A full-rigged sailing ship may have four masts: from fo'c'sle to stern – a foremast, mainmast, mizzen mast and jigger mast.

Master	Navigator of a ship. In a small ship, he could also be the captain. In larger ships, there was a captain and a master.
Mizzen	*See* Masts *and* Sails
Reef	A ridge of rock or coral concealed below the sea's surface; part of a sail which can be reefed to reduce the sail area by tying it in with reef-points (cords sewn to the sail)
Rigging	The ropes and, in modern ships, wires, which support the masts and sails when spread, or are used to hoist, lower and manage sails
Sails	The number spread can vary from one (e.g. a mizzen sail on a drifter or trawler to help keep the bows into the wind) to 25 or more in a square-rigged ship. Each has a name to identify it according to its position from bowsprit to jigger and from deck to skysail (refer to manual of seamanship or encyclopedia).
Schnorkel	A device used by some German U-boats to take in air without surfacing, enabling them to remain under water for long periods
Schooner	A sailing ship with foremast and mainmast, rigged fore and aft
Ship-of-the-line	Line-of-battle-ship *q.v.*
Shrouds	The rigging which supports a mast athwartships (*see* Stays)
Sloop	A single-masted sailing vessel, rigged fore and aft
Spar	Any pole of wood or metal used in rigging
Stays	The rigging which supports a mast fore and aft
Straddle	A gunnery term describing a salvo which falls across the target on the bearing aimed without necessarily hitting it
Strake	A fore and aft line of plates or planks forming part of the hull
Tacking	Making way under sail into the wind by altering course so that the wind comes alternately from port or starboard, i.e. on the port or starboard tack
Tholepin	A wooden peg inserted vertically in a boat's gunwale to provide a fulcrum for an oar
Transom	The flat vertical stern of a boat
Trice	To haul up by rope
Waist	The lowest part of a ship's upper deck between the fo'c'sle and quarterdeck or aftercastle
Warp	The same as 'kedge' *q.v.*, except the rope or cable may be attached to a fixture other than an anchor
Wear, wore	Tack by steering to bring the stern through the wind intentionally, whereas gybing is the same movement performed suddenly (or unintentionally due to a change of wind or steering error)
Weigh (anchor)	To raise from the seabed
Whip	A length of rope rove through a block or pulley secured to a yard, for lifting purposes
Yard	A spar slung from a mast to suspend a sail; a yardarm is the tapering end of a yard

Bibliography

Adam, Frank *Clans, Septs and Regiments of the Scottish Highlands* (Edinburgh, W. & A.K. Johnston, 1934)

Aitchison, Peter *Children of the Sea: The Story of the Eyemouth Disaster* (East Linton, Tuckwell Press, 2001)

Armstrong and Osborne (eds) *Echoes of the Sea: An Anthology* (Edinburgh, Canongate, 1998)

Baird, Bob *Shipwrecks of the Forth* (Glasgow, Nekton Books, 1993)

Baird, Bob *Shipwrecks of the West of Scotland* (Glasgow, Nekton Books, 1995)

Bennett, Geoffrey *Cowan's War* (London, Collins, 1964)

Boswell, James *Journal of a Tour to the Hebrides* (London, Penguin Books, 1984)

Brooks, G. *The Trial of Captain Kidd* (Wm Hodge & Co. Ltd, 1930)

Brown, Gordon *Maxton* (Edinburgh, Mainstream Publishing, 1986)

Bryant, Arthur *Samuel Pepys* (3 Vols) (London, Collins, 1949)

Campbell, Vice-Admiral Gordon, VC *My Mystery Ships* (London, Hodder & Stoughton, 1928)

Carter, George *Outlines of English History* (London, Relfe Brothers, 1924)

Chalmers, W.S. *The Life and Letters of David Beatty* (London, Hodder and Stoughton, 1951)

Chronicle Communications Ltd, London *Chronicle of Britain and Ireland* 1992

Churchill, Winston S. *The Second World War* (6 Vols) (London, Cassell & Co. Ltd, 1951)

Cochrane, Thomas, Tenth Earl of Dundonald *The Autobiography of a Seaman* (London, Richard Bentley & Son, 1890)

Coull, James R. *The Sea Fisheries of Scotland* (Edinburgh, John Donald Publishers, 1996)

Cunningham, A.B. *A Sailor's Odyssey* (London, Hutchinson & Co., 1951)

Devine, T.M. *The Scottish Nation 1700–2000* (London, Penguin Books, 1999)

Fraser, Antonia *Mary Queen of Scots* (London, Weidenfeld & Nicolson Ltd, 1969)

Fry, Michael *The Scottish Empire* (East Linton, Tuckwell Press, 2001)

Galt, John *The Steamboat* (Edinburgh, William Blackwood, 1822)

Graham, Eric J. *A Maritime History of Scotland: 1650–1790* (East Linton, Tuckwell Press, 2001)

Grimble, Ian *The Sea Wolf* (London, Blond & Briggs, 1978)

Harper, J.E.T. *The Truth about Jutland* (London, John Murray, 1927)

Johnson, Dr Samuel *A Journey to the Western Isles of Scotland* (London, Penguin Books, 1984)

Kennedy, Ludovic *Nelson's Band of Brothers* (London, Odham's Press, 1951)

Laughton, Sir T. Knox *British Sailor Heroes* (London, Bickers & Son, 1930)

Leach, Nicholas *For Those in Peril* (Kettering, Silver Link Publishing and RNLI, 1999)

Lewis, Michael *The Navy of Britain* (London, George Allen & Unwin, 1948)

Lindesay, Robert Lindesay of Pitscottie *The History and Cronicles of Scotland*, edited by Aeneas

J.G. Mackay (Edinburgh 1899–1911)

Lloyd, Christopher *Lord Cochrane: Seaman, Radical, Liberator* (New York, Henry Holt & Co., 1947)

Lockhart, G.W. *The Scots and Their Fish* (Edinburgh, Birlinn Ltd, 1997)

Mackay, James *I Have Not Yet Begun to Fight: A Life of John Paul Jones* (Edinburgh, Mainstream Publishing, 2000)

Mackenzie, Agnes Mure *Scottish Pageant* (4 Vols) (Edinburgh, Oliver & Boyd, 1949)

Mackenzie, Agnes Mure *The Passing of the Stewarts* (Edinburgh, Oliver & Boyd, 1958)

Mackie, R.L. *A Short History of Scotland* (Edinburgh, Oliver & Boyd, 1930)

Mackie, R.L. *King James IV of Scotland* (Edinburgh, Oliver & Boyd, 1958)

Masefield, John *Sea Life in Nelson's Time* (London, Methuen & Co., 1905)

Mathew, David *Scotland under Charles I* (London, Eyre & Spottiswood, 1995)

Miller, James *Salt in the Blood* (Edinburgh, Canongate, 1999)

Moyse-Bartlett H. *A History of the Merchant Navy* (London, George H. Harrap & Co., 1937)

Munro, Neil *Para Handy* (Edinburgh, William Blackwood, 1980)

Prebble, John *The Highland Clearances* (London, Penguin Books, 1969)

Ritchie, Robert C. *Captain Kidd and the War against the Pirates* (Harvard University Press, 1986)

Rixson, Denis *The West Highland Galley* (Edinburgh, Birlinn, 1998)

Rodger, N.A.M. *The Safeguard of the Sea* (London, W.W. Norton & Co., 1999)

Roughhead, William 'The Riddle of the Ruthvens; and other Studies', *Juridical Review*, 1919

Shackleton, Sir Ernest *South: The Story of the 1914–1917 Expedition* (London, William Heinemann Ltd, 1919)

Sherburne, J.H. *The Life of Paul Jones* (London, John Murray, 1825)

Smout, T.C. *A History of the Scottish People 1560–1830* (London, Collins, 1969)

Stevenson, Robert Louis *The Amateur Emigrant* (London, Hogarth Press, 1984)

Stevenson, Robert Louis *Memories and Portraits* (London, Chatto & Windus, 1887)

Stewart, William *Fishing in Scotland from the Sixteenth Century to the Present Day* (Lossiemouth, The Lossie Printers, 2001)

Vian, Sir Philip *Action This Day* (London, Frederick Muller, 1960)

Wilkins, Frances *Strathclyde's Smuggling Story* (and others in the series) (Wyre Forest Press, 1992)

Wills, Elspeth *Scottish Firsts: Innovation and Achievement* (Edinburgh, Mainstream Publishing, 1987)

Wilson, Barbara Ker *Scottish Folk-Tales and Legends* (Oxford, Oxford University Press, 1954)

Winton, John *Cunningham: The Greatest Admiral since Nelson* (London, John Murray, 1998)

Ziegler, Philip *Mountbatten* (London, Guild Publishing, 1985)

Index